Butterflies of Houston
and Southeast Texas

Corrie Herring Hooks Series
Number Thirty-two

Butterflies of
Houston
& Southeast Texas

John & Gloria
Tveten

Photographs and Illustrations
by the Authors

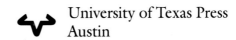

University of Texas Press
Austin

Frontispiece: A tiger swallowtail, Papilio glaucus,
sips nectar from the blooms of wild black cherry.

First edition, 1996

Requests for permission to reproduce material from this work should be
sent to Permissions, University of Texas Press, Box 7819, Austin, TX
78713-7819.

♾ The paper used in this publication meets the minimum requirements
of American National Standard for Information Sciences—Permanence
of Paper for Printed Library Materials, ANSI Z39.48-1984.

Library of Congress Cataloging-in-Publication Data

Tveten, John L.
Butterflies of Houston and southeast Texas / John & Gloria Tveten ;
photographs and illustrations by the authors — 1st ed.
        p.   cm. — (Corrie Herring Hooks series ; no. 32)
Includes bibliographical references and index.
ISBN 0-292-78142-3 (cloth). — ISBN 0-292-78143-1 (pbk.)
1. Butterflies—Texas—Houston.   2. Butterflies—Texas—Houston—
Identification.   3. Butterflies—Texas.   4. Butterflies—Texas—
Identification.   I. Tveten, Gloria A., date.   II. Title.   III. Series.
QL551.T4T945   1996
595.78′9′0976414—dc20   95-50198

To our son Michael,
who shares our interest in nature.

Contents

Acknowledgments

This project began many years ago, when a patient father indulged his young son's love of butterflies and other insects. He built display cases, provided books and equipment, and was always ready for collecting trips into the fields and forests of the Midwest. To the late Tuko Tveten we owe an enormous debt of gratitude.

With our son Michael, this interest in insects continued into a third generation. He has been a companion on many fieldtrips, a partner in countless discoveries and delights, and a source of valuable information as he continued an education in entomology. It is to him that we dedicate this book.

Many other butterfly enthusiasts have contributed greatly to our work. Roger Peace accompanied us on several photographic trips in Southeast Texas and shared the excitement of rearing adult butterflies from their larvae. We thank Geyata Ajilvsgi, Charles Bordelon, Dale Clark, and Hoe Hin Chuah for sharing their extensive knowledge of local butterflies and for suggesting locations for particular species. Don Olhausen, Martha Henschen, Randy Beavers, and Valerie Karime provided both butterfly larvae and plants for study, while botanists Charles Peterson and Larry Brown offered assistance in identifying larval food plants.

We thank Raymond Neck for several discussions on butterfly taxonomy and nomenclature and Steve Williams and Richard Orr for copies of their checklists for the Houston area. Mike Rickard contributed his personal butterfly list and the benefit of his years of experience in Southeast Texas. He also read the completed manuscript and offered many helpful suggestions for improvements. His extensive knowledge and contributions have been invaluable.

James Smith provided information on butterfly distributions in Brazoria County and helped us locate several species that occur less frequently in the immediate Houston area. He also read the manuscript and offered us the benefit of his wide field experience.

Nancy Greig, too, provided useful comments and suggestions for the improvement of the initial manuscript.

We thank those who provided photographs to supplement our own: Geyata Ajilvsgi (amymone), Carlos Hernandez (zebra), George Krizek (Cassius blue and twin-spot skipper), and Michael Tveten (great purple hairstreak).

Finally, we owe an enormous debt of gratitude to the University of Texas Press for their faith in this project.

*Butterflies of Houston
and Southeast Texas*

Introduction

The study of butterflies has long been the province of the professional or serious amateur collector. The insects are captured and carefully mounted, their wings spread for display. Identification then becomes a matter of systematic comparison with photographic or painted illustrations depicting all the species of a given region. Specialists even dissect the bodies of certain species to verify by microscopic examination their identities, allowing, at the same time, a careful study of taxonomic relationships. There are numerous manuals and field guides available for the serious butterfly collector. Some depict representative butterflies from around the world; others treat the species of North America, the eastern or western states, or even a specific state or region. Many of these sources are listed in the bibliography.

Recently, however, there has been a dramatic turn toward butterfly watching as a rewarding outdoor pastime, much like the way the popularity of bird watching is sweeping the country. The butterflies are observed in their natural habitats, appreciated for their gemlike beauty and lilting flight, and then allowed to continue on their way. Hikers and campers, gardeners, birders and wildflower enthusiasts, nature photographers—all are discovering that butterflies can add enjoyment to their pursuits. Most people will want to identify the species they see, to put a name on their new discoveries and learn more about the habits of these fascinating insects. That is the purpose of this book.

Identification, of course, can be difficult in the field. Some butterflies do not allow a close approach, or they might fly before distinctive features can be seen. Some diagnostic field marks are visible only at close range or when the wings are widely spread, as with mounted specimens. Many butterflies sit with wings tightly closed, failing to reveal the upperwing patterns usually portrayed in field guides intended for collectors. Here, however, we show live butterflies

A great southern white, Ascia monuste, *completes its entire life cycle in a patch of saltwort along the Texas coast near Freeport.*

in their natural positions, sometimes with wings spread widely, often with them closed above their backs. In many cases, the underwing pattern is most diagnostic, particularly within the confusing array of small blues, hairstreaks, and skippers. Not every butterfly can be identified conclusively in the field, but with patience the careful observer can soon learn the species of the area.

We have designed this book specifically for Houston, Texas. All of the common butterfly species are described and illustrated, as well as most of those that occur less frequently. It is not possible to include every individual that might stray into the region on rare occasions, for vagrant or wind-blown butterflies sometimes turn up far from their normal range. Texas has repeatedly been termed a "biological crossroads," and we see influences from all directions, including tropical butterflies that range across the Rio Grande from Mexico and sometimes wander farther north. Most of the butterflies seen in Houston and the surrounding Southeast Texas area, however, will be found on the pages of this book.

We have an advantage in treating a limited area. Many of the problems in butterfly identification stem from the large number of similar species that occur in varied habitats across the country. Scores of confusing crescents and checkerspots, hairstreaks, or skippers confront the beginning butterfly enthusiast from the pages of the standard field guides. In most cases, only a few inhabit any given region, and the choices in a local book are limited and less intimidating.

We have no quarrel with butterfly collecting. Indeed, our interest was first kindled through that hobby. Many problems of classification and taxonomy can be solved only by collecting, and much remains to be learned from the collections of museums and qualified individuals. Such activities have no effect on butterfly populations when pursued in moderation, for most species lay their eggs almost immediately after emerging and seldom live for more than a few days or weeks. Only when rare species are confined to limited habitats is there a need for restrictions on insect collecting. Most people, however, prefer to enjoy and learn about butterflies as part of the natural scene. It is to them that this book is directed, hoping it will stimulate interest in the beautiful and fascinating creatures with which we share our world.

What Is a Butterfly?

Perhaps the most frequent question asked about butterflies is: "How do they differ from moths?" There is no straightforward, all-inclusive answer. In general, butterflies are active almost exclusively by day; moths tend to be nocturnal. The antennae of butterflies end in pronounced clubs or swellings, while those of moths have no clubs and are usually feathered or threadlike. Butterflies lack the frenulum, a coupling device that hooks together the forewing and hindwing of most moths. There are, however, small groups that do not fit these nice categories.

Butterflies and moths combine to form the scientific order Lepidoptera, a word coined from the Greek *lepis*, "scale," and *ptera*, "wing." Their thin parchment wings are covered with tiny overlapping scales both above and below, making possible different colors and patterns on opposite sides of each wing.

Butterflies, in turn, comprise two superfamilies: Papilionoidea, the "true butterflies," and Hesperioidea, the skippers. The latter tend to be robust, heavy-bodied insects with distinct hooks at the tips of their clubbed antennae. Most are small and drab, and they fly with the quick, darting movements from which they take their name. Both superfamilies are included in this book.

Butterfly Numbers and Distribution

Estimates vary as to the number of butterflies found throughout the world. Most authors cite between fifteen thousand and twenty thousand species, although classification changes constantly. Much remains to be learned about the relationships of various populations. Some valid species look much alike, while other species have geographical or seasonal forms that are very different in appearance. About seven hundred butterfly species are found at least occasionally in the United States and Canada. Many are common residents across large portions of the continent; others appear as rare strays from Mexico or the West Indies.

Roughly one hundred species occur regularly in Houston and the neighboring areas of Southeast Texas. Some are eastern forest species and reach the southwestern corner of their range in the wooded portions of northern Harris County. Others wander eastward from the more arid Hill Country or northward along the coast in summer from deep South Texas and the Rio Grande Valley.

Because butterflies are tied to specific larval food plants, they have definite preferences in habitat. Some wander widely as adults, perhaps to feed at nectar plants in backyard flower gardens. Others rarely leave their own special niches. Pine woodlands, salt marshes, and prairie grasslands all have their own unique butterflies. Finding them involves learning their individual requirements.

Scientific and Common Names

Most professional biologists and serious students of plants and animals use the scientific names, a system devised by eighteenth-century Swedish botanist Carl von Linné, or Carolus Linnaeus. In Linnaeus' system, every species has a two-part Latin name. Current usage places that name in italic for publication. The first part is always capitalized and indicates the genus, a group of very closely related organisms. The second part is not capitalized and describes the individual species. There can be only one pair of names for any life-form, and no two plants or animals share the same scientific name.

Unfortunately, no such list is inviolable, and even the scientific names change from time to time. Some changes occur as we learn more about butterfly populations and their relationships; others, as the result of scientific precedent. Thus, not all authors agree on the proper nomenclature. In general, we have followed the Lepidopterists' Society's *A Catalogue/Checklist of the Butterflies of America North of Mexico*, by Lee Miller and F. Martin Brown, published in 1981, and its supplement, edited by Clifford Ferris in 1989. In a few cases, we have adopted recent changes to that system.

Common names for butterflies present an even greater problem, for there has been no standard system. One reference, for example, may call a common Houston species the "ocola skipper," while another gives it the name "long-winged skipper."

In an attempt to standardize such nomenclature, Jacqueline Miller published *The Common Names of North American Butterflies* in 1992, using a general consensus from current field guides and butterfly manuals. She also listed other commonly used names. Also in 1992, the English Names Committee of the recently formed North American Butterfly Association (NABA) adopted a slate of common names, seeking to standardize the system even more and to use names that impart additional information about close relationships and important features.

In order to be consistent with the nomenclature in most of the field guides now in use, we have, in general, followed Miller's system. When the NABA choice seems to have particular merit, however, we have adopted it instead. All such common names are listed under each species account, and all are included in the index.

The Butterfly Life Cycle

Most animals change significantly during their lifetimes, but few do so as dramatically as the lepidoptera. In a complete metamorphosis, butterflies pass through four major stages—egg, larva, pupa, and adult—undergoing amazing transformations at each step.

Aristotle's description of the process, as quoted by Gray in a 1954 issue of *The Lepidopterists' News*, captures the wonder with which he viewed it. The fourth-century B.C. Greek philosopher wrote of the butterflies he called "psyches":

> Psyches develop from caterpillars which grow on green leaves . . . ; first they are less than grains of millet, then they grow into small grubs and in a few days into little caterpillars; after this they grow more and become quiescent and change their shape and are called chrysalides and have a hard shell; but they move if they are touched. They are attached by spider-silky filaments; they have no mouth or any other obvious organs; after no long passage of time the shell bursts open and out fly the winged creatures which we call psyches.

Figure 1: Life cycle of the tiger swallowtail

The metamorphosis occurs with amazing rapidity, a complete life cycle often taking no more than a month. A butterfly egg usually hatches in about five days, and the caterpillar progresses through several molts in two or three weeks before pupating. Eight to ten days later, a perfect adult butterfly emerges from the pupa, ready to repeat the cycle.

During the warm spring and summer months, many of our species go through several such cycles, raising two or more successive generations of butterflies in a single season. Most, however, have a resting stage during part of the year, usually because of cold winter temperatures. Triggered by changes in the length of the daylight period, eggs or pupae enter a stage of arrested development called diapause, resuming their development again in the spring, when emerging caterpillars or adults can find an adequate food source. Adults or partially grown larvae may also hibernate during periods of cold weather, emerging occasionally from their shelters on warm winter days to feed.

EGG: Female butterflies lay their eggs either singly or in groups, usually on the leaves or new growth of appropriate larval food plants. While adult butterflies sip nectar from a wide variety of flowers, the caterpillars have a much more limited diet. Many are confined to a single plant genus or family. The female butterfly detects the proper host visually and then lands to sample it with sensory cells on her legs or antennae. She will lay dozens, perhaps hundreds, of eggs during her short life.

Butterfly eggs take a variety of shapes, sizes, textures, and colors. Some are spherical; others are conelike or spindle-shaped, often with minute ridges or sculptured ornamentation. If they begin to develop immediately, they normally hatch within a week.

LARVA: A young caterpillar's first meal often consists of the remainder of its eggshell; it then proceeds to feed on tender plant material. Young leaves and flower buds provide nutritious fare. If several eggs were laid together, the larvae feed communally through their early stages, usually skeletonizing the leaves until they can eat the tougher veins. Later, most wander off alone to complete their development and find a site in which to pupate.

The caterpillar body consists of the head, three thoracic segments, and ten abdominal segments. The thorax carries three pairs of true legs typical of all insects. They will also be found on the adult. Four pairs of prolegs on abdominal segments provide the major means of larval locomotion, but they will not be preserved in the adult butterfly. The larva breathes through small holes, or spiracles, on the sides of the thorax and abdomen; the head is equipped with minute eyes, a silk spinneret, and powerful chewing mandibles.

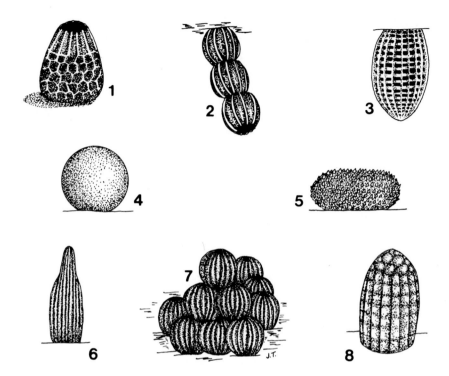

Figure 2: Butterfly eggs
1. Pearl crescent
2. Question mark
3. Monarch
4. Spicebush swallowtail
5. Spring azure
6. Little sulphur
7. Tawny emperor
8. Gulf fritillary

A varied array of setae, or short "hairs," stiff spines, and fleshy filaments adorn many caterpillars.

Because an insect's tough chitinous skin does not grow or stretch, the larva must shed its skin several times as it grows. It usually goes through five different stages, called instars, from hatching until pupation. The old skin loosens and splits open, and the caterpillar crawls out with a new skin and head capsule. The color and ornamentation may change with each new instar.

Few caterpillars feed in the open, fully exposed to predators and parasitic insects. Many seek shelter by folding leaves or gathering and tying them together with silk, while others hide by day under bark or at the base of plants and emerge at night to feed. Camouflage patterns and branching spines offer a degree of protection, and a few species consume toxic chemicals in their food plants and advertise their distastefulness with bright warning colors.

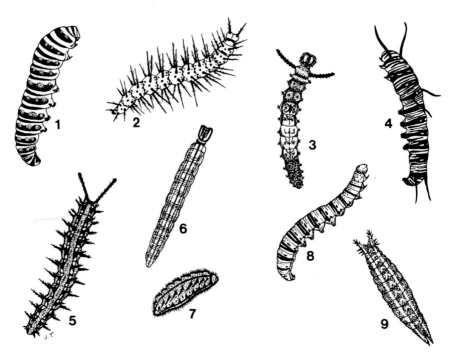

Figure 3. Butterfly larvae
1. Black swallowtail
2. Zebra
3. Viceroy
4. Queen
5. Variegated fritillary
6. Clouded skipper
7. Gray hairstreak
8. Cloudless sulphur
9. Tawny emperor

The larval stage of a butterfly can prove as interesting as the adult itself. It is often the longest lived of the stages, and it is the one in which all of the growing occurs. Once a butterfly emerges from its pupa and expands its wings, it will grow no more.

PUPA: On reaching maturity, the final-instar larva stops eating and selects a suitable pupation site, sometimes wandering far from its food plants. During its last day as a caterpillar, it may also change color and expel fluid to become shorter and plumper. Some species choose to pupate on the ground amid the leaf litter; others remain in their leafy nests. Many larvae hang head downward from silken pads or rest suspended in girdles of silk.

Once the caterpillar is securely in place, the skin splits and rolls down, revealing the fresh chrysalis beneath. In one quick movement as the skin is discarded, a hook, called the cremaster, at the tip of the abdomen is anchored

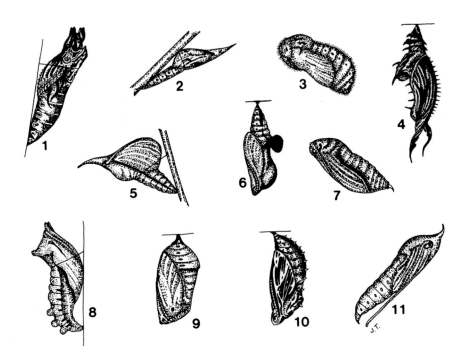

Figure 4: Butterfly pupae
1. Giant swallowtail
2. Falcate orangetip
3. Gray hairstreak
4. Zebra
5. Cloudless sulphur
6. Viceroy
7. Silver-spotted skipper
8. Pipe-vine swallowtail
9. Monarch
10. Variegated fritillary
11. Brazilian skipper

securely in the silk pad. Over the next few hours the pupa will harden and change shape slightly, assuming a characteristic appearance that serves to identify the butterfly developing within. Because the inert chrysalis provides a tasty morsel for birds and other predators, it is usually camouflaged in brown or green, blending with the leaves or twigs on which it rests. If disturbed, it may twitch violently from side to side.

ADULT: Development of the butterfly can sometimes be observed through the translucent pupal shell, the wing pattern becoming gradually apparent. On the day of eclosion, the adult forces its way quickly out of the pupal case and hangs on the empty shell to expand its folded wings, slowly pumping body fluid through the soft veins. Once expanded, the butterfly rests for an hour or more before the fragile wings harden enough to support flight. During the expansion and hardening process, the wings can be easily damaged.

An adult butterfly does not grow; once it expands after emerging, it remains the same size throughout its short lifetime.

Life expectancies of butterflies vary dramatically. Some adults live only a few days; a week or two is typical for many species. Autumn generations of some butterflies, however, live for several months, hibernating through the winter to mate and lay their eggs the following spring. The famous monarch, of course, migrates southward for the winter and retraces at least part of its route in spring before producing another brood.

The adult has only a sucking proboscis rather than chewing mouthparts. As a result, butterflies cannot consume solid food. Many obtain energy by sipping sugar-rich nectar from flowers. Others drink fluids from tree sap, rotting fruit, bird droppings, animal dung, or carrion. Some species, particularly the males, gather at mud puddles or damp sand to imbibe water rich in dissolved salts and other nutrients. Hill's laboratory experiments clearly show that the availability of carbohydrates increases longevity in several butterfly species. Given only water to drink, small lycaenids lived only three or four days; with 10-percent honey solution, they survived for fifteen to twenty days.

The lives of butterflies revolve around warm sunlight, nectar, and actively growing plants on which the females can lay their eggs. The timing of the various broods has evolved to take advantage of all three conditions.

Because butterflies are cold-blooded, they must warm their bodies and powerful flight muscles to a certain level before they can fly. This is accomplished by basking in the sun. Some species spread their wings widely to the warming rays; others hold them closed above the body but turn until they are perpendicular to the sun. The latter are usually darkly colored below, a factor that aids in energy absorption. In cool weather or on cloudy days, butterflies may not fly at all. They roost at night, usually with wings tightly closed, in some sheltered niche or beneath an overhanging leaf. Most perch alone, but a few species congregate at nightfall in large communal roosts.

The Struggle for Survival

Butterflies face constant danger throughout all four stages of their development. Weather, of course, plays an enormous role in their lives. Many species cannot survive extreme cold, and early freezes catch some broods unprepared. Migrants that wander northward may not survive the winter and must recolonize the region every year. Heavy rains and strong winds take their toll by damaging fragile wings; washing eggs, larvae, or pupae from their precarious perches; or destroying larval and adult food resources.

Birds, mice, lizards, spiders, and other predators hunt adult butterflies as

Figure 5: Adult butterflies
1. Question mark
2. Great purple hairstreak
3. Zebra swallowtail
4. Silver-spotted skipper
5. Southern pearly eye
6. Monarch
7. Snout butterfly
8. Dog face
9. Gulf fritillary

well as caterpillars and chrysalides. Predation on lepidoptera by other insects is a major factor. Praying mantids, dragonflies, wasps, stinkbugs, and a variety of six-legged carnivores do not draw the line at feeding on others in their class. At times it seems as if much of the natural world runs on caterpillar power.

Viruses and fungal diseases often wipe out entire colonies of lepidoptera larvae, spreading rapidly when the caterpillars become too numerous and crowded. Parasites play the largest regulatory role. Some tiny insects lay their own eggs within the shells of butterfly eggs, their larvae emerging in place of the intended caterpillars. Tachinid flies and ichneumonid, braconid, and chalcid wasps lay their eggs on or within the bodies of caterpillars. The larval flies and wasps live and feed within their still ambulatory prey, which do not die until the parasites have matured, thereby assuring a fresh and ample food supply.

The power of flight, of course, enables adult butterflies to escape many threats, but they are subject to constant danger from equally agile birds. Other predators lie in wait wherever butterflies choose to feed or roost.

At all stages in their life histories, butterflies depend on a variety of protective mechanisms. Some larvae are protected by an armament of spines or by distasteful body fluids containing toxic chemicals sequestered from the plants they eat. Others are adept at building shelters, and many carry camouflage to the extreme. It is a delicate balance, this constant struggle against enormous odds, but butterflies manage to endure as long as they can find their all-important food plants and selected habitats.

Studying and Enjoying Butterflies

BUTTERFLY WATCHING: This rapidly growing hobby requires no equipment beyond a book for identification and, perhaps, binoculars with close-focusing capabilities. Such binoculars bring the butterfly into closer and sharper view while the watcher remains at a distance. Glassberg, in his excellent book for the northeastern region, *Butterflies through Binoculars*, recommends Minolta "Pocket" binoculars that focus down to a distance of six feet or less. Some butterfly watchers, Glassberg notes, prefer 7X or 8X models; his personal choice is 10X, enlarging the image ten times. Many of the models used by bird watchers do not focus closely enough, making them of limited utility for the smaller butterflies. Any binoculars, no matter how inexpensive, will be of some assistance; the most important objective is to enjoy the adventure of the hobby.

Butterflies occur virtually everywhere, offering added interest to family outings and vacations. A remarkable number live or feed in backyard flower gardens, and several of these are on the wing on warm, sunny days almost throughout the year in Houston. Because each species has special habitat requirements and peak flight times, each outing may provide something new.

Even the novice butterfly watcher can contribute to scientific studies by careful observation. The life histories and larval food plants of many species remain unknown, while few regions have complete checklists of local species. By keeping dated records of butterflies and their numbers, along with individual habits and plant preferences, one can assemble much new and useful data.

COLLECTING: Collecting has played a major role in accumulating the knowledge of butterflies we now have. It is the only way to study in careful detail their structure and variation and to compare individuals and populations. As noted earlier, collecting has little impact on butterfly abundance, for most mate and lay eggs shortly after emerging and then die within a few days. Collecting rare or threatened species, or catching large numbers from a single population, obviously should be avoided.

Butterfly collecting, however, requires considerable effort, not only in properly mounting each specimen, but in maintaining the collection and protecting it from dermestid beetles and other museum pests that make inroads into collectors' treasures.

Every specimen collected must be properly labeled; without data it is scientifically useless. Each label should contain the state, county, locality, date, and collector's name. Other useful information includes the elevation, weather conditions, plant associations, and so forth.

Butterflies may be collected with nets or raised from larvae. Lepidopterists also attract moths to bait traps and to lights at night. There are many books to aid the beginning collector, some of which are listed in the bibliography. Detailed equipment and techniques are beyond the scope of this book, however, and we encourage the reader to enjoy butterflies as living creatures and to observe their role in nature.

REARING BUTTERFLIES: Caterpillars of many butterfly species are relatively easy to find. Gulf fritillary larvae, for example, feed on passion-vines throughout the Houston area, while tawny emperor larvae browse on the leaves of hackberry trees. In almost every habitat, from backyard gardens to dense woodlands, at least a few caterpillars will be eating away at the grasses, wildflowers, shrubs, and trees. The larval food plants of each butterfly are listed in the species accounts.

It is possible to observe caterpillars in their original locations, but many will be lost to parasites and predators. Others will wander off to pupate unseen, and it is difficult to follow a larva through its final stages. For this reason, many people enjoy raising butterflies in captivity, releasing them after they emerge. It is, of course, the best way to obtain perfect specimens for a collection or for close-up photography.

Caterpillars can be placed singly or in small numbers in a variety of containers. Plastic boxes or wide-mouth jars work well and allow close observation. Screen cages or jars with netting over the top also prove useful, but larval food plants should then be kept in small vials of water to prevent them from drying out. Each container must be cleaned at least once a day and fresh leaves provided; plant cuttings can usually be kept in a plastic bag in the refrigerator if there is no live plant nearby. As the caterpillars mature, twigs can be added as pupation sites.

Rearing butterflies requires time and effort, but it can be a rewarding experience. Many larval hosts remain to be discovered, and the behavior of various caterpillars can be amazingly complex. This also provides a dramatic, hands-on way of introducing children to the world of nature.

PHOTOGRAPHING BUTTERFLIES: As noted above, rearing butterflies from their larvae provides fresh and undamaged specimens for photography. Newly emerged adults do not fly immediately after unfurling their wings, and they can then be transferred carefully to a suitable and photogenic outdoor location or to an indoor setup. The entire life cycle can be documented on film, providing an excellent photo essay.

A single lens reflex camera is almost essential for good close-up photography. Indoor work with insects of any kind requires flash equipment, while outdoor work usually requires longer lenses. In order to obtain large enough images, most butterfly photographers rely on macro lenses of various lengths.

Most of our butterflies were photographed with either 50mm or 100mm macro lenses. To obtain the depth of field and sharp detail necessary to illustrate both the field marks and the delicate beauty of the subjects, we often resorted to flash techniques. Close-ups were taken with a ring-light flash calibrated with the magnification as marked on the barrel of the macro lens.

Good photographs can be achieved with all kinds of cameras, lenses, and techniques. As with any such hobby, however, the main reward is enjoyment and understanding. With proper documentation, some of those photographs may also reveal new and unusual facts about even our most common butterflies.

Butterfly Gardening

More and more people are planting their yards and gardens to encourage and attract wildlife, and even a small area can harbor an amazing variety of butterflies. Of the several books on that subject, one of the best for the Houston area is Geyata Ajilvsgi's excellent and beautifully illustrated *Butterfly Gardening for the South*.

To attract the maximum number of butterfly species, both nectar plants and larval food plants must be provided. The two are not the same. Most caterpillars will feed only on a very narrow range of hosts, usually those within a single genus or family. Adult butterflies, on the other hand, visit a wide range of blossoms in search of nectar, although many have their own particular favorites based on flower shape, color, or nectar content.

Among the best nectar plants for Southeast Texas are lantanas, butterfly bush (*Buddleia*), button-bush, milkweeds, pentas, phlox, verbenas, purple coneflower, asters, zinnias, and marigolds. Some are hardy native perennials;

others are annuals or more tropical species that must be replanted each year. With an assortment of plants, however, there will be blooms to attract butterflies from early spring until frost.

Larval food plants are much more specific, and they are listed in the individual species accounts later in this book. Dill, parsley, and fennel provide food for black swallowtail caterpillars; pipe-vines attract the namesake pipe-vine swallowtails. Finding these plants as they wander in search of nectar, females lay their eggs and ensure a future crop of butterflies as well.

Local dealers can assist with suitable plants for specific soil types and growing conditions, while nature centers and arboretums often have special native-plant sales and offer advice on the ones most attractive to butterflies and other wildlife. It goes without saying, of course, that chemical pesticides have no place in a butterfly garden; butterflies are insects too.

Butterfly Conservation

Butterfly populations in North America have undergone profound changes through the years. Some species have virtually disappeared; others have become more abundant across sections of their former range or have expanded into new territories. These trends accompany major land-use changes as forests are cleared and marshes drained. Urban and suburban environments offer a different selection of larval hosts and nectar plants than do native prairies and woodlands. Even the removal of fencerows from agricultural fields and the loss of railroad rights-of-way lead to the loss of butterflies, for these were major corridors of native plants. Pesticide spraying and pollution have had an undeniable effect, again not only on the insects themselves but also on the plants they consume.

Butterfly gardening provides one way to counteract some of these losses. Small plots throughout a neighborhood cannot make up for the loss of a virgin prairie or the clear-cutting of a timbered tract, but they may be the last retreat for several species. As with most of our wildlife, the question is not what happened to a declining species; the question is what happened to the habitat.

Many conservation organizations have taken an active interest in butterfly preservation, as have the societies of professional and amateur lepidopterists. Individuals and communities across the country must also become involved. It will take a concentrated effort to maintain present population levels, but the rewards are rich indeed.

Swallowtails

FAMILY PAPILIONIDAE

The swallowtail family contains our largest and most impressive butterflies. Between 550 and 700 species occur around the world, depending on the classification followed. The majority are tropical, but at least a few species can be found in almost every type of habitat. More than two dozen inhabit North America, with seven occurring regularly in the Houston area. All of the latter appear in this book.

Local swallowtails are instantly recognizable by their large size and by the namesake tails on the hindwings; however, family members in other regions may lack those tails. The unifying element in their classification is a unique pattern of veins in the wings. Two different subfamilies compose the Papilionidae in North America. One, Papilioninae, contains all of the Texas species. The other, Parnassiinae, contains a group of butterflies called parnassians that occur only in the far North and in the western mountains.

Adult swallowtails feed readily at flowers or land to sip water and dissolved mineral salts at patches of damp sand or mud. While feeding, they often beat their wings rapidly, perhaps because their great size causes slender flower stalks to bend.

Swallowtail eggs are usually spherical and pale green, laid singly on the food plants. They darken as they mature, and the tiny larvae can be seen within. Young caterpillars often exhibit a pattern thought to mimic an inedible bird dropping, while older ones molt to more dramatic colors that may include false eyespots for defense. They are smooth-skinned or have fleshy tubercles, lacking the sharp spines that adorn many other caterpillars.

All swallowtail larvae possess a fleshy, forked organ called the osmeterium (spelled "osmaterium" by some authors) that can be extruded from a slit behind the head when the larva is disturbed or threatened. Connected to a scent

The bulging eyespots on a Palamedes swallowtail caterpillar, Papilio palamedes, *presumably mimic the head of a snake.*

1. Tiger swallowtail

2. Giant swallowtail, larva with osmeterium extended

gland, the osmeterium gives off a powerful, sickeningly sweet odor thought to help repel predators and parasites. Recent research suggests it contains compounds found in ant pheromones and may work best against those biting insects. Only caterpillars of the Papilionidae have these retractable osmeteria.

Swallowtail pupae normally bear camouflage colors of brown or green. The posterior end of the chrysalis is attached to a button of silk by a set of tiny hooks called the cremaster, while a girdle of silk supports the pupa upright on the branch or other support. All of our swallowtails overwinter in the pupal stage.

The name "papilio" was first used by Linnaeus for all of the butterflies when he published his tenth edition of *Systema Naturae* in 1758. That great work provides the starting place for all zoological nomenclature. Placing butterflies in the genus *Papilio*, Linnaeus chose specific epithets from Homer to honor the heroes of the Trojan War. He soon ran out of heroes, however, and resorted to characters from Greek and Roman mythology. Later, *Papilio* became the accepted genus name for only the swallowtails. Present-day taxonomists have gone much farther in separating even our few species of Papilionidae into several different genera.

Pipe-Vine Swallowtail
Battus philenor
Pipevine swallowtail, Blue swallowtail

The lovely pipe-vine swallowtail is one of the most abundant and widespread swallowtails in the Houston area and throughout Southeast Texas. Although it appears almost completely black at a distance, its hindwings glisten with an iridescent blue-green that shimmers in the sunlight. On the underside of the hindwing, it flashes a row of prominent orange spots on an iridescent blue field.

Battus philenor larvae feed on various species of pipe-vines, sometimes called Dutchman's pipe, of the genus *Aristolochia*. These include such native plants as the large-leaved, high-climbing *A. tomentosa* and smaller herbs like *A. serpentaria* and *A. reticulata* that are common in East Texas woodlands. In addition, they make frequent use of exotic pipe-vine species that are widely grown as ornamentals. Several other food plants have been reported, but some of them may be in error.

The caterpillars sequester in their bodies toxic compounds from the pipe-vines. Consequently, those larvae and the resulting adults are distasteful to birds, their chief predators. In addition, rows of red-orange spots on the abdomen of the adult connect to glands that produce an acrid odor when squeezed. Its tough body allows the butterfly to survive a predator's "taste test," often without great harm.

Because of this unpalatability, the pipe-vine swallowtail serves as the "model" in one of the best-known cases of Batesian mimicry. Spicebush and black swallowtails, the black female form of the tiger swallowtail, and the red-spotted purple are all thought to derive some protection from their resemblance to *philenor*.

The genus name, *Battus*, according to Opler and Krizek, is that of "a regal Greek family" from Cyrene in North Africa. *Philenor* comes from the Greek meaning "conjugal," or "fond of her husband."

A wide-ranging species, the pipe-vine swallowtail occurs from the Great Lakes states to the Desert Southwest and southern Mexico. Although the larvae feed almost exclusively on pipe-vine, the adults readily visit a variety of different flowers. They seem to prefer those with pink, purple, or orange hues.

The closely related polydamas swallowtail, *B. polydamas*, also called the "gold rim," occurs from South Texas to Argentina. It lacks the prominent tails of the pipe-vine swallowtail and has a row of yellowish spots on each wing. *Polydamas* occasionally ventures northward to Houston, and even farther, but it is extremely rare in our area and should never be expected.

SIZE: 2¾–4 inches, occasionally larger.
DESCRIPTION: Black with hindwings iridescent blue-green.
SIMILAR SPECIES: Other black-colored swallowtails have different spot patterns. Red-spotted purple lacks tails.
SEASON: March–November; several broods.
LARVA: Reddish brown to black, with fleshy tubercles and filaments.
FOOD PLANTS: Various pipe-vines of the genus *Aristolochia*.

1. Dorsal

2. Pair mating, ventral

3. Larva, black form

4. Larva, red form

Zebra Swallowtail

Eurytides marcellus
Pawpaw butterfly

The zebra swallowtail can be mistaken for no other local butterfly as it flits through the woodlands. Extremely long, slender tails stream out behind, and the pale greenish white wings are crossed by black stripes. Red and blue spots further ornament the upperside, while a bright red stripe crosses the underside of the hindwing. The sexes are similar; however, pronounced seasonal variations occur. Butterflies that emerge in early spring are smaller and paler, with shorter tails, while summer broods are larger and darker.

The striking zebra swallowtail ranges throughout the eastern United States but is rare in the North and more abundant in the deep South. Unfortunately, it seldom strays far from the moist woodland habitats where various species of pawpaw grow. It does not adapt well to land clearing or to urban and suburban environments. Thus it is not usually found in Houston, although we have seen it nearby in Chambers and Liberty counties and south of Conroe in Montgomery County. In spite of its rarity within the city, it is too large and too spectacular to ignore in this book. Butterfly enthusiasts should find it throughout much of the year in the forests of East Texas.

The zebra swallowtail was first placed in the genus *Papilio* with all other swallowtails and then was classified as *Graphium marcellus*, the name employed in many older books still in use. It is a member of a worldwide group of about 140 species of "kite swallowtails," most of which are tropical in their distribution. *Marcellus* is the only black-and-white striped species that occurs this far north, although another has been reported at least once in South Texas as a stray from Mexico. Eurytus, according to Opler and Krizek, was a king of Oechalia, while Marcellus was a Roman surname.

The female zebra swallowtail lays her eggs singly on the underside of pawpaw leaves, utilizing both dwarf pawpaw and the larger common pawpaw in Texas. Larvae are notoriously cannibalistic and will eat others found on the same plant. Most butterfly books describe the caterpillar as pea-green with alternating yellow and black bands, but a dark chocolate-brown form with orange and white bands is also common in East Texas. The pupae may be either green or reddish brown, but that color does not relate to the color of the larva. The brown caterpillar pictured here produced a lime-green chrysalis.

Zebra swallowtails fly close to the ground with shallow wingbeats and an erratic flight often described as "batlike," moving more quickly and elusively than it first appears. They feed at a variety of flowers, hanging with rapidly beating wings as they sip the sweet nectar. Males regularly patrol territories near the host plants in search of females, and they may also congregate in small groups at mud puddles or moist stream banks.

SIZE: 2½–4 inches.
DESCRIPTION: White with black stripes; long, slender tails.
SIMILAR SPECIES: Tiger swallowtail is yellow with black stripes. No other black-and-white swallowtail occurs in Houston.
SEASON: March–December. Most common in spring and summer.
LARVA: Two color forms: green with yellow and black bands, or dark brown with orange and white bands.
FOOD PLANTS: Common pawpaw and dwarf pawpaw, as well as other *Asimina* species where they occur.

1. Dorsal

2. Ventral

3. Larva, green form

4. Larva, brown form

Black Swallowtail

Papilio polyxenes
Eastern black swallowtail, American swallowtail

A butterfly of open fields and farmlands, the black swallowtail occurs frequently in urban yards and gardens. It visits a variety of flowers for nectar but seems particularly partial to milkweeds, thistles, and clover. Larvae feed on numerous members of the parsley family, including cultivated carrots, parsley, dill, celery, and fennel. It also utilizes prairie parsley, a common wildflower in the Houston area.

Adults are sexually dimorphic. Although both sexes have black wings bordered with small yellow spots, the wings of the male are also crossed by another band of larger spots that is absent or reduced in the female. Iridescent blue scaling is more prominent on the hindwings of the female, and she is one of several butterflies thought to receive protection by mimicking the distasteful pipe-vine swallowtail.

The first two larval instars resemble bird droppings, as do many of the swallowtail larvae, but later stages range from leaf-green to almost white, with broad black bands dotted with orange or yellow. When abundant, these "parsley-worms" may cause damage to garden crops, but most city gardeners welcome the colorful caterpillars and the lovely adults they will produce.

The butterflies thermoregulate by "dorsal basking," a common trait among many species. When the air is cool, they perch close to or on the ground, with black wings spread and abdomen raised to absorb the heat from the sun. As the temperature rises, the butterflies perch higher and lower the abdomen to shade it, flying more frequently to perch or feed. Most courtship and mating activity takes place from midday through late afternoon.

The eastern *Papilio polyxenes* belongs to a complex group of swallowtails that is more prevalent in the western states. In that region, several similar species and a host of subspecies and forms make iden-

1. Male, dorsal

2. Female, dorsal

3. Larva

tification a much more difficult task.

The genus name, *Papilio*, comes from the Latin for "butterfly" and was first applied by Linnaeus as the genus for all known butterflies. This species takes its name from Polyxena, the daughter of Priamos, King of Troy, in Homer's *Iliad*.

SIZE: 2½–4 inches.

DESCRIPTION: Black wings with rows of yellow spots separated by blue scaling.

SIMILAR SPECIES: Pipe-vine and spice-bush swallowtails have different patterns. Western relatives do not occur in Houston.

SEASON: February–November; several broods.

LARVA: Green to whitish, with black bands dotted with yellow.

FOOD PLANTS: Carrot, parsley, dill, celery, fennel, prairie parsley, and other members of the parsley family, Apiaceae.

Giant Swallowtail
Papilio (Heraclides) cresphontes

As its name implies, the giant swallowtail is the largest of all North American butterflies, although it is occasionally rivaled by female tiger swallowtails. Lepidopterists and authors do not agree on the name for this largely tropical genus. Some place it in *Papilio*; others separate it as *Heraclides*. Similar species occur farther south, and one, the thoas swallowtail, *P. thoas*, ranges northward from the Mexican border to Houston and beyond. It is extremely rare in this area, however, and is almost impossible to distinguish in the field.

Both sexes of the giant swallowtail have dark chocolate-brown wings with yellow markings. A broad diagonal band of yellow spots crosses the forewing and extends onto the base of the hindwing. The underside is mostly yellow.

A widely distributed species, this handsome swallowtail ranges from the eastern U.S. to the Southwest and thence southward through Mexico, Central America, and most of South America. It shares the southern portions of its range with several similarly marked tropical species. A strong flier, it also wanders northward as far as Canada.

The caterpillars of most swallowtails have a mottled, "bird-dropping" pattern in their early instars, but the larva of the giant swallowtail retains that pattern throughout. It is a shiny, wet-looking brown, with mottled whitish saddles across its body. When disturbed, it extends its red, forked osmeterium from behind its head to release a pungent odor. The chrysalis is mottled gray-brown and bears a remarkable resemblance to a broken twig.

Larvae feed on cultivated citrus, lime prickly-ash, Hercules'-club, hop-tree, and other members of the rue family, Rutaceae. The female butterfly may lay four to five hundred eggs that hatch into large, voracious caterpillars. These "orange dogs" occasionally become pests in citrus groves. In the Houston area, we have found the caterpillars on all of the above plants as well as on the spiny trifoliate orange that is widely naturalized in local woodlands.

The giant swallowtail takes its scientific name from Cresphonte, one of the Heraclids who claimed to be descendants of Hercules in Greek mythology. Now this butterfly of almost mythical proportions visits backyard gardens throughout our area. It utilizes nectar from a variety of blossoms, but Ajilvsgi suggests butterfly bush (*Buddleia*) and lantana as two of its favorites.

SIZE: 4–6 inches.
DESCRIPTION: Dark brown with bands of yellow spots.
SIMILAR SPECIES: Tropical relatives of similar appearance are not expected in Houston.
SEASON: Almost throughout the year; several broods.
LARVA: 2½ inches; brown-and-white, "bird-dropping" pattern.
FOOD PLANTS: Cultivated citrus, trifoliate orange, lime prickly-ash, Hercules'-club, common hop-tree.

1. Dorsal

2. Ventral

3. Larva

Tiger Swallowtail
Papilio (Pterourus) glaucus
Eastern tiger swallowtail

The tiger swallowtail appears to have been the first North American insect portrayed in art by European visitors to this continent. John White, the commander of Sir Walter Raleigh's third expedition to Virginia, painted it on Roanoke Island in 1587. With its bright yellow wings crossed by black stripes, the butterfly is unmistakable.

Similar forms found in the western states and in the North are now recognized by most authors as distinct species. These two, the western tiger swallowtail, *Papilio rutulus*, and the Canadian tiger swallowtail, *P. canadensis*, do not occur in the southeastern states or in our area. The two-tailed swallowtail, *P. multicaudatus*, ranges into West Texas but is not to be expected in the Houston region.

Thus it appears that identification of the tiger swallowtail should be a simple matter. There is, however, a complicating factor: males are always yellow, but females may be either yellow or black. The black form is rare in the northern portions of the tiger swallowtail's range, but it may predominate in the South. Both occur in Houston. In most cases, enough of the striped pattern is visible against the darker background to be recognizable, especially on the underside of the wings.

The coloration is apparently caused by a gene on the Y chromosome, so that each female is the color of her mother. The characteristic is not transmitted to males. The black form is thought to derive added protection by mimicking the inedible pipe-vine swallowtail. Field studies have shown that males prefer yellow females as mates, but the black females are less vulnerable to attack by birds. The two effects balance, and both color forms persist in nature.

1. Male, dorsal

2. Black female, dorsal

3. Dark female, dorsal

Tiger swallowtails inhabit deciduous woodlands and stream corridors, where they often fly high amid the vegetation. Males patrol their routes in search of females, with most courtship and mating occurring in late afternoon. In spite of their preference for wooded areas, the butterflies are frequently found within the city, where they visit a wide variety of flowers. Azaleas, honeysuckles, buttonbush, milkweeds, and thistles appear to be among their favorites.

Females lay their eggs singly on a wide variety of trees and shrubs throughout their range, but we have found them most commonly on ash and black cherry in this region. Young larvae have the characteristic "bird-dropping" pattern; mature larvae are green with two large eyespots on the swollen thorax. They feed primarily at night and rest during daylight hours on silken pads laid down within rolled leaves. The chrysalis may be brown, tan, or green. Adult butterflies will probably live no more than two weeks after emerging, but they will have started the process over again. In spite of their short lives, they will soon be followed by another brood.

4. Dark female, ventral

SIZE: 3½–5½ inches.

DESCRIPTION: Male yellow with black stripes. Female similar, or black with striped pattern partially obscured.

SIMILAR SPECIES: Other tiger-striped swallowtails do not normally occur in Houston. Dark female somewhat resembles the spicebush and pipe-vine swallowtails.

SEASON: March–November; probably three broods.

LARVA: Early stages brown and white; later stages green with false eyespots.

FOOD PLANTS: Ash, black cherry. Many others reported.

5. Larva

Spicebush Swallowtail

Papilio (Pterourus) troilus
Green-clouded swallowtail

The spicebush swallowtail, along with the tiger and Palamedes swallowtails, is placed in the broad genus *Papilio* by some present-day authors and in the more limited grouping *Pterourus* by others. A recent checklist published by the North American Butterfly Association takes the former taxonomic stand, while lists from the Lepidopterists' Society support the latter. Such discrepancies illustrate the lack of uniformity in both scientific and popular butterfly nomenclature. Troilus, the source of the spicebush swallowtail's specific epithet, was the son of Priamos, King of Troy, in the *Iliad*.

The broad, black hindwings of the adult butterfly are bordered with pale greenish, crescent-shaped spots. Hindwings of the male are clouded with a blue-green band, while those of the female have a blue shading. Two bands of large orange spots mark the underside of both sexes. *Troilus* is considered one of several species that receive some degree of protection by mimicking the pipe-vine swallowtail.

It is the caterpillar of this common insect, however, that often attracts the most interest. Once it has molted from its earlier instars and shed its "bird-dropping" camouflage, it is bright green with enormous, staring "eyes." Two large orange spots on the enlarged thorax are centered with black "pupils" and appear quite realistic. It would be easy to see how they might intimidate a potential predator that fears it has tackled too ferocious a prey. Those "eyes," of course, are merely ornamentation; the functional eyes are tiny dots on the much smaller head. Behind the eyespots are another pair of orange patches and then a series of blue dots down the abdominal segments of the larva.

Before pupation, the green caterpillar

1. Male, dorsal

2. Female, dorsal

3. Ventral

4. Larva

turns bright yellow but retains its characteristic pattern. It then wanders about looking for a place to attach itself and transform into a chrysalis. A number of butterfly larvae undergo such confusing short-term color changes, and this pre-pupation state is not mentioned or depicted in many books currently in use.

Spicebush and sassafras are usually mentioned as the larval food plants of the spicebush swallowtail, and these are, indeed, the primary ones in the woodlands of East Texas. In Houston and the surrounding suburban areas, however, the introduced camphor-tree plays a major role. The trees are widely planted in residential neighborhoods, and many harbor developing broods of spicebush swallowtail larvae. The larvae feed primarily at night, hiding during the day within a rolled leaf stitched with silk. Red bay is also listed as a food plant, but in our area it seems to be utilized much more heavily by the Palamedes swallowtail.

The spicebush swallowtail inhabits woodlands, forested swamps, and stream banks from the Canadian border to the Gulf Coast and central Texas, but it also frequents yards and gardens within the city. It visits a variety of flowers, beating its wings slowly as it clings to the blossoms and uncoiling its long proboscis to sip nectar from their throats.

SIZE: 3½–4½ inches.

DESCRIPTION: Male hindwing washed with blue-green; female, with blue. Underside of hindwing with two rows of orange spots.

SIMILAR SPECIES: Compare with patterns of black and pipe-vine swallowtails and with the black female of the tiger swallowtail.

SEASON: March–November.

LARVA: Green with large eyespots.

FOOD PLANTS: Spicebush and sassafras in woodlands, camphor-tree in residential areas. Red bay and sweet bay also reported.

Palamedes Swallowtail
Papilio (Pterourus) palamedes
Laurel swallowtail

The large, broad-winged Palamedes swallowtail is a spectacular butterfly of the wooded southeastern swamps, ranging around the Atlantic and Gulf coasts from southern New Jersey to Texas and sparingly into Mexico. A strong flier, it may also wander far inland. In the wetlands, it nectars avidly at such common wildflowers as pickerel-weed and iris, but it also favors azaleas and thistles. It may even soar through backyard gardens, seeking other seasonal blooms. Newly emerged males congregate in large numbers at mud puddles to sip water and dissolved mineral salts.

Named for Palamedes, son of Nauplius, mythical King of Euboia, the Palamedes swallowtail is placed by some authors in the genus *Papilio* and by others in the genus *Pterourus* with the tiger and spicebush swallowtails and their close relatives.

The sexes are marked alike, their brownish black wings rimmed with yellow spots and crossed by another broad yellow band. The underside of the hindwing has a unique narrow orange stripe at the base, parallel to the abdomen, that distinguishes this species from all other dark swallowtails when it perches with closed wings or flutters at a flower.

The caterpillar is green with two large eyespots, much like those of the spicebush swallowtail. The fake "eyes" seem to protrude more, however, and the orange spots behind them are darker, as is the reddish underside of the entire larva.

Red bay is the major larval food plant in eastern Texas and throughout most of the range. Sassafras is apparently used on occasion, as is sweet bay, although some larvae would take neither in laboratory experiments. Cultivated avocado is also mentioned by some authors. As with several other swallowtail caterpillars, those

1. Dorsal

of *palamedes* rest during the day on a pad of silk on the upperside of a leaf, rolling the edges of the leaf upward to provide concealment.

SIZE: 3½–5½ inches.

DESCRIPTION: Blackish, with broad yellow band.

SIMILAR SPECIES: Male black swallowtail has spotted abdomen, lacks basal orange stripe below.

SEASON: April–December; two or three broods.

LARVA: Green with large eyespots. More red below than spicebush swallowtail.

FOOD PLANTS: Red bay. Sassafras, sweet bay, and avocado also reported.

2. Larva

3. Ventral

Whites and Sulphurs

FAMILY PIERIDAE

A large family of nearly worldwide distribution, the Pieridae are most diverse in the tropics. Some, however, fly even above the Arctic Circle, and others inhabit high mountaintops, adapting to a very short summer season with chill winds and low nighttime temperatures. Most authors count approximately eleven hundred species throughout the world, but others list as many as two thousand, illustrating the lack of a uniform taxonomy. Approximately sixty occur in North America.

Most pierids are medium to small butterflies with white, yellow, or orange wings. They are usually sparsely marked with black. It was probably one of the common yellow European species, the sulphurs, that first led to the name "butterfly."

Many family members show strong sexual dimorphism, with males and females having different markings. Under ultraviolet light, they also exhibit other patterns that are apparently useful to them in species and sex recognition and in courtship. Butterflies see in the ultraviolet portion of the spectrum, detecting wavelengths that are invisible to human eyes.

In addition to sexual differences, species may have distinctive seasonal forms. In temperate regions, butterflies from the spring brood may appear quite different from those that develop in the summer. In the tropics, the forms correspond to wet and dry seasons.

North American pierids fall into three subfamilies, although some authors combine the first two. The Pierinae contains the "whites," their white wings marked with black; the Anthocharinae contains the "orangetips" and "marbles," whose white wings are often tipped with orange and marbled below with green; and the Coliadinae contains the yellow "sulphurs," spelled "sulfurs" in some publications.

A little sulphur, Eurema lisa, *sips nectar from a colorful penta in the authors' backyard butterfly garden.*

All of the adult butterflies feed on flower nectar. In addition, males flock around mud puddles and stream banks, a social behavior the females rarely exhibit. Males patrol an area regularly in search of potential mates, usually seducing them with fragrant pheromones. Pierids tend to have short larval periods, developing rapidly and producing several overlapping broods during the warm seasons of the year. Some are also strong fliers known for long-distance, directional mass flights, although the actual dynamics of these migrations remain to be determined. As a result, many of the Pieridae are widely distributed over a large range.

The eggs of the whites and sulphurs are long and spindle-shaped, while the pupae are attached to silken mats and suspended by girdles of silk. The head of the pupa, or chrysalis, has a pointed projection.

Caterpillars lack the ornamentation displayed by many other families. They are usually green and covered with very short setae, or hairs. Larvae of the sulphurs feed primarily on legumes, family Fabaceae, while the majority of the whites and orangetips utilize plants of the mustard family, Brassicaceae. Some of the latter become pests on cabbage and other cultivated crops. They are apparently distasteful to potential predators because they incorporate mustard oils into their body tissues.

1. Checkered white, female   2. Cloudless sulphur, male

Checkered White

Pontia protodice
Common white

The checkered white was formerly placed in the genus *Pieris*, but most references now include it in *Pontia*. The latter takes its name from an area along the western edge of the Black Sea. A wide-ranging species, the checkered white occurs across much of the U.S. and northern Mexico. Some authors suggest, however, that it was more common before being displaced by the introduced cabbage white. Such population trends are difficult to follow because the butterflies are strong fliers, capable of expanding into new regions or increasing their range northward sporadically during the summer season. Thus their abundance and the limits of their range vary from year to year.

The checkered white is not one of the more common butterflies in Houston.

Despite its wide distribution, it is absent from much of Louisiana and eastern Texas, ranging into our area occasionally from the west.

The sexes differ markedly. Females are heavily checkered above with black or charcoal-brown, the underside of the hindwings lightly shaded with yellow-green or tan along the veins. Males are less profusely marked, with lightly checkered forewings and plain white hindwings. Broods in the spring and fall, during shorter photoperiods, are smaller and more heavily patterned, usually with gray-green veining on the underwings.

Checkered whites lack the scent glands of many other butterflies and identify their mates by ultraviolet reflection rather than by pheromones. Females reflect more UV light because of different wing pigments, and the males therefore chase those adults that reflect the appropriate pattern.

Females lay their yellowish, spindle-

1. Female, dorsal

2. Female (left) and male, ventral

3. Larva

shaped eggs on a wide variety of plants in the mustard family. Virginia peppergrass and others in the genus *Lepidium* are among the most popular, but cultivated cabbage, broccoli, and cauliflower are also used. Thus the checkered white can become a pest on such agricultural crops.

The caterpillar is blue-green or purplish green with four yellow stripes and numerous small black tubercles. Feeding on the buds, flowers, seed pods, and tender leaves of their many food plants, the larvae grow rapidly and produce several overlapping broods of butterflies each year.

The checkered white prefers open, weedy fields and roadsides, where the adults visit a wide variety of flowers for nectar. They also flock to mud puddles to sip the salt-rich solutions. Like most butterflies, they are short lived, and they will typically survive no more than a week. During that time, however, they will have mated and begun a new generation soon to follow.

SIZE: 1¼–2 inches.
DESCRIPTION: Female heavily checkered on upperside; male lightly marked on forewings only.
SIMILAR SPECIES: Similar western relatives do not occur in Houston. See also cabbage white and falcate orangetip.
SEASON: March–November; several overlapping broods.
LARVA: Blue-green, with yellow stripes and black dots.
FOOD PLANTS: Virginia peppergrass and many other wild mustards, cabbage, broccoli, cauliflower.

Cabbage White

Pieris rapae
Cabbage butterfly, European cabbage butterfly

One of the best-known and most widely distributed of all North American lepidoptera, the cabbage white is an immigrant to this continent. A few specimens were first collected near Quebec, Canada, in 1860. Brown and Heineman suggest the species was probably introduced shortly before that on cabbages included among the food stores of a ship arriving from Europe. By 1881, it had spread westward to the plains and southward to northern Florida. In a few more years, it had crossed the grasslands and mountains to colonize Montana and Colorado. There is some evidence that it may also have been introduced on the West Coast at about the same time.

Now the cabbage white blankets most of the continent, from central Canada to the southern states. It remains largely absent, however, from the southern portions of Florida, Louisiana, and Texas. We include it among the butterflies of Houston because it occasionally appears around the city and because of its ecological significance. We have encountered it a few times in vegetable gardens north and west of Houston. These populations, like the original immigrants, may well have arrived as eggs, larvae, or pupae on farm produce. The species occurs more commonly in the central and northern portions of the state.

The cabbage white ranges widely in Europe, Asia, and northern Africa. It has also been introduced to Australia. The genus, *Pieris*, was the name of a mythical Greek muse, while *rapae* comes from the Latin *rapa*, for "turnip." Some authors place the species in the genus *Artogeia*.

The chalky white wings of the butterfly are tipped with black above. The male has a single small black spot on the fore-

1. Ventral

wing; the female, two. The tip of the forewing and the hindwing beneath are uniformly shaded with pale yellow or yellow-green.

As its name implies, the cabbage white includes the cabbage among its larval food plants. However, its voracious caterpillars feed on almost any wild or cultivated member of the mustard family and can become pests in crops of broccoli, Brussels sprouts, cauliflower, radishes, turnips, and collards. Plants in the caper family and nasturtiums are also widely used.

There are two or three broods in the northern portions of the range, as many as seven or eight in the South. Indeed, the cabbage white flies almost throughout the year in warm climates. The female may live for up to three weeks and lay as many as seven hundred eggs before she dies. The peak in egg production occurs about one week after she emerges from the chrysalis.

Eggs are laid singly on the host leaves, and tests show that the female seeks out plants in vigorous growth, with succulent leaves and abundant protein for the developing young. The pungent mustard oils provide the stimulus for egg laying and feeding, and caterpillars in the laboratory have eaten filter paper and other substances soaked in these strong oils. The larvae are green or bluish green with narrow yellow stripes and are covered with short hairs.

Cabbage whites inhabit open areas, including weedy fields, roadsides, and urban or suburban gardens, visiting a variety of flowers for nectar. Although their flight appears slow and erratic, they sometimes travel many miles, especially when assisted by strong winds. They are thus capable of quickly establishing new colonies, where they can become pests on cultivated crops. A tiny braconid wasp is one of the major parasites of the caterpillar and helps keep populations in check. Parasitic wasps and flies play that

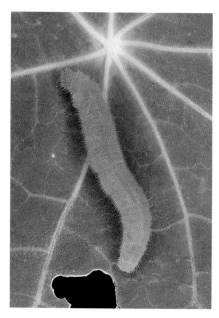

2. Larva

role in controlling many of our lepidoptera, fine-tuning the delicate balance of nature.

SIZE: 1½–2 inches.

DESCRIPTION: White with dark tip on forewing and one (male) or two (female) black spots. Underside of hindwing yellowish.

SIMILAR SPECIES: Checkered white has checkered pattern above, with underwings patterned along the veins. Falcate orangetip has sickle-shaped forewings, green pattern along veins below.

SEASON: Throughout most of the year; many broods.

LARVA: Green with thin yellow stripes; covered with short hairs.

FOOD PLANTS: Most wild and cultivated Brassicaceae: cabbage, cauliflower, Brussels sprouts, radish, turnip, collard, mustard, peppergrass, nasturtium.

Great Southern White
Ascia monuste
Southern white

The great southern white, as its name implies, is a southern species that ranges across much of tropical America. It occurs commonly throughout the year in the Rio Grande Valley and in Florida and then expands northward along the coasts in summer, breeding as it goes and generating new broods that will not survive the winter. It also reaches far inland on occasion. It is during these migrations that *Ascia monuste* is most likely to be seen in the Houston area. It occurs more frequently along the coast near Freeport or Galveston.

Larger than the checkered and cabbage whites, the male great southern white is pure white with jagged, scalloped black margins on the upperside of the forewings. The hindwings beneath are creamy yellow. Females are dimorphic, with a much darker form emerging during the longer days of spring and summer. It is heavily clouded with black scaling both above and below. The late fall form resembles the white male, but with more black on the margins and a dark spot on the forewing.

Most abundant in the salt marshes and coastal dunes, the larvae of the great southern white feed on saltwort (*Batis*) and sea-rocket, also called beach cabbage (*Cakile*). Inland, they consume Virginia peppergrass and a wide variety of other plants in the mustard family. They may also infest cultivated cabbage, broccoli, Brussels sprouts, cauliflower, radish, and nasturtium. The caterpillars vary greatly in color, but are usually yellow or orange with stripes of dark gray or purplish green.

The larvae and resulting adults are apparently distasteful to many predators because of the assimilation of strong mustard oils and thus join a large group of white butterflies similarly protected. Their common color and pattern are an

1. Male, dorsal

2. Male (left) and female mating, ventral

example of a phenomenon called Müllerian mimicry, in which a number of protected species evolve a common appearance so that predators more quickly learn to avoid them. This is quite different from Batesian mimicry, in which a palatable species gains protection by mimicking the pattern of a distasteful one.

Scott documents the migration of the great southern white in detail. The flights apparently take place in response to crowding. Females mate soon after emerging, and the migrations usually start at nine or ten o'clock the following morning. Some mass flights last only a few hours, but others continue for as long as ten hours the first day and several hours the next, ranging as far as one hundred miles. The butterflies fly steadily along, rarely stopping to feed at flowers. They appear to follow natural routes such as beaches and roads, but not all strike off in the same direction. Once a route is selected, however, the migrants

follow it faithfully, flying from three to ten feet above the ground.

Not all individuals migrate. Some merely disperse locally, while others strike out for new territory. Reaching their destination, the females lay their yellow, spindle-shaped eggs singly or in groups on the leaves of an appropriate food plant. Adapted to a beach or salt-marsh environment, those eggs can tolerate short immersions in salt water. Tagging studies show that adult males normally live about five days, while females live eight to ten days. By that time, however, they have left another generation, perhaps to continue the annual dispersal farther north.

3. Female, dorsal

4. Female, dorsal

5. Female, dorsal

6. Larva

SIZE: 1¾–2½ inches.

DESCRIPTION: Male white with jagged black forewing margin. Female variously clouded with gray.

SIMILAR SPECIES: Checkered white and cabbage white are smaller and have different black markings.

SEASON: Mainly late summer and fall in our area; all year in deep South Texas.

LARVA: Orange or yellow, with gray or purplish green stripes.

FOOD PLANTS: Saltwort, sea-rocket, Virginia peppergrass, cabbage and related vegetable crops in the family Brassicaceae, nasturtium.

Falcate Orangetip
Paramidea midea
Falcate orange tip, Falcate orange-tip

There is presently a great deal of disagreement about the nomenclature applied to this pretty little spring butterfly. Most books now in use give it the scientific name *Anthocharis midea*, while older publications call it *A. genutia*. Miller and Brown, in *A Catalogue/Checklist of the Butterflies of America North of Mexico*, however, place the falcate orangetip in the genus *Falcapica*. Ferris prepared a supplement to that checklist in 1989, applying the genus *Paramidea* and noting that it predated *Falcapica* and thus took scientific precedence. Miller, in *The Common Names of North American Butterflies* (1992), adopts Ferris' stand, but many recent authors disagree and prefer *Anthocharis*. We have used the name applied in the amended checklist of the Lepidopterists' Society by Ferris.

The common name, too, illustrates the lack of uniform standards for butterfly names. Unlike the authors of bird books, who have long followed the edicts of the American Ornithologists' Union, writers on butterflies have no single standard. Miller's list of common names was endorsed by the Lepidopterists' Society, while the new North American Butterfly Association uses a different set of names. Thus the forms "orangetip," "orange tip," and "orange-tip" all appear in print.

Whatever we choose to call it, the falcate orangetip is unmistakable. The forewings are hooked, or falcate, and those of the male are tipped with orange. The tip is also bordered with small black marks, and a single black spot adorns the cell of the forewing. Females lack the orange wingtips, but the black markings remain. The underside of the hindwing is broadly marbled with green in both sexes. Other orangetips and marbles occupy various regions of the country and are similarly marked beneath, but none occurs in the Houston area.

The falcate orangetip is one of the first butterflies of spring, emerging as early as the last few days of February in this area and flying through the early weeks of March. About the time the yellow jessamine blooms along the trails, it lights the open woodlands with its bright, gossamer wings. Even cool daytime temperatures do not deter it, although it prefers to fly in dappled sunlight. We have watched a wood filled with fluttering butterflies grow quiet when a cloud obscures the sun. The orangetips quickly hang beneath the leaves until sunlight returns.

Males patrol a regular route among the trees, flying with a slow, fluttering, erratic beat. Females are less visible as they frequent patches of their food plants, members of the mustard family. Many mustards are used throughout the orangetip's range, but bitter-cresses, *Cardamine* species, are among its favorites. In East Texas, we find the eggs and larvae primarily on spring-cress, *Cardamine rhomboidea*.

Several authors note that females can detect other butterflies' eggs on a host and never lay more than one egg per plant. However, on many occasions we have found several eggs or small larvae on a single plant. The orange, spindle-shaped egg is usually laid on the pedicel at the base of the flower, and the developing larva consumes flowers, buds, and developing seed pods. It is seldom found feeding on the leaves. The caterpillar is striped with blue and green and dotted with small black tubercles. It also has a wide white stripe down each side and an orange stripe on the back. The slender, thornlike chrysalis has a long spike on the head.

Range maps in recent butterfly books indicate the falcate orangetip is absent from southern Louisiana and southeast

1. Male, ventral

2. Larva

Texas, its range circumventing the Houston area to reach the coast farther south and continuing to the Rio Grande Valley. However, we have found it to be fairly common in early spring in western Chambers County along the Trinity River bottom and in northern Harris County. We even encounter it occasionally in Houston's Memorial Park.

The delightful little falcate orangetip appears as a harbinger of spring, sipping nectar from the earliest spring flowers. It quickly raises its single brood and is gone for the remainder of the year. The pupa formed in March will remain until the following spring, and some butterflies may not emerge for yet another year.

SIZE: 1⅜–1¾ inches.
DESCRIPTION: Hooked forewing tipped with orange in male; underside of hindwing marbled with green in both sexes.
SIMILAR SPECIES: Other white butterflies are larger, without falcate wings.
SEASON: March; single brood.
LARVA: Green with blue, white, and orange stripes.
FOOD PLANTS: Spring-cress and other wild mustards.

Orange Sulphur
Colias eurytheme
Alfalfa butterfly

The orange sulphur, also called the alfalfa butterfly, is one of the most widely distributed and most abundant species in North America. Although rare east of the Appalachians before 1890, it has colonized virtually all of the East Coast and now occurs from the Atlantic to the Pacific and from Canada to central Mexico. It inhabits open fields, marshes, and roadsides throughout the Houston area. Multiply brooded, the orange sulphur appears almost continuously from March to November or December and nectars at a succession of flowers through the year.

The male is orange above with solid black borders. A black spot ornaments the forewing cell; a red spot, the hindwing. The wings beneath are more greenish yellow, the hindwing containing a silver, pink-edged spot, usually with another smaller satellite spot beside it. Females are dimorphic. The orange form is similar to the male, but with the black borders containing orange spots. A white form has greenish white wings with the same pattern.

Seasonal forms also exist. Those emerging after the short photoperiods in early spring are smaller and lighter and have narrower dark borders. They may, in fact, look much like the clouded sulphur, *Colias philodice*, which has yellow wings. That species, too, ranges across most of the continent. Normally all forms of the orange sulphur have some orange shading, but hybrids also occur, and the situation can be confusing. That complication is not a problem in our area, however, because the clouded sulphur is not normally found in eastern or southern Texas.

The orange sulphur lays its eggs on a variety of plants in the pea family, Fabaceae. Alfalfa is a favorite, but white sweet-clover, white clover, and vetches also prove popular. The butterflies are strong fliers that cover long distances, and they readily colonize new areas with cultivated legume crops, at times becoming an agricultural pest. The caterpillars are bright green with a white line along each side, the stripes bordered below with black.

The breeding biology of the ubiquitous orange sulphur has been studied extensively, and Scott provides a summary of the intricate system. Nitrogen that goes into the orange pigment of the normally colored female is instead used by the white female to produce more stored fat and larger eggs that lead to faster development. Males apparently prefer orange females for mating, but the white ones produce new broods more rapidly. They have a reproductive advantage in northern populations where the season is short, and they are more plentiful there than in the South, where the orange form dominates.

Ultraviolet reflectance also plays an important part in courtship and mating of the orange sulphur, since butterfly eyes are sensitive to those wavelengths. Only the male reflects UV light from the upper surface of the wings, and the female must see that UV pattern to accept her mate. The male, on the other hand, is attracted to the greenish yellow color on the underside of the wings and is repelled by ultraviolet reflection. In addition, the male produces a pheromone that induces the female to take a mating position. Even when the visible wing color of the male was changed in laboratory experiments, he remained acceptable to the female as long as the UV reflectance pattern was preserved.

The male clouded sulphur does not reflect ultraviolet, a factor that would normally prohibit interbreeding with a female orange sulphur. Experiments show, however, that females less than an hour old cannot distinguish between the two.

1. Male, dorsal

2. Female, dorsal

3. Male, ventral

Thus most hybrids of this type occur with newly emerged females. The process usually produces sterile female offspring.

There is a smaller barrier to interbreeding between a male orange sulphur and a female clouded sulphur. The male chooses his mate by color of the underwings alone, and the female does not distinguish the difference in the male's UV pattern. This type of hybridization takes place often where both species occur, and the sex ratio of the resulting offspring is normal. Because the hybrid female tends to mate with a male orange sulphur, and because the genes governing color and UV reflectance are all on the male's X chromosome, those chromosomes do not ordinarily end up in the other species. The two species, the orange and clouded sulphurs, thus remain distinct despite hybridization.

4. Female, ventral

SIZE: 1½–2½ inches.

DESCRIPTION: Male orange with black border; silver spot below. Female orange or white, with spotted black border.

SIMILAR SPECIES: Clouded sulphur and other *Colias* not normally found in Houston. Sleepy orange has no hindwing spot.

SEASON: March–November; several broods.

LARVA: Green with white lateral stripe.

FOOD PLANTS: Alfalfa, sweet-clover, white clover, vetch, other members of the family Fabaceae.

5. Larva

Dog Face
Colias (Zerene) cesonia
Southern dogface, Dog's head butterfly

Some taxonomists place the dog face in the genus *Colias* with many of the other sulphurs; others segregate it in the more limited *Zerene*. All of the common names, of which there are many in the literature, reflect the profile of a dog's head on the forewing. Both sexes are yellow, with broad black borders outlining the "poodle," but the female has more diffuse dark markings and a less sharply defined face. A black spot provides the eye. The wings are sharply pointed, even slightly falcate, not rounded as are those of the other sulphurs. Spring and summer broods are yellow beneath; the underwings of the winter brood are flushed with rosy pink. Rare white females or yellow ones lacking the black border have been collected, but we have seen neither in the Houston area.

The dog face ranges from the southern states through Central and South America. It has several broods each year, the last one in the fall delaying reproduction until the following spring. These overwintering butterflies can appear whenever temperatures are warm enough. A strong flier, the dog face colonizes the northern states during the summer months, even reaching irregularly into Canada. Most of these immigrants fail to breed or produce only one more generation, dying out again as winter comes.

The male dog face attracts his mate with a vivid UV pattern on his wings and with fragrant pheromones. The mated female lays her eggs on a variety of plants in the family Fabaceae, including false indigo (often called lead plant), prairie clover, white clover, and alfalfa. Farther south, in Corpus Christi State Park, we found the larvae abundant on Texas kidneywood. The mature caterpillars are highly variable, but most are green, usu-

1. Male, dorsal

2. Male, ventral

3. Larva

ally marked with yellow and black crossbars or longitudinal lines.

Dog face butterflies stop at a variety of flowers to sip nectar, but they are fast fliers and soon dart off again. Both sexes, however, frequent wet patches of earth, and they may remain almost motionless there for hours. Bailowitz and Brock describe this activity well: "During the heat of the day they often participate in puddle parties."

SIZE: 2–2¾ inches.

DESCRIPTION: Yellow, with sharply pointed wings. Broad black border of forewing outlines a dog's head in profile, a black spot providing the eye. Female with markings more diffuse.

SIMILAR SPECIES: Other large sulphurs have rounded wings.

SEASON: March–December; occasional all year.

LARVA: Green, variable. Usually with yellow and black stripes or crossbars.

FOOD PLANTS: Family Fabaceae: false indigo, prairie clover, white clover, alfalfa, others.

Cloudless Sulphur
Phoebis sennae
Cloudless giant sulphur

This giant sulphur is one of the more common and distinctive Houston butterflies. It occurs virtually throughout the year, and even on warm winter days it may come sailing through suburban yards and gardens, looking for nectar-filled flowers at which to feed. It visits a wide variety of blossoms, but seems particularly fond of lantana, Turk's-cap and other native mallow species, cultivated hibiscus, red tropical sage, zinnia, and goldenrod. An inhabitant of open, weedy fields and roadsides, it also congregates at mud puddles for moisture and salts.

Larger than the other common sulphurs, the male is clear lemon-yellow above, without the dark borders that characterize the smaller pierids. It has elongated forewings that give it a strangely triangular shape when perched, an appearance that is immediately distinctive. Females range in color from darker yellow to white, the latter form being more common in the summer and the former in the winter. Females have the margins of the upperside lightly bordered with dark spots, and both sexes have a single or double pink-rimmed silver spot in the center of the hindwing beneath.

Several other tropical giant sulphurs range into South Texas, and these may occasionally stray northward to Houston. We include the large orange sulphur, *Phoebis agarithe*, in this book, and the orange-barred sulphur, *P. philea*, is also recorded as a rare visitor to the area. Both have more orange on the upperside of the wings and are more heavily marked than the cloudless sulphur.

A strong flier, the cloudless sulphur migrates far beyond its normal year-round range. A native from Argentina through tropical America to the southern states, it moves northward in the spring and summer. Breeding as it goes, it may even reach the Canadian border. Most of these migrants perish with the cold, but as autumn approaches, some of the last brood begin a return migration, arriving back in the South to survive the winter. Brown and Heineman also report large flights of cloudless sulphurs hundreds of miles out over the Caribbean Sea, perhaps moving from island to island or striking out for South America.

Scott records in detail the courtship behavior. The male patrols a regular route in search of a female, then hovers over her as she lands, touching her with his wings and legs to release seductive pheromones. An unreceptive female spreads her wings and raises her abdomen to prevent mating. After mating with a willing female, the male flies off, the female still dangling passively beneath him.

Females deposit their eggs on legumes such as partridge pea and various species

1. Male, ventral, emerging from pupa

2. Larva

of senna. The latter are placed in the genus *Cassia* in most references; however, Hatch, Gandhi, and Brown, in their 1990 *Checklist of the Vascular Plants of Texas*, divide that former genus into *Chamaecrista* and *Senna*. Indeed, the scientific name of the cloudless sulphur comes from "senna," the common name for most of its food plants. The genus *Phoebis* is the namesake of Phoebe, daughter of Gaea and sister of Apollo.

Larvae of the cloudless sulphur vary from bright green to yellowish and are dotted with small black tubercles. Yellow stripes usually adorn the sides, along with blue spots or short transverse bands. The easily recognizable chrysalis is strongly pointed at both ends, and the deep wing cases give it a hunchbacked appearance. It, too, varies greatly in color, from green to pink, sometimes banded with yellow.

Several subspecies of the cloudless sulphur have been described. The nominate *P. s. sennae* occurs in the Caribbean,

while *P. s. eubule* ranges throughout the southeastern states. *P. s. marcellina* reaches South Texas from the tropics and is darker and more heavily marked beneath. These subspecies combine with various color forms of the female to present a very complex system. Most amateur butterfly enthusiasts will be satisfied with simply calling them all "cloudless sulphurs," enjoying their bright, year-round beauty.

SIZE: 2¼–3 inches.
DESCRIPTION: Male unmarked lemon-yellow above; females either yellow or white, with limited dark markings not forming a continuous border.
SIMILAR SPECIES: Other rare giant sulphurs more orange.
SEASON: Throughout the year.
LARVA: Green, with yellow side stripes, black dots, and variable blue markings.
FOOD PLANTS: Senna species, partridge pea.

Large Orange Sulphur
Phoebis agarithe
Orange giant sulphur, Cloudless orange

1. Male, ventral

This large, showy butterfly is not a regular resident of Houston. It ranges throughout much of lowland tropical America, from Peru northward to South Texas and Florida, and occasionally strays to our area and beyond in mid to late summer. Less migratory than the cloudless sulphur, it is nevertheless a strong flier and has been reported on rare occasions from as far north as South Dakota and Wisconsin. The large orange sulphur moves most frequently through central Texas, and we have seen it along wooded stream banks and in patches of flowers in the Hill Country near Austin. Williams reports it in small numbers from Victoria and Calhoun counties, but specimens have also been captured near Huntsville.

The male is a clear, unmarked golden orange above. Females vary from yellow-orange to creamy white, the latter form shaded with salmon-pink scales. The forewing of the female, both above and below, and the underside of the male's forewing bear a distinctive straight, continuous submarginal row of dark smudges. This line of spots is broken and offset on the orange-barred sulphur, *Phoebis philea*, and the argante giant sulphur, *P. argante*, two other large tropical species that stray northward less frequently than does *P. agarithe*.

The large orange sulphur frequents a wide variety of flowers, including those of suburban gardens, and descends readily to sip moisture at puddles. Larval food plants include woody legumes placed by many authors in the mimosa family, Mimosaceae. Other botanists consider this group to be a subfamily of the Fabaceae. Members of the genus *Pithecellobium*, which contains the Texas ebony, appear to be the most frequent hosts, but *Inga* and *Cassia* (now *Senna*) are also listed in several references.

An uncommon Houston visitor, the large orange sulphur would be easily missed among the much more abundant cloudless sulphurs. Its large size and great beauty, however, make it worth the painstaking search.

SIZE: 2¼–2¾ inches.
DESCRIPTION: Male unmarked yellow-orange above. Female yellow-orange or pinkish white, with straight line of spots on forewing above and below. Winter brood more heavily marked than others.
SIMILAR SPECIES: Male cloudless sulphur is lemon-yellow; female lacks diagonal line of dark forewing spots. Orange-barred sulphur and argante giant sulphur have dark spot row broken and offset on forewing below.
SEASON: Rare vagrant in summer and fall.
LARVA: Green, with yellow stripe on side edged below with black or dark green.
FOOD PLANTS: Woody legumes including *Pithecellobium*, *Inga*, and perhaps *Senna* species.

Little Sulphur
Eurema lisa
Little yellow

This charming little yellow pierid occurs abundantly throughout the Houston area in virtually every season of the year. Ajilvsgi calls it "probably the South's most plentiful butterfly." Some recent authors have placed it in the genus *Pyrisitia*, but Ferris suggests in his 1989 supplement to the Lepidopterists' Society checklist that *Pyrisitia* is best considered a subgeneric name under *Eurema*.

The little sulphur is sexually dimorphic. The male is bright yellow with solid black borders on the upperside. Females are paler yellow (or less frequently white) with reduced, irregular borders on the hindwings. A tiny black spot or dash on the upper forewing and a diffuse reddish brown patch near the margin of the hindwing beneath are unique to this species. Other small yellow *Eurema* sulphurs that might rarely stray into the region lack those diagnostic marks.

A resident of dry fields, roadsides, and open woodland margins, the little sulphur lays its eggs on various plants of the family Fabaceae. Several senna species are common hosts, and partridge pea and powderpuff are used extensively in Houston. Ajilvsgi adds bluebonnets and deer pea vetch to the list, while some authors cite clovers as alternate food plants. The caterpillar is bright grass-green, with one or two white lines along each side.

As with many of the common whites and sulphurs, mating behavior is well documented. Males patrol regular routes throughout the warm daylight hours, flying even on cloudy, windy days. The slow, rather erratic flight is usually low to the ground. Only the male reflects ultraviolet light, and he avoids other butterflies that also reflect, thereby narrowing his search. Locating a female, he releases pheromones from scent patches of special wing scales called androconia. These male pheromones are essential in making the female receptive, causing her to lower her abdomen, exposing it beneath her folded wings. Once mated, the pair flies off still connected, the male carrying his "bride."

We watched a colony of several dozen little sulphurs at a patch of powderpuff, *Mimosa strigillosa*, in western Chambers County during late October. A low, sprawling vine, powderpuff is abundant along roadsides and bayou banks throughout the Houston area, undoubtedly serving as an abundant host for this common butterfly species. The males patrolled back and forth above the foliage, while the females fluttered slowly from plant to plant, laying single pale yellow, bottle-shaped eggs on the upper side of tender young leaves near the growing tip. The sensitive leaflets then closed around each egg, effectively hiding it from view. Later, when the tiny green larvae hatched, they, too, were almost impossible to see among the overlapping, finely divided compound leaves.

The little sulphur occupies a permanent range from tropical America and the West Indies to the southern United States. Each spring, however, adults begin a northward movement, stopping to breed along the way and generating others that take up the quest. Some will reach Minnesota and Maine, although this southern species cannot survive a freeze. As fall approaches, many return to the South, but others perish in their new home. The process will begin anew the following spring.

Enormous numbers of migrating little sulphurs have been documented by several authors. Howe reports, "They sometimes fly over the Caribbean and the Atlantic in huge flocks numbering in the millions." According to Pyle (1981), "Columbus is supposed to have witnessed from the decks of the Santa Maria

1. Male, dorsal

2. Female, yellow form, dorsal

3. Female, white form, dorsal

4. Female, yellow form, ventral

58 / *Whites and Sulphurs*

5. Larva

one such mass movement, probably consisting of this species or the cloudless giant sulphur."

SIZE: 1¼–1½ inches.

DESCRIPTION: Male bright yellow with black border. Female yellow or white with reduced border on hindwings. Small black dot on forewings.

SIMILAR SPECIES: Other small *Eurema* sulphurs lack black dot.

SEASON: Virtually all year; many broods.

LARVA: Green, with white stripe on side.

FOOD PLANTS: Senna, partridge pea, and powderpuff most common in Houston.

Mexican Yellow
Eurema mexicanum
Mexican sulphur, Wolf-face sulphur

The Mexican yellow enters the Houston area as a rare midsummer or fall vagrant from the South and West. A largely tropical butterfly, it ranges from northern South America to the Desert Southwest. It occurs as a resident species nearly year-round along the lower Gulf Coast of Texas and up the Rio Grande to the Trans-Pecos. As is the case with many of the Pieridae, it then stages long-distance migrations during the summer breeding season, perhaps as a result of overcrowding. Wandering widely through the Great Plains, the Mexican yellow occasionally reaches the Canadian border. Those long-distance travelers, however, fail to survive the winter.

Both sexes have pale creamy wings, the male with a darker yellow band along the upper margin of the hindwing. The black forewing border outlines the profile of a dog's head, and the hindwing extends into a short, triangular tail. In the fall form, the hindwings are more reddish beneath.

The Mexican yellow flies close to the ground, frequenting mud puddles and seeps for moisture and sometimes congregating in large numbers within its normal range. It prefers dry, open hillsides and desert scrub, visiting overgrown fields as it moves northward. The caterpillar is green, but little has been published about the life history. Most books list *Cassia* (now *Senna*) as the food plant, but Opler suggests those reports may be in error. He cites acacia and *Diphysa*.

Until recently, authors used *E. mexicana* as the scientific name of the Mexican yellow. Ferris, however, noted in 1989 that the name should be corrected to *E. mexicanum* to conform to the International Code of Zoological Nomen-

1. Male, dorsal

2. Male, ventral

clature. Most new publications follow that form.

SIZE: 1½−2 inches.

DESCRIPTION: Creamy yellowish white, with black forewing border outlining a dog's head. Hindwing with short tail.

SIMILAR SPECIES: Dog face butterfly larger, brighter yellow, and lacks tails.

SEASON: Rare vagrant in late summer and fall.

LARVA: Green.

FOOD PLANTS: Acacia, senna, and *Diphysa* reported. Needs further study.

Sleepy Orange

Eurema nicippe
Rambling orange, Nicippe sulphur

Although it might be encountered virtually throughout the year in Houston, the sleepy orange is most abundant in late summer and fall. There are probably four or five different broods, the last one overwintering as adults. While butterflies emerging during the spring and summer may live no more than a week, those of the winter brood live five or six months, laying their eggs when springtime temperatures begin to rise and food plants become available.

The sleepy orange ranges throughout the West Indies, Mexico, and the southern United States. The summer broods migrate northward, colonizing the northern states and occasionally reaching well into Canada. Other individuals may also migrate southward as far as Costa Rica.

Bright orange wings with irregular black borders identify both sexes of the sleepy orange. A yellow form is very rare. Both sexes have a black spot in the forewing cell, but the borders of the female's wings are more diffuse than those of the male. The color of the wings beneath varies dramatically with the season. Summer adults are orange-yellow, while those of the winter brood are tan, brown, or brick-red, variously mottled with darker spots.

An inhabitant of fields, roadsides, and open woodlands, the sleepy orange congregates at mud puddles and wet sand to drink but utilizes flowers less frequently than do many others of the family Pieridae. Larval food plants are usually listed as "various species of *Cassia*," but that genus has recently been split into *Senna* and *Chamaecrista*. Several sennas and the common partridge pea of the latter genus prove most popular in this region. Numerous reports of clovers as larval

1. Male, dorsal

2. Ventral

3. Larva

food plants are apparently based largely on laboratory experiments.

Both the scientific and common names vary a great deal within the available literature. This species was placed by Miller and Brown in the genus *Abaeis*, and several authors subsequently followed that nomenclature. Ferris' supplement to the Lepidopterists' Society checklist, however, again relegates *Abaeis* to subgeneric status and reinstates *Eurema*. The specific epithet, *nicippe*, owes its origin to a Roman poet of the third century B.C.

Klots, Howe, Scott, and Ferris and Brown all comment on the unsuitability of the time-honored common name "sleepy orange." This butterfly, they assert, is anything but sleepy, flying erratically in zigzag fashion when disturbed. Pyle (1981), however, suggests the name may have come from the butterfly's habit of hibernating through the coldest days of the southern winter. Emmel (1991)

has yet another interpretation. The sleepy orange, he notes, may have gained its name from the wavy black spot on the forewing that looks to some observers like a closed eye.

SIZE: 1⅜–2 inches.

DESCRIPTION: Orange with irregular black borders, spot on forewing; color variable beneath.

SIMILAR SPECIES: Orange sulphur has more regular borders and a silver spot on the hindwing beneath; female has light spots in the black border.

SEASON: Throughout much of year; most common in summer and fall.

LARVA: Green, with short downy hairs; light stripe on side.

FOOD PLANTS: Partridge pea, senna species.

Dainty Sulphur
Nathalis iole
Dwarf yellow

This smallest of all North American whites and sulphurs has a wingspan of only an inch. It is also the only pierid to feed in the larval stage on plants of the aster family rather than on members of the pea or mustard families. The chrysalis lacks the head spike of other pierids, and the adult butterfly differs in wing venation and other structural features. So distinctive is this tiny sulphur that some taxonomists feel it should be accorded a separate subfamily of its own.

The forewings are elongated, giving the dainty sulphur a different shape from others with which it might be confused. Both sexes are yellow above with black markings, although the wings of the female are more heavily dusted with dark scaling. Occasional white or orange forms are rare. The underside of the forewing is yellow at the base with black spots. Summer broods have the underside of the hindwing pale yellow; the winter brood is dusky green below.

The dainty sulphur is a year-round resident from Guatemala and the West Indies northward to Florida and the southwestern states, including Texas, where it inhabits dry, open areas such as weedy fields and sandy coastal flats. Flying just a few inches above the ground, it sips nectar from a number of different flowers, especially those of the Asteraceae, and congregates at mud puddles and patches of damp sand.

For some unknown reason, the Florida population is not highly migratory, but that of the Southwest expands northward during the summer months. Migrating along stream corridors and colonizing weedy patches, the tiny butterflies breed rapidly and continue on their way. Pyle (1981) notes that the dynamics of the migration remain to be explored, and it

1. Dorsal

2. Greenish winter form, ventral

is not yet clear whether individual adults fly long distances or whether the successive broods leapfrog along the route. Whatever the mechanism, dainty sulphurs reach the northern tier of states by the end of summer, only to perish in the winter cold. The northward flow will begin again the next year.

The caterpillars of the dainty sulphur develop on dogweeds, sneezeweeds, shepherd's needle, garden marigold, and other low plants of the aster family. Most references also list common chickweed as a larval food plant, but some authors suggest this needs further verification, since chickweed is a member of the Caryophyllaceae, a family far removed from the Asteraceae.

The dainty sulphur, one of our smallest butterflies, takes its scientific name from Iole, daughter of Eurytus, the mythical king of Oechalia. Hercules killed Eurytus when the king refused to allow him to marry Iole.

SIZE: ¾–1⅛ inches.

DESCRIPTION: Yellow, with black tip and bar on forewing.

SIMILAR SPECIES: Barred yellow, *Eurema daira*, is larger, lacks black spot in cell of forewing, not greenish beneath. Little sulphur is larger, lacks bar on rear edge of forewing.

SEASON: Throughout most of the year; most common from midsummer through late fall.

LARVA: Green, with purple stripe on back, fused black and yellow stripe on side, and pair of red tubercles behind the head.

FOOD PLANTS: Dogweeds, sneezeweeds, shepherd's needle, marigold, other small Asteraceae. Common chickweed and others reported.

Gossamer-Winged Butterflies

FAMILY LYCAENIDAE

This huge, worldwide family contains between four thousand and six thousand species, depending on the taxonomy followed. More than one hundred occur in North America. Most are small in size, and one, the western pygmy blue, *Brephidium exile*, ranks as our tiniest butterfly.

Members of four separate subfamilies compose the Lycaenidae in the United States: the harvester, coppers, hairstreaks, and blues. Four other subfamilies inhabit other parts of the world. All share a characteristic wing venation and the fact that the male butterflies have the front pair of legs reduced in size and largely nonfunctional for walking. Females have six normally developed legs.

Although small, many of the adults are brilliantly colored, with two different types of scales on the wings. The brown and gray colors owe their origin to normal pigmented scales, but the iridescent blue, green, purple, and fiery orange that characterize many of the lycaenids are generated structurally by light refraction within other specialized scales. Males and females of the same species may differ markedly in the color and pattern of their wings above, but they usually look alike beneath.

The eggs of the lycaenids are flattened and highly sculptured, shaped like sea urchins or turbans. The small larvae are short and slug-shaped, with retracted heads and bodies covered with fine, short hairs. They often feed on flowers or immature fruits rather than on the leaves of plants. Typically green or brown, some of these caterpillars have evolved unique relationships with ants. They depend on the ants for protection from other small predators and in return reward their protectors with sugary secretions called "honeydew." To this end, they have evolved abdominal glands that produce the secretions, and the ants herd them as "cattle." When an ant wishes to "milk" a larva, it

A gray hairstreak, Strymon melinus, *dines at the colorful blooms of Texas lantana, a favorite butterfly nectar plant.*

rubs the gland with its antennae, stimulating release of a tiny drop of sweet liquid.

The typical lycaenid chrysalis is short and stout, attached to its substrate by a fine silken girdle. When disturbed, the body of the pupa may flex, causing membranes between the segments to produce faint creaking sounds. It is thought that these noises may help to ward off potential small predators and parasites. Winter is usually spent in the egg or pupal stage, although the caterpillars of some lycaenids hibernate when partially grown.

Most of the gossamer-winged butterflies perch with tightly closed wings, opening them only in flight or occasionally when basking in the sun. Members of each subfamily, however, look much alike on the upperwing surface, and they are best identified by careful examination of the underwing patterns.

HARVESTERS, subfamily Miletinae: Although few in number, the harvesters are virtually worldwide in distribution. Only one species, however, occurs in North America. It is unique among our butterfly fauna in having a carnivorous caterpillar that feeds on woolly aphids rather than on plant material.

COPPERS, subfamily Lycaeninae: Coppers range primarily through the north temperate regions of the world, including the northern and western United States. None occurs in our area, however. Encountered elsewhere, they can usually be recognized by their small size and the brilliant coppery orange color on the upper surface of the wings, although some species deviate from that model.

HAIRSTREAKS, subfamily Theclinae: The hairstreaks are particularly abundant in the New World tropics, but many species occupy territories in our region and throughout the United States. They take their name from thin, hairlike lines crossing the under surfaces of the wings. Most also display slender tails on the hindwings, although some lack that distinguishing characteristic.

Hairstreaks are fast-flying butterflies that dart about so quickly and erratically that they are extremely difficult to follow. Pugnacious males defend territories around their perches and fly out to investigate any intruder. When perched, sometimes upside-down, hairstreaks rub their hindwings together while keeping their forewings tightly closed. The slender tails apparently resemble antennae, an illusion further heightened by colored eyespots near their bases. By drawing attention to its "false head," the little butterfly may convince a hungry bird or other vertebrate predator to grasp the wrong end, thereby allowing a quick escape in the opposite direction.

Tropical hairstreaks rank among the most brilliant and colorful of all butterflies, but most of our species are plain brown or gray above. The key to

1. Gray hairstreak

2. Ceraunus blue, male

identification lies in the pattern of lines and spots exposed on the underwings as the butterfly perches quietly. Some are extremely wary and difficult to approach, however, and the observer will often be forced to classify them simply as "hairstreak species."

BLUES, subfamily Polyommatinae: The fragile-looking little blues are concentrated in the Old World tropics and in the north temperate zone, including alpine meadows of the western U.S. About thirty-two species inhabit North America, with several ranging into the Houston area. They take their name from the clear blue upperwings of many of the males. Females tend to be more brownish or have wider dark borders on blue wings. As with most of the other local lycaenids, the pattern of spots on the underwings serves to separate the species.

The blues possess a weaker, more fluttery flight than their relatives, but they can dart away quickly when alarmed. Unlike most of their gossamer-winged relatives, male blues often gather at mud puddles or wet sand to sip moisture, salts, and amino acids useful in building body proteins. When basking, they open their wings to flash the azure color that distinguishes them from all other small butterflies.

Harvester
Feniseca tarquinius
Wanderer, Alder butterfly

The harvester is unique among our butterflies in having carnivorous caterpillars that feed on woolly aphids; larvae of all other North American species consume the leaves, stems, flowers, or fruits of plants. Adult butterflies seldom stray far from their host aphid colonies and do not visit flowers for nectar. Instead, they use an unusually short proboscis to sip honeydew from the aphids and to take fluids from tree sap, carrion, and dung. Freshly emerged butterflies also imbibe moisture at mud puddles and patches of wet sand.

About fifty species of harvesters occur around the world, primarily in Africa and Asia. Only *Feniseca tarquinius* inhabits North America. This small butterfly is bright orange above with brownish black borders and spots. Below, it is pale orange-brown with darker brown spots bordered with faint white rings. It perches with wings tightly closed, the males defending territories and patrolling areas near their favorite perches in search of females.

Mated females normally lay their eggs in colonies of woolly aphids, and hatching occurs within three or four days. Caterpillars vary in color from green to pinkish but are usually greenish brown with faint olive stripes. Long white hairs adorn their bodies. Perhaps because of its rich diet, the larva develops with amazing rapidity, completing all four growth stages in as little as eight days. The brownish chrysalis, held in place with a girdle of silk, bears a remarkable resemblance to a monkey's head. Within seven to eleven days, another adult emerges, completing an entire life cycle in only three weeks. Consequently, there can be several broods of harvesters each year in the South.

The range map in Opler's recent *A Field Guide to Eastern Butterflies* does not show the harvester as occurring in the immediate Houston area. The species ranges from southern Canada through the eastern states to Florida and South Texas, but its indicated range circumvents the Gulf Coast of Louisiana and Texas. We have found the harvester, however, in several locations in Houston, and it turns up virtually every year in our backyard in Baytown, particularly in early to mid July. There it swirls around our patio, perching on various plants, or even on the brick wall, darting off at our approach.

Most authors cite aphids found on alder or beech as primary larval foods and list hawthorn, ash, and several others as alternates. None of these tree species occurs in our yard, and we suspect the caterpillars are feeding on abundant aphids or scale insects on cedar elms. The immature stages can be very difficult to find, since the larvae usually live inside small silk webs liberally covered with aphid carcasses, perhaps as a defense against ants.

The genus name, *Feniseca*, according

1. Dorsal

2. Ventral

Great Purple Hairstreak
Atlides halesus
Great blue hairstreak

This largest and most spectacular of all our lycaenids hints at the splendor of tropical hairstreaks. Klots suggests it has "the most brilliant, changeable coloring of any of our butterflies." Several authors argue against the time-honored name of "great purple hairstreak," noting that the color of the wings above is a bright iridescent blue rather than purple. They suggest a more appropriate name is "great blue hairstreak," but checklists by both Miller and the North American Butterfly Association bow to precedent and retain the old name. We continue that practice here for uniformity. The species takes its scientific name from Stephen Hales, an English botanist.

The blue wings of *Atlides halesus* above are bordered with black; those of the female are duller and with the blue areas more restricted than in the male. Two tails, the lower one longer than the upper one, adorn each hindwing. The wings beneath are dark charcoal-gray or black, with a slight purplish cast. Iridescent gold and blue spots ornament the rear edge of the hindwing; the wing bases and the lower surface of the abdomen are bright red-orange.

The great purple hairstreak ranges from the central states southward to Guatemala. Its larva is our only butterfly caterpillar that feeds on mistletoe. Green with a covering of short green or orange hairs, it is well camouflaged and difficult to find. The pupa hibernates under loose bark or at the base of the host tree.

Adult males establish territories around trees containing mistletoe and return to them regularly, especially on warm afternoons. Perching in the treetops, they await passing females. Their flight is rapid and erratic, but they are attracted readily to flowers, where they can be approached closely. Goldenrods, rag-

to Opler and Krizek, comes from the Latin for "a person who mows," in the same context as the common name, "harvester." Presumably it denotes the systematic harvesting of aphids and their honeydew. This species is the namesake of Lucius Tarquinius Superbus, an Etruscan king of Rome.

SIZE: 1⅛–1¼ inches.
DESCRIPTION: Orange above with brownish black pattern. Orange-brown below with darker spots rimmed by white rings.
SIMILAR SPECIES: Coppers do not occur in the Houston area. Metalmarks have patterns of small spots and lines both above and below and perch with wings open.
SEASON: March–September. Seems to be most common in Houston in July.
LARVA: Greenish brown, with faint lines and long whitish hairs. Usually lives in silk web in aphid colony.
FOOD PLANTS: Carnivorous on woolly aphids.

1. Ventral (*photo by Michael Tveten*)

worts, and other members of the family Asteraceae seem to be particularly attractive to the butterflies, but Ajilvsgi lists many others as favorite nectar plants.

Whittaker made a careful study of the habits of the great purple hairstreak in Texas, using study sites near Austin and Laredo. He found that the females scattered their eggs widely over the host American mistletoe, with as many as twenty-two eggs on a single plant, although they were not laid in clusters. Newly emerged caterpillars ate tender young leaves or rasped the surface of older leaves, while larger caterpillars chewed through old leaves, occasionally defoliating the entire plant. Whittaker noted no interactions between the larvae and any of the ant species that he found on the mistletoe. He therefore suggests that the butterfly utilizes mistletoe for its nutritive qualities rather than for any protection by ants, as is evident among several other lycaenid species.

As is the case with many other lepidoptera, Whittaker also found the chief source of mortality to be hymenopteran parasitoids. Small chalcid and braconid wasps emerged from the butterfly eggs, larvae, and pupae. The cryptic camouflage of the great purple hairstreak's early stages may protect it from larger predators, but it proves less effective against other predatory or parasitic insects that share its treetop niche.

SIZE: 1¼–1¾ inches.

DESCRIPTION: Large, iridescent blue above with black borders, two tails on each hindwing. Black below with red spots on wing bases and abdomen.

SIMILAR SPECIES: White-M hairstreak, *Parrhasius m-album*, is smaller, lacks red spots below. Rickard reports *P. m-album* from Bellaire and Memorial Park in Houston, "especially on goldenrod in the fall." He also cites widespread observations in the wooded areas of Harris and Fort Bend counties.

SEASON: March–November; several broods.

LARVA: Green, with short greenish or orange hairs.

FOOD PLANTS: Mistletoe species only.

Soapberry Hairstreak
Phaeostrymon alcestis
Alcestis hairstreak

The soapberry hairstreak occurs from Kansas southward through Oklahoma and central Texas into Mexico, with a separate population in Arizona. It is generally absent from extreme eastern and southeastern Texas and ranges into the Houston area as a casual visitor from the west. It seldom wanders far from sources of its larval food plant, western soapberry, *Sapindus saponaria* var. *drummondii*. Many older references also list the introduced chinaberry, *Melia azedarach*, as a host, but those reports are undoubtedly in error. The confusion may have resulted from the fact that "chinaberry" serves as an alternate common name for soapberry in some sections of the country. The type specimen of the soapberry hairstreak was described by W. H. Edwards from near Dallas, Texas, in 1871.

Both sexes of the soapberry hairstreak are plain, warm brown above with two tails on each hindwing. Below, a submarginal band of red-orange crescents extends along the hindwing and onto the forewing. Also diagnostic is the postmedian band on the hindwing, which is jagged and takes the form of a sharply defined "VW" mark.

The soapberry hairstreak is apparently single-brooded and appears from April through June, the eggs laid during one season hatching the following spring. Current sources, including Opler and Pyle (1981), note that the early stages are "not reported" or "undescribed." However, we reared this butterfly from larvae found at Fort Lancaster State Historic Site in Crockett County, Texas, on April 28, 1983.

The fully developed caterpillar was

1. Ventral

2. Larvae

bright green with two strongly marked, parallel white lines down the back and another along each side. Short, white hairs covered the body. Found feeding avidly on a small soapberry tree near the park headquarters, several larvae subsequently produced jade-green pupae in captivity. Adults emerged about eight days later.

SIZE: 1⅜ inches.
DESCRIPTION: Plain brown above, with two pairs of tails. Hindwings beneath with postmedian band forming sharp "VW"; row of red-orange crescents extending onto forewing.
SIMILAR SPECIES: Other similar hairstreaks lack combination of "VW" mark and extended red-orange band.
SEASON: April–June; single brood.
LARVA: Green with white stripes and short white hairs.
FOOD PLANTS: Western soapberry.

Banded Hairstreak
Satyrium calanus

The banded hairstreak is the most abundant of a complex of *Satyrium* species found in eastern North America, and it is the one most likely to occur in the immediate Houston area. The hickory, striped, King's, and Edwards' hairstreaks are all similar in appearance and sometimes present identification problems, even for the experienced collector. Minor differences in the underwing patterns are usually diagnostic, but would be extremely difficult to observe in the field. *S. calanus*, however, appears frequently in woodlands and oak-shaded yards and parks throughout our region, while the others seldom range this far south and west. Rickard reports the striped hairstreak, *S. liparops*, from Houston's Memorial Park "during the spring hairstreak flights."

Blackish brown above, the banded hairstreak has two pairs of tails, the upper ones much shorter than the lower ones. A postmedian band of dark, white-edged dashes crosses the hindwing below, and the large blue spot near the tails lacks a red cap. These latter two features usually serve to separate the species from similarly marked hairstreaks.

The banded hairstreak ranges from southern Canada to Florida and south-central Texas. Opler notes that it is geographically variable and that there may be more than one species, a problem that requires further study. Our form was previously known as *Satyrium falacer*, an epithet now relegated to subspecies status under *S. calanus*.

The pale green eggs are laid on the twigs of oaks, hickories, or walnuts, and the developing larvae first eat flower catkins before consuming tender leaves. They range in color from green to brown or pinkish gray, ornamented with oblique white lines. We have found several color variations within a single brood of cater-

1. Ventral

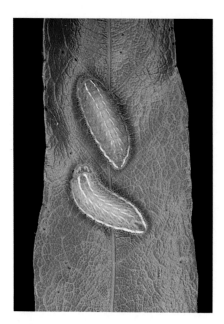

2. Larvae, green and gray forms

pillars on a willow oak in our backyard. Some references suggest the adults appear in May and June in Texas, but we found pupae in late March and the butterflies emerged the first week in April. The flight time and abundance of the banded hairstreak vary from year to year. There is apparently a single brood, and it is the eggs that hibernate through the winter.

Male butterflies bask in the sunlight on shrubs and low limbs through much of the day, waiting for passing females. They are pugnacious, aggressive insects and dart out to "tussle with intruders," as one author puts it. Several males may chase each other in a whirlwind of wings, then break off the chase to perch again, each in his own territory.

Banded hairstreaks readily visit flowers, and Clench conducted a thorough study of their nectar favorites several decades ago. He found that milkweeds and white sweet-clover ranked high on the list, with tall, white flowers generally proving more popular than shorter plants or those with yellow or violet blooms.

Calanus, like many other hairstreaks, frequently lands head downward on its perch. While resting, it rubs its hindwings together while holding its forewings still. It has long been argued that this behavior enhances a "false-head" defense in which the slender tails look like antennae and the eyespots on the hindwings appear to be true eyes. Presumably this pose entices predators to seize the wrong end of the butterfly, tearing loose a small portion of the wings while the intended prey darts off in the opposite direction.

Robbins, in a detailed analysis of this proposal, further notes that the anal angle of the hindwing is frequently everted at right angles to give a three-dimensional appearance, and the tails are crossed so that their white tips flicker in the light. The wings of some hairstreaks have conspicuous lines converging toward the tails, further drawing attention to this area. As evidence that such a "false-head" theory may be correct, Robbins cites a high incidence of damage to the rear margin of the wings, presumably from bird beaks, and several field observations in which lizards invariably attacked the butterflies from the rear.

SIZE: 1–1¼ inches.
DESCRIPTION: Dark blackish brown above. Hindwing beneath crossed by line of dark, white-edged dashes. Blue tail spot without orange cap.
SIMILAR SPECIES: Several others are less abundant in Houston. They have dark spots instead of dashes or an orange cap on the blue tail spot.
SEASON: April–May; single brood.
LARVA: Green, brown, or pinkish gray; with oblique white lines.
FOOD PLANTS: Oaks, hickories, walnuts.

Northern Hairstreak

Fixsenia ontario
Texas hairstreak, Autolycus hairstreak

This pretty little butterfly is part of a highly variable complex over which taxonomists still argue. Populations range from southern Canada to Florida and Texas and sparingly westward, varying dramatically in the length of the tails, the amount of orange on the wings above, and the extent of the orange and blue spots on the hindwing below.

Older references placed these hairstreaks in the genus *Euristrymon*, but Clench subsequently rescinded his action in erecting that genus and they were returned to *Fixsenia*. Some authors now favor placing them in *Satyrium*. We have chosen to follow the checklists of Ferris and Miller in using *Fixsenia*.

Further disagreement arises at the species level. The northern hairstreak, *F. ontario*, and the southern hairstreak, *F. favonius*, have long been considered separately, with the latter occurring in Florida and the extreme Southeast and several populations of the former ranging across the rest of the country. Recent authors, however, seem inclined to combine them as subspecies of a single species, using the name *favonius* because it has scientific priority. Again, we have chosen to follow Ferris and Miller, retaining the distinction between the forms and calling this butterfly the northern hairstreak, *Fixsenia ontario*.

As if that were not confusing enough, the form occurring in our region is distinctive in having large orange patches on the upper side of both wings. From a type specimen collected in Dallas, Texas, it was named subspecies *autolycus*, although whether it is then a subspecies of the northern hairstreak or the southern hairstreak remains the subject of some argument. For simplicity, it might be best to call our orange-spotted population the

1. Ventral

"Texas hairstreak," ignoring for now the taxonomic confusion.

Beneath, the northern hairstreak looks like many of its close relatives, but the black-and-white midline forms a large "W" near the tails, and several red-orange spots border the hindwing. In flight or when basking, however, our Texas form flashes large rusty orange patches on the wings above. This serves to distinguish it from several more abundant species in the Houston area.

Apparently single-brooded, the caterpillars hatch in early spring from eggs laid on oak twigs the previous year. In studies of several hairstreak species in North Carolina, Gifford and Opler found that females of *F. ontario* oviposited only on twigs that would produce male catkins. Upon emerging, the tiny larvae bored into individual flowers and fed on pollen, leaving the outer flower parts uneaten. Older larvae also consumed

2. Larva

leaves. A few references cite both oaks and hawthorns as larval food plants, but most authors list only various species of oaks. Emerging from chrysalides in April or May, adults inhabit oak woodlands and edges. They perch on their host trees but visit a variety of flowers for nectar, most commonly in late afternoon.

Scott, among others, describes the caterpillar as being yellowish green with darker green dorsal stripes and a yellow stripe along the side. However, he considers both the southern and northern hairstreaks to be a single species, and that description is usually given for the typical *F. favonius*. Gifford and Opler noted that their larvae of *F. ontario* were always pale green. We also found the caterpillar of the Texas form to be pale green, lacking the stripes but dotted profusely with tiny yellowish spots.

SIZE: ⅞–1⅛ inches.
DESCRIPTION: Large rusty orange patches on wings above.
SIMILAR SPECIES: Hairstreaks with similar underwings lack orange patches above.
SEASON: April–May.
LARVA: Pale green dotted with yellow.
FOOD PLANTS: Several oak species.

Red-Banded Hairstreak
Calycopis cecrops

One of the prettiest of our small hairstreaks, *Calycopis cecrops* is dark gray-black or brownish black above with patches of deep, iridescent blue that flash in flight. The blue on the male is usually restricted to the hindwings near the tails; that of the female is more extensive and may extend onto the forewings. Beneath, the black-and-white line that crosses the gray-brown wings is widely bordered inwardly with red or red-orange. That broad band extends across both the hindwing and the forewing and gives the species its common name. The scientific name stems from the Greek Kekrops, the first king of Attica and founder of Athens.

As Gifford and Opler note in a paper on the natural history of hairstreaks, "The habits of *Calycopis cecrops* are bi-zarre." Females lay their eggs on the underside of dead leaves near the base of appropriate food plants, where the eggs and newly emerged larvae are hidden from view. The caterpillars later crawl up to feed on flowers and leaves. Sumacs, wax myrtle, crotons, and oaks have all been listed as larval food plants, and Gifford and Opler successfully raised red-banded hairstreaks on both sumac and wax myrtle.

Those authors, however, describe the caterpillar as "dull blackish brown" in all its instars, while Heitzman and Heitzman describe it as "yellowish green with a bluish green dorsal line and a heavy covering of brownish hairs." We have been unable to find larvae in this area, although freshly emerged butterflies swirl through our yard and around our patio from spring until late fall. Of the listed food plants, we have only oak nearby, and it is possible that the larvae feed high

1. Typical *cecrops*, ventral

2. Form with narrow red band, ventral

in the trees out of sight. Small larvae among the detritus on the ground would be almost impossible to see.

Male butterflies perch on the leaves of trees and shrubs, waiting for passing females. They seem to be most active in late afternoon. Both sexes visit a variety of flowers for nectar and sip moisture from damp earth. There are apparently at least three broods in the Houston area, producing fresh adults from March into November. The larvae are slow to develop, and broods overlap through the year. Some larvae may also hibernate before finishing their development.

The red-banded hairstreak ranges across the southeastern corner of the U.S., from Long Island to Missouri and Kansas and southward to Florida and Texas. It occupies the eastern third of our state, where its range overlaps that of the dusky-blue hairstreak, *C. isobeon*. It appears likely that these two sibling species interbreed in the Houston area, or that they are forms of a single species. That problem is discussed further in the following account.

SIZE: ¾–1 inch.

DESCRIPTION: Gray-black with blue patches above. Postmedian line edged with wide red band below.

SIMILAR SPECIES: Dusky-blue hairstreak has narrow red band on forewing, larger red-orange cap on black spot between tails.

SEASON: March–November.

LARVA: Descriptions vary (see text).

FOOD PLANTS: Sumacs, wax myrtle, crotons, oaks. Eggs laid beneath dead leaves on ground.

Dusky-Blue Hairstreak
Calycopis isobeon
Dusty-blue hairstreak, Beon hairstreak

Both *Calycopis isobeon* and the preceding *C. cecrops* occur in the Houston area, forming a confusing complex that demands more detailed study. According to most references, several distinctive differences exist in the underwing patterns of the two species. The dusky-blue hairstreak has a larger red-orange cap on the black spot between the tails than does the red-banded hairstreak, the extent of the orange exceeding that of the black. The red-orange postmedian band is also narrower on the dusky-blue hairstreak, particularly on the forewing, where it thins dramatically. Pyle (1981) also notes that the red-orange band tends to "bleed through" the black and white into the tail area of the hindwing. Slightly smaller size and more extensive blue areas above also characterize the typical *C. isobeon*.

The dusky-blue hairstreak ranges from central and southeastern Texas to northern South America, only occasionally straying farther north and east. The red-banded hairstreak ranges from eastern Texas through the southeastern states. Thus the two species overlap in our area, and many of the specimens we have encountered appear to be intermediate between them.

In the northern part of the region, from Montgomery and Liberty counties northward into the Big Thicket, we find the typical *cecrops*, with a broad red band and small cap on the black tail spot. South and west of Houston, we encounter specimens of *isobeon* with a narrow red-orange forewing band and large red-orange cap. Most of the butterflies examined in Houston and Baytown, however, have a narrow red-orange band that bleeds through into the tail area below like *isobeon* and a small red-orange cap on the black tailspot like *cecrops*. In many cases, there is no cap at all on the

1. Ventral

2. Ventral

tailspot, yet the colored forewing band is very narrow. These specimens match neither of the typical forms.

Ehrlich and Ehrlich, in their 1961 field guide, stated that the two nominate species "are similar and may be difficult to separate, though unquestionably distinct." More recently, however, Opler (1992) notes that some dusky-blue hairstreaks in southern Texas "appear to be intergrades between this species and the red-banded hairstreak, suggesting that they are the same species." Certainly there seems to be a gradual transition between the typical forms through the Houston area, and clear identification awaits more detailed taxonomic work.

The caterpillar of the dusky-blue hairstreak is reportedly dark brown, with two black dorsal lines and long brown hairs. Opler suggests it eats dead leaves, fruits, and detritus on the ground, especially under sumacs and other members of the family Anacardiaceae. Scott also states that laboratory larvae eat both fresh and dead leaves, seeds, and berries of dozens of different plant families, "even poison ivy, bread crumbs, hair follicles, dead insects, and fellow larvae."

SIZE: ¾–1 inch.

DESCRIPTION: Gray-black with blue patches above. Postmedian line edged with red-orange band below. Large red-orange cap on black tail spot.

SIMILAR SPECIES: Red-banded hairstreak has wider red-orange band, especially on forewing, and smaller red-orange cap on black tail spot. Intermediates between the two are common in Houston.

SEASON: March–November.

LARVA: Brown, with two black dorsal lines and brown hairs.

FOOD PLANTS: Dead leaves and fruits.

Olive Hairstreak

Mitoura grynea
Cedar hairstreak

The small, tailed olive hairstreak can be confused with no other butterfly in the Houston area. Dark brown above, it has lighter rust-colored patches that are more extensive in the spring brood than in the summer. The hindwings beneath are rich apple-green, with two white marks near the base and an irregular white line edged inwardly with reddish brown.

The olive hairstreak ranges from New England to Florida and Texas, occurring wherever eastern red cedar grows. Females lay their eggs on nothing else, and the butterflies seldom stray far from stands of that tree. Consequently, this pretty little butterfly is not common within the city, but we have found it nearby in Montgomery and Chambers counties. It inhabits open woodlands, pastures, and abandoned farmland, seeming to find stands of red cedar wherever they have been planted or chance to spring up.

Formerly known as *Callophrys gryneus*, the olive hairstreak is now placed in the genus *Mitoura*. The specific epithet has recently been altered to *grynea* to conform to the International Code of Zoological Nomenclature. According to Opler and Krizek, it was named after Grynea, a town in Mysia in northwest Asia Minor. Several similar species, or named subspecies, occur in both the eastern and western states, but this is the only one expected in our region of Texas. Each of those separate taxa makes use of its own species of juniper.

Perched with folded wings on red cedar, *Juniperus virginiana*, the olive hairstreak blends perfectly with the foliage. The butterfly collector's standard method of finding it is to rap sharply on the tree trunk, sending hairstreaks swirling out in rapid, erratic flight. They fly about for a moment and then land again, often on the same perches they left. Both sexes visit flowers for nectar, but they do so less frequently than many other hairstreak species. The butterflies seem most active in the afternoon, when mating takes place. There are apparently at least three overlapping broods in Texas, with the first adults appearing in March and others continuing into September or October. Individual butterflies live approximately one week.

SIZE: 7/8 – 1 1/8 inches.
DESCRIPTION: Brown above with rusty patches. Apple-green below with white markings bordered by reddish brown.
SIMILAR SPECIES: None in Southeast Texas.
SEASON: March–September; several overlapping broods.
LARVA: Emerald-green, with white chevrons.
FOOD PLANTS: Eastern red cedar.

1. Ventral

2. Larva

Henry's Elfin
Incisalia henrici
Woodland elfin

The elfins compose a small group of short-tailed or tailless brownish hair-streaks. Some authors place them in the genus *Callophrys*, combining them with the olive hairstreak and its relatives that others assign to *Mitoura*. In general, the elfins appear early in the spring and have but one brood a year. They occur more abundantly in the northern states than in the South.

A widely distributed but very local species, Henry's elfin ranges throughout much of eastern North America, from southern Canada to Florida and Texas. Houston is located along the southern fringe of that range, and Henry's elfin occurs only as an infrequent stray from East Texas or from the central portion of the state.

The upperside of this small, short-tailed hairstreak is brown; the underside, dark brown on the basal portions of the wings and lighter on the outer portions. The dividing line is relatively straight on the forewing but much more irregular on the hindwing, where it is usually white at each end. Fine blue-gray scaling gives the outer edges of the wings below a frosted appearance. The sexes are alike, the male lacking the stigma, a scent patch on the upper side of the forewing, possessed by most male elfins.

Various authors have reported a wide range of food plants for Henry's elfin. Redbud, blueberries and huckleberries, hollies, wild plum, black cherry, and vi-burnum are all utilized, although butter-flies in a given region seem to prefer one specific host. Roy Kendall found *Incisa-lia henrici* feeding on Texas persimmon in central Texas, while Ajilvsgi adds Texas mountain laurel and Texas bluebonnet to the list. Most authors report that the female lays her eggs singly in the flower clusters and the caterpillars feed on flow-

1. Ventral

2. Larva, green form, with parasite egg

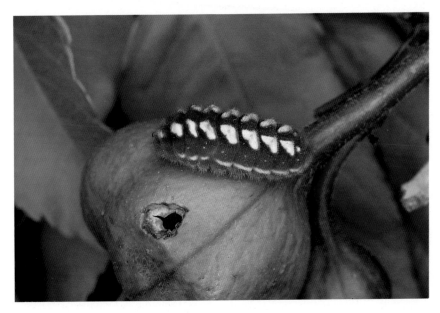

3. Larva, red form

ers and developing fruits. Gifford and Opler, however, documented Henry's elfins in North Carolina laying eggs on the leaves of hollies, where the larvae consumed young leaves just bursting from the buds. Those authors describe the larvae as green; most others note the color varies from green to red-brown or maroon, usually with lighter markings.

We found several caterpillars of Henry's elfin on Mexican buckeye. Some were burrowing into the green seed pods, while others were eating leaves of the same tree. The former were deep maroon in color; the latter, bright green, all with white markings of varying size. Neither color form would adopt the food of the other, but the two produced identical adult butterflies. It is interesting to speculate whether the chemical composition of the fruits and leaves determines the color of the larvae.

There is a single brood of Henry's elfins each year. Adults appear from late February to May, emerging from hibernating pupae. Well camouflaged amid the foliage of their host trees and shrubs, they can sometimes be seen nectaring at flowers or sipping moisture at mud puddles.

SIZE: ⅞–1⅛ inches.

DESCRIPTION: Brown above. Base of hindwing beneath much darker than outer portion, with irregular postmedian line.

SIMILAR SPECIES: Frosted elfin, *I. irus*, possible as stray from farther north in Texas. Hindwing less distinctly two-toned.

SEASON: February–May; single brood.

LARVA: Green to maroon, with white markings.

FOOD PLANTS: Redbud, blueberries and huckleberries, hollies, wild plum, black cherry, viburnum, Mexican buckeye, Texas persimmon, Texas mountain laurel, Texas bluebonnet.

Eastern Pine Elfin

Incisalia niphon
Pine elfin, Eastern banded elfin, Banded elfin

Plain brown above, the female more tawny than the dark brown male, the eastern pine elfin is strikingly banded and barred with rich brown and black beneath. It also lacks the tails characteristic of most of our hairstreaks. No other small hairstreak found in our region is so boldly marked, although a similar species, the western pine elfin, occurs in the Rocky Mountain states. The wing margins are checkered black and white, giving them a scalloped appearance.

The eastern pine elfin is placed by some authors in the genus *Callophrys* with the other elfins and the green cedar hairstreaks. The species, according to Opler and Krizek, takes its name from the Greek *nipha*, meaning "snow." It is perhaps an allusion to the early spring emergence of the elfins, even in northern latitudes. *Incisalia niphon* ranges from Canada to Florida and East Texas, appearing in our state in March and April. Although there is but one brood each year, the butterflies emerge from hibernating pupae over a staggered period of several weeks.

Pine elfins, as the name suggests, depend on pines as larval food plants. Thus they reach the southern edge of their range in Houston and occur more frequently northward into the East Texas Piney Woods. Near the city, they would be expected in northern Harris and Montgomery counties. Research documents loblolly and shortleaf pines as food plants, along with several other of the "hard" pines. No mention is made in the literature of slash pine, however, and the replacement of native pine species with plantations of imported trees may have a negative effect on colonies of butterflies.

Pine elfins are rarely seen except when

1. Ventral

nectaring at flowers or sipping from mud puddles and moist sand. Startled, they fly high into the treetops, where males perch in wait for females. They sit in patches of sunlight with closed wings tilted from the perpendicular to absorb the maximum radiant energy, counteracting the cool air of early spring. Most active from midday until late afternoon, they seldom move far from open woodlands and clearings where small to medium-sized pines occur.

Females lay their pale green eggs singly on the new growth of young trees, and the hatchling larvae bore into the needle sheath. Later they consume the entire leaf. Pale green with two cream stripes along each side and a light transverse bar behind the head, the caterpillars are well camouflaged among the pine needles.

SIZE: ¾–1⅛ inches.
DESCRIPTION: Brown above. Underside boldly banded with brown and black, fringes checkered.
SIMILAR SPECIES: None in our area.
SEASON: March–April; single brood, but staggered emergence.
LARVA: Green, with cream-colored stripes.
FOOD PLANTS: Pines.

Gray Hairstreak
Strymon melinus
Common hairstreak, Melinus hairstreak

While most butterflies are specialists in their habitats and larval food plants, the gray hairstreak is a generalist in almost every sense of the word. It is the most widespread and abundant of our hairstreaks, occurring in the U.S. from coast to coast and from sea level to at least nine thousand feet. Recolonizing the northern latitudes every spring and summer, it ranges from South America northward to Canada, the larvae feeding on the flowers and fruits of a wide variety of plants. We found caterpillars consuming the flowers of Turk's-cap in Houston's wildflower gardens and burrowing into the green fruits of fragrant sumac in the Basin of Big Bend's Chisos Mountains.

The gray hairstreak is dark gunmetal-gray above with an orange spot on each hindwing near the base of the long, slender tail. The wings beneath are paler pearl-gray, although butterflies of the early spring brood are smaller and darker than those found in summer. Bright orange and blue patches ornament the tail region below, and the postmedian black-and-white line is relatively straight and usually edged inwardly with orange.

Larvae utilize scores of different food plants in at least twenty different families, although they seem partial to members of the pea and mallow families. They normally eat the fruits and flowers; less frequently, tender young leaves. When abundant, they can become pests on commercial crops of cotton, beans, and corn. These habits have earned the caterpillars the colloquial names of "cotton square borer" and "bean lycaenid." They range in color from yellow to green to reddish brown, often with lighter oblique marks along the sides. However, the larvae we have found across Texas have been entirely green and covered with short hairs.

Gossamer-Winged Butterflies / 87

1. Dorsal

2. Ventral

3. Larva

The gray hairstreak occurs from at least February to November in the Houston area. There appear to be three or four generations each year, but the broods are not synchronized and emerge at various times, perhaps because the rate of development varies on different hosts. Adults frequent fields and roadsides, open woodlands, and even residential parks and yards, nectaring at a wide variety of flowers. Unlike most hairstreaks, they bask in the sunlight with wings spread widely, but they also sit and rub their hindwings together in typical hairstreak fashion.

Males perch on the leaves of shrubs and trees in the afternoon, waiting for passing females. Opler and Krizek note that they perch low to the ground in the spring and move higher as the year progresses, perhaps seeking cooling breezes as temperatures rise. Mated pairs have been seen only at night, according to those authors, and females oviposit in midafternoon. They lay their pale green eggs singly on buds or newly opened flowers.

Several subspecies of this common insect have been described and named across the continent. Emmel (1991) suggests that if any butterfly besides the familiar monarch deserves to be named the national butterfly, the abundant and widespread gray hairstreak would be a strong candidate.

SIZE: 1–1¼ inches.
DESCRIPTION: Dark gray above with orange tail spot. Light gray below with orange and blue patches near tails.
SIMILAR SPECIES: Other hairstreaks browner, lack orange spot on dark gray hindwing above.
SEASON: February–November; several overlapping broods.
LARVA: Variable; most frequently green.
FOOD PLANTS: Scores of different plants in many families. Usually consumes flowers and fruits.

Western Pygmy Blue
Brephidium exile
Pygmy blue

The western pygmy blue is appropriately named, for it is the smallest butterfly in North America, if not in the entire world. With a wingspan of about one-half inch, it is easily overlooked by the casual observer. However, its delicate beauty and gemlike markings make it well worth searching for. It is not uncommon in the greater Houston area, particularly around Galveston Bay and in the marshes and dunes along the Gulf.

The wings of the western pygmy blue are mostly brown above, usually with some blue scaling at their bases. Females average slightly larger and browner than the males. The hindwing beneath is whitish at the base, and the outer fringes of the wings are white. These features distinguish *Brephidium exile* from the eastern pygmy blue, *B. isophthalma*, which has brown wing bases below and brown fringes. A submarginal row of black spots centered with metallic green scales further ornaments the ventral hindwing of both pygmy blues.

Much confusion exists over the classification of what most authors currently treat as two distinct species in the genus *Brephidium*. The western form, which ranges from the Texas coast across the Desert Southwest to California, is called the "western pygmy blue" or simply "pygmy blue." It has long been classified as *B. exilis*, but the name has recently been changed to *exile* to conform to the code for zoological nomenclature.

The "eastern pygmy blue" ranges from Florida and the southeastern Atlantic Coast to eastern Louisiana. It was formerly called *B. pseudofea*, but that taxon has now been relegated to a subspecies under *B. isophthalma*. Scott considers all forms to be members of a single species, an argument that has not been widely accepted.

Williams, in his checklist of the butterflies of Southeast Texas, concurs with Scott. He suggests that both forms occur in the checklist area and that *pseudofea* (now *isophthalma*) "is the race which occurs on the coast west at least to Galveston Co." Rickard also reports the eastern form from Harris County, as well as from Sabine Pass and the Bolivar Peninsula.

However, most of the specimens we have taken around Galveston Bay appear to be typical of the western form, *exile*. These fragile butterflies are easily damaged and worn, the whitish scaling rubbing off the underwing bases and the fringes wearing away. They then look more like the eastern *isophthalma*.

In examining a colony of pygmy blues near Rockport in Aransas County, we did find some individuals that closely fit the description of the typical eastern form. One of those is illustrated in this account, along with the western form. These individuals, as in *isophthalma*, had uniformly brown hindwings below and dark fringes. This problem obviously deserves further study along the Texas coast.

The pygmy blue, whatever its classification, inhabits coastal marshes and dunes, roadsides, and waste places throughout the region. In deep South Texas it occurs throughout the year; farther north, it has several broods from at least May until November. It flies weakly and low to the ground, but its tiny size makes it almost impossible to follow. It usually visits small flowers, its short proboscis dictating its choice of nectar plants.

Larvae are yellowish green with numerous small brown tubercles. They consume species of saltbush, pigweed, glasswort, and other salt- and alkali-tolerant plants that grow profusely along the coast and across arid inland regions.

1. Typical *B. exile*, ventral

2. *Isophthalma*-like form, ventral

SIZE: ⅜–¾ inch, females usually larger than males.

DESCRIPTION: Brown above, with blue wing bases. Underside of hindwing whitish at base; fringes white.

SIMILAR SPECIES: Eastern pygmy blue has brown fringes and hindwing entirely brown below. See also patterns of other blues.

SEASON: At least May–November; most abundant in autumn.

LARVA: Yellow-green, with brown tubercles.

FOOD PLANTS: Saltbushes, pigweeds, glassworts, others.

Cassius Blue

Leptotes cassius
Tropical striped blue, Striated blue, West Indian blue

This tiny blue averages only a little larger than the pygmy blue. It ranges northward from South and Central America to southern Florida and deep South Texas, where it may be found almost throughout the year. From that base it occasionally wanders as far as the central states, but it is never abundant outside its subtropical habitat. The cassius blue should be looked for in the Houston area in summer and fall, but it is easily mistaken for the somewhat larger but similarly marked marine blue, *Leptotes marina*.

Males are pale blue above; females are more whitish with broad, dark margins. So delicate and translucent are the wings that the underwing pattern shows through from below. The underside is striped with white and tan bands, much like the pattern of the marine blue, but the stripes are more broken and leave a blank area on the forewing at the outer portion of the trailing edge.

Several subspecies have been named throughout the cassius blue's large range. The "striated blue," *L. cassius striatus*, occurs from Panama to South Texas and beyond, while the "West Indian blue," *L. cassius theonus*, is found in the West Indies and Florida. Our subspecies, *striatus*, has a purplish cast to the blue above and more closely resembles the marine blue.

An inhabitant of weedy fields and residential areas, the cassius blue nectars at a wide variety of flowers and lays its eggs among the buds of ornamental leadwort (*Plumbago*), milk pea, lima and string beans, rattlebox, and other members of the legume family. The developing larvae then feed on the blossoms and fruits. Green with a russet cast, the caterpillars are tended by ants that feed on the "honeydew" secretions from abdominal

1. Ventral (*photo by George Krizek*)

glands. Association with the defensive ants probably serves to protect the caterpillars from parasites and small predators.

SIZE: ⅝–⅞ inch.
DESCRIPTION: Pale blue or whitish above. Underwings crossed by broken white and tan bands.
SIMILAR SPECIES: Marine blue larger, with violet-blue cast. Undersides of both wings have more continuous brown lines.
SEASON: All year in South Texas, wanders northward in summer and fall.
LARVA: Green, with russet cast.
FOOD PLANTS: Plumbago, milk pea, lima and string bean, rattlebox, other Fabaceae.

Marine Blue
Leptotes marina
Striped blue

The marine blue is lilac-blue above, the female duller than her mate and with brownish borders. Only the smaller cassius blue, *Leptotes cassius*, shares *L. marina*'s "zebra striped" underwing pattern. The pale brown lines of the marine blue, however, are continuous across the forewing. Two prominent submarginal black spots rimmed with metallic silver-blue scales gleam like jewels on the hindwing below.

The marine blue ranges from Guatemala through Mexico to the southwestern states, where it flies year-round from South Texas to California. The type specimen was described from Vera Cruz, Mexico. From its stronghold in the mesquite thorn-scrub, deserts, and canyons of the Southwest, *L. marina* moves northward each summer, sometimes reaching far into the midwestern states. These migrants cannot withstand the winter, but they may establish short-lived breeding colonies for the season. The marine blue appears in the Houston area as early as April and remains sparingly until October or November, but it is not one of our more common lycaenids.

The pretty little butterflies frequent stream beds and sip moisture from the mud, but they also inhabit weedy fields and urban gardens. Females lay their delicate green eggs on flower buds of a wide variety of plants, primarily those in the family Fabaceae. Alfalfa, clover, milk-vetch, sweet pea, false indigo, acacia, wisteria, and various bean species all serve as larval food plants, as does leadwort, or plumbago.

Brown (1990) published an interesting account on the urban biology of *L. marina* in southern California. In San Diego County, cape plumbago has been introduced from South Africa and is

1. Male, dorsal

2. Ventral

widely planted as a garden ornamental, becoming the primary larval host of the marine blue within the cities. The hatching larvae bore into the buds near their bases and feed primarily on reproductive tissue, rarely eating the flower petals. They were never observed to feed on foliage.

All of the caterpillars encountered in the field were closely associated with Argentine ants. Three to five ants on a single plant inflorescence, notes Brown, always indicated the presence of one or more larvae. In laboratory experiments, however, larvae developed normally in the absence of ants. The only nectar sources adults were observed to use were the small white flowers of Brazilian pepper. Although the butterflies swarmed around the larval hosts, they were not seen to take nectar from them.

The marine blue, suggests Brown, "is one of few native North American butterflies that has benefited from the activities of man by its remarkable switch to a new larval host introduced from South Africa and to a nectar source and an ant introduced from South America." None of these is closely related to the butterfly's native resources. It is probably this adaptability that has allowed the marine blue to expand its ecological range into urban environments.

SIZE: ⅝–1 inch.

DESCRIPTION: Lilac-blue above, with no white. Pale brown stripes continuous across both wings beneath; two black submarginal spots with iridescent blue scaling.

SIMILAR SPECIES: Cassius blue is smaller, with female whitish above. Brown stripes below broken, absent in forewing corner.

SEASON: April–November; irregular.

LARVA: Green to brownish, often with dark brown stripes or spots.

FOOD PLANTS: Many legumes, leadwort (plumbago).

Ceraunus Blue
Hemiargus ceraunus
Southern blue, Antillean blue

The male ceraunus blue is blue above with narrow black borders, while the female is browner with blue only on the wing bases. Both sexes have a postmedian row of white-rimmed brown dashes crossing the underside of the wings. *Hemiargus ceraunus* looks much like the Reakirt's blue, *H. isola*, but it lacks the latter's chain of prominent round, white-rimmed, black spots across the forewing beneath.

The ceraunus blue may well be the most widespread and abundant blue in the Americas; however, it occurs irregularly as far north as the Houston area. A tropical species originally described from Jamaica, it ranges from the southern U.S. through the West Indies and Central America to South America. Three different subspecies occur in the U.S., the Texas one being *H. ceraunus zachaeina*, the "zachaeina blue." *H. c. antibubastus*, the "Florida blue," is found in Florida, while *H. c. gyas*, "Edward's blue," or the "gyas blue," inhabits the Desert Southwest through California and Arizona. The nominate subspecies, *H. c. ceraunus*, is restricted to the West Indies. All vary slightly in their markings. The specific name, according to Opler and Krizek, comes from the Greek *keraunos*, meaning "thunder and lightning." Those authors do not suggest a reason for the selection.

The ceraunus blue flies all year in extreme South Texas and wanders northward in the summer. It is not as common in Houston as Reakirt's blue, although small concentrations are sometimes encountered. The similarity of the two species makes field identification more difficult, although the bold black spots of Reakirt's blue can usually be seen at close range. The broods have not been well defined, and some authors suggest that

1. Ventral

there may be a longer-lived winter form followed by several generations of a summer form.

Adults nectar at a variety of flowers but seem to prefer members of the Asteraceae. Males patrol during most warm daylight hours in search of females, inhabiting thorn-scrub woodlands, fields, and beach dunes. The females lay their eggs on a wide variety of herbaceous and woody legumes, including partridge pea, mesquite, acacia, loco-weeds, and various beans. Caterpillars are highly variable, ranging from green to yellow to red, all with short silver-white hairs.

SIZE: ¾–1 inch.

DESCRIPTION: Male blue above; female largely brown. Wings beneath crossed by row of white-rimmed brown dashes.

SIMILAR SPECIES: Reakirt's blue has a chain of large round, white-rimmed, black spots on forewing below.

SEASON: Summer and fall; irregular.

LARVA: Variable. Green, yellow, or red with short white hairs.

FOOD PLANTS: Numerous herbaceous and woody legumes (Fabaceae).

Reakirt's Blue

Hemiargus isola
Mexican blue, Solitary blue

The male Reakirt's blue is lilac-blue above; the female, browner with blue wing bases. The key to identification of this common species, however, is the row of prominent round, white-rimmed, black spots on the forewing beneath. No other small blue butterfly carries these distinctive marks. The outer margin of the forewing is also straighter than in related species, giving Reakirt's blue a slightly squarish shape.

Hemiargus isola ranges from Costa Rica to Texas and the southwestern states. The nominate subspecies is confined to the central highlands of Mexico; our subspecies is *H. i. alce*. Reakirt's blue flies throughout most of the year in South Texas, Arizona, and southern California, wandering northward in summer to colonize the midsection of the country. Some vagrants reach even the northern states and Canada. It is doubtful, however, that any of these migrants survive the winter.

Reakirt's blue may appear in Houston from March or April until November, but we have found it most abundant after early June. An inhabitant of weedy fields and roadsides, it flies close to the ground and sips nectar from a variety of flowers. It also visits mud puddles and moist sand, as do most of the lycaenids, but it seems to be largely solitary in its habits, thereby accounting for one of its alternate common names.

The complete life cycle is poorly known, according to most references, and the caterpillar has not been described in the scientific literature. We have failed to find it by looking on reported food plants in our area. Male butterflies patrol erratically for most of the day in search of mates, and the females lay their eggs at midday on flower buds of acacias, mesquite, clovers, sweetclovers, indigoes, and a number of other members of the Fabaceae. The larvae consume flowers and immature fruits and are reported to be attended by ants.

SIZE: ¾–1⅛ inches.
DESCRIPTION: Row of round, white-rimmed, black spots on underside of forewing is distinctive.
SIMILAR SPECIES: Ceraunus blue has a line of dark dashes rather than round spots on forewing beneath.
SEASON: March–November; most abundant June–October.
LARVA: Not described.
FOOD PLANTS: Variety of legumes in family Fabaceae.

1. Ventral

Eastern Tailed Blue
Everes comyntas
Tailed blue

Everes comyntas is one of the most abundant butterflies in many portions of the eastern United States. It occurs from southern Canada to Florida and Texas and from the Atlantic Ocean to the Rocky Mountains. Another population ranges from the Desert Southwest through Mexico and Central America to Costa Rica. Strangely isolated colonies also exist in coastal Oregon and California, perhaps as the result of introductions. A sister species, the western tailed blue, *E. amyntula*, occurs in Canada and throughout the western states. It does not inhabit our area of Texas, where the eastern tailed blue is the only member of the subfamily with short, slender tails on the hindwings. *E. comyntas* is less abundant in Southeast Texas than farther north, but it is fairly common throughout the Houston area from March until November.

Males are lavender-blue above; females are brown, the early spring broods with blue at the base of the wings. Below, both sexes are pale grayish white with distinct black spots. Two large orange spots ornament the outer margin of the hindwing near the base of the tail. The fragile tails are distinctive, but may be damaged or worn on some specimens.

The eastern tailed blue flies weakly and low, scarcely rising above the grass tops in the open, sunny environments it prefers. It inhabits weedy fields, roadsides, and gardens, and is one of the few butterflies that seem to have profited by human encroachment. Its short proboscis limits its feeding to open or short-tubed flowers, but it visits a wide variety of small blossoms. Swarms of tailed blues also congregate around mud puddles to sip water with its dissolved minerals and amino acids. Like many of the hairstreaks, the tailed blue rubs its hindwings

1. Ventral

2. Larva

together when perched, perhaps diverting potential predators away from its more vulnerable foreparts.

Male tailed blues patrol for prospective mates throughout the warm daylight hours, and most mating takes place from late morning until midafternoon. Females lay their pale green eggs singly among the flower buds of clovers, sweetclovers, medics, vetches, lupines, and a wide variety of other herbaceous legumes. The caterpillars then feed on the flowers and developing fruits, more rarely on tender leaves. Green with a dark dorsal stripe and fainter dark side stripes, they develop quickly through four instars before pupation. Successive generations often switch from one food plant to another as the blooming season advances, and the last generation in the fall spends the winter as mature caterpillars and pupates in the spring.

SIZE: ¾–1 inch.
DESCRIPTION: Tails diagnostic. Male blue above; female brown. Pale grayish white below with black spots and two orange patches near base of tail on hindwing.
SIMILAR SPECIES: No other blue in our region has tails.
SEASON: March–November.
LARVA: Green, with dark dorsal stripe.
FOOD PLANTS: Many herbaceous plants in family Fabaceae.

Spring Azure
Celastrina argiolus
Azure blue, Common blue

The spring azure is one of the most abundant butterflies across large portions of the United States, and, as its name suggests, it is one of the first to appear in spring. Indeed, Williams notes that it "could actually be dubbed the Midwinter Azure in Southeast Texas, for it appears during warm spells in January and February." By May it has largely disappeared, to be replaced by several other species of blues that emerge later in the year. The spring azure is not a common butterfly in Houston, however. It occurs more frequently in the deciduous woodlands just to the north of our immediate area.

Confusion reigns over the appropriate name or names for the spring azure. Old references use the scientific name *Lycaenopsis argiolus* or *L. pseudargiolus*. More recent authors seem almost evenly split between *Celastrina argiolus* and *C. ladon*. Opler, Miller, and Ferris employ the former; Pyle, Glassberg, and others use the latter. We have adhered to the checklists published by Miller and Ferris, while realizing the final word has not been heard.

This problem in nomenclature stems from the fact that the Old World holly blue is designated as *C. argiolus*. Those authors who feel the American form is merely a subspecies of the Eurasian butterfly retain the name. Others consider it a separate and distinct species and call it *C. ladon*. Both classifications are widely used at the present time.

Whatever its proper scientific name, the New World spring azure ranges from Canada south of the tundra through the U.S. and mountains of Central America to Columbia. In the U.S. it is absent only from peninsular Florida, the southern plains, and much of the Texas Coast.

In addition to the nomenclatural de-

1. Male, dorsal

2. Ventral

bate, we face an even more difficult problem involving the many distributional and seasonal forms of the spring azure. Glassberg describes it as "a bewildering complex of species and forms." He asserts, "We are still far from unraveling the whole story." The dusky azure and the Appalachian blue have already been separated from the complex, but neither of those occurs in Texas. Opler notes that there may still be as many as three species covered by what we now call *C. argiolus*. *Ladon*, the specific name preferred by some, seems prophetic: Ladon was the dragon with one hundred heads in Greek mythology. He guarded the gardens of the Hesperides and was killed by Hercules. It may well take a Herculean effort to sort out the taxonomy of this little butterfly.

The spring azure is identified by the grayish underside of the hindwing marked with dark spots and a row of marginal crescents enclosing small dots. There are no orange patches or prominent spots filled with iridescent, metallic scaling. In the early spring form, the wings are darker gray with heavier markings; the later forms have pale grayish-white underwings with smaller, less distinct spots. The male is clear sky-blue or violet-blue above, while the female is duller with at least some black color framing the forewing.

The spring azure flies higher than many of the other blues, usually at least three or four feet above the ground, visiting a variety of flowers. Newly emerged males also congregate at mud puddles to sip liquids. Most active from midafternoon until nearly dusk, the males patrol clearings and the edges of deciduous woodlands in search of mates. Females lay their eggs on the buds and flowers of dogwood, black cherry, viburnums, blueberries and huckleberries, and a wide variety of other trees and shrubs. The larvae vary in color from yellow-green to

pink, often with a dark dorsal stripe and oblique side stripes.

The number of broods differs in various parts of the country. In the South, there are apparently at least two full broods and then another spread out until fall, the latter with a rapidly decreasing frequency of emergence. Opler and Krizek note that the individual adult is short-lived, surviving no more than four days. On the average, they suggest, the female emerges and mates on the first day, lays eggs on the second day, and rarely survives through the third or fourth day.

SIZE: ¾–1¼ inches.

DESCRIPTION: Highly variable. Male blue above; female with black border on forewing. Pale gray beneath, with dark spots and row of crescents on margin of hindwing.

SIMILAR SPECIES: Tailed blue has obvious tails and orange patches. Compare other underwing patterns.

SEASON: January–October; rare after May.

LARVA: Yellow-green to pink, with dark dorsal stripe.

FOOD PLANTS: Dogwood, black cherry, viburnums, blueberries and huckleberries, many others.

Metalmarks

FAMILY RIODINIDAE

The metalmarks take their name from small flecks and patches of scales that gleam like burnished metal on their wings. Some authors place them in the subfamily Riodininae within the Lycaenidae, but there are several anatomical differences. The antennae of the metalmarks are unusually long, and the wing venation is not the same. As is the case with lycaenids, however, the forelegs of the males are greatly reduced and are not used for walking. Females have six functional legs. A few authors, particularly in older European literature, use the family name Nemeobiidae.

Approximately thirteen hundred species of metalmarks have been identified, most in the American tropics. Many are wildly colorful, and some have tails like miniature swallowtails or are otherwise "outrageously shaped and decorated," as D'Abrera describes them. He calls the metalmarks "delightful and riotously ornamented creatures." In spite of their great beauty and variety, the metalmarks compose the most neglected of all butterfly families. Individuals mimic lepidoptera of almost every other family, including the skippers and moths, and their classification is extremely complex. In addition, many are fast fliers that inhabit the upper levels of tropical forests, where they are very difficult to study and catch. Others perch on the underside of leaves and remain undetected. Although enormously diverse, they probably occur in relatively low numbers.

Only two dozen metalmark species occur in North America north of Mexico, primarily in the southern and southwestern states. While tropical species may be extremely colorful, most of our metalmarks are more drably. cloaked in brown and orange with black markings. On closer examination, however, the metallic scales gleam like silver threads woven through a delicate tapestry.

The eggs of the Riodinidae are highly variable, but many have a flattened

A little metalmark, Calephelis virginiensis, *perches with wings spread wide. Metallic-looking scales give rise to its name.*

"sea-urchin" shape. The caterpillars are flattened and stout, but less sluglike than those of the Lycaenidae. Highly variable in color, they normally bear dense tufts of long, fine hairs, an unusual characteristic among butterfly larvae. The short, stout pupae may hang from a support by the cremaster at the end of the abdomen, or they may be hidden away on the ground, often at the base of the food plant.

Metalmarks are quite specific in their ecological requirements and seldom wander far from their colonies. They readily visit flowers for nectar and normally perch with open wings spread widely, unlike most other butterflies.

Several species of metalmarks occur in southern and central Texas, and these may occasionally stray toward the Houston area. The only species to be expected in our region, however, is the little metalmark, *Calephelis virginiensis*.

1. Little metalmark

Little Metalmark
Calephelis virginiensis
Virginia metalmark

1. Dorsal

This tiny butterfly ranges along the southeastern Atlantic coastal plain and around the Gulf, reaching its western limits near Houston in Southeast Texas. It is the only metalmark in most of that region. Williams notes that there are no records in recent years near Houston, and that a colony found by Rickard (1967) may no longer exist. However, the little metalmark could easily be over-looked and should be searched for near the coast and in grassy areas amid open, sandy pine woodlands in the northern portion of our area. We photographed the species in Hardin and Tyler counties north of Beaumont.

Several similar metalmarks occur in southern and central Texas, but these are less likely to reach Houston. The little metalmark is best identified by the com-bination of its small size, uniform rusty orange-brown color of the wings above, and dark wing fringes devoid of white checkering. Black markings are heaviest in the basal area of the wings above, and metallic, silvery bands cross the wings and trace the outer margins. The wings below are a slightly brighter orange.

The little metalmark visits a number of flowers for nectar, utilizing mainly short-tubed members of the Asteraceae. It sits with its wings spread wide, and males perch on low vegetation through the sunny daylight hours, waiting for pro-spective mates. Several broods are re-ported for Texas, with adults flying from March until November. However, we have not personally encountered the little metalmark before early May.

Pale green with rows of long, white hairs, the caterpillar feeds on bull thistle (also called yellow thistle) in Texas. Ac-cording to Opler and Krizek, this un-usual larva hides under a host leaf during the day and emerges to feed on top of the leaf at night and on cloudy days, making it extremely difficult to find. The pupa is attached to the lower leaf surface by a silken button and girdle.

SIZE: ⅝–¾ inch.
DESCRIPTION: Orange-brown with black spots and metallic silver lines. Fringes dark, not checkered.
SIMILAR SPECIES: Other metalmarks are extremely unlikely in our area.
SEASON: Reportedly March–November.
LARVA: Green, with long white hairs.
FOOD PLANTS: Bull thistle.

Snout Butterflies

FAMILY LIBYTHEIDAE

This is the smallest of our butterfly families, containing only ten or twelve species. It is also a cosmopolitan group, however, with one or more species in each of the world's temperate and tropical regions. Such worldwide distribution suggests an ancient lineage, and snout butterflies have been found in fossil shales in Florissant, Colorado, dating back 35 million years. Some authors now place this small group of butterflies in a subfamily Libytheinae within the larger family Nymphalidae. Checklists by Ferris and Miller, however, retain family status for Libytheidae, and we use that classification here. Whatever the taxonomic merits of the two points of view, there seems to be instructional value in separating groups of insects that are unique and readily identifiable by the beginner.

The snout butterflies take their name from the unusually long labial palpi, the mouthparts that protect the proboscis. These project far out in front of the head and give the appearance of a beak or snout, although they have no obvious special function. The forewings are hooked, with their tips abruptly squared off. Like the lycaenids and metalmarks, male snout butterflies have the front legs reduced and nonfunctional, while females have three normal pairs of walking legs. Adults often perch motionless on twigs, where the cryptic underwing pattern mimics dead leaves. Scott notes that the "snout" then resembles a leaf stalk and suggests that it evolved to perfect the leaflike camouflage.

Most snout butterflies feed on hackberries, *Celtis*, although the Japanese species utilize members of the rose family. Eggs are laid in small groups on the leaves, and the cylindrical caterpillars are usually green with yellow streaks. They resemble somewhat the larvae of the whites and sulphurs. Pupae hang

A cryptic, dead-leaf pattern provides camouflage for a perching snout butterfly,
Libytheana bachmanii.

1. Snout Butterfly

from a silk button, however, without the silken girdle employed by the Pieridae. Snout butterflies readily visit flowers for nectar. Many are known for staging mass migrations, dispersing from areas of high population density.

Snout Butterfly

Libytheana bachmanii
American snout, Eastern snout butterfly

The snout butterfly can be confused with no other species. Its labial palpi extend far forward from the head into a long beaklike snout from which it takes its name, and its forewings are hooked and abruptly squared off at the tips. The forewing above has white spots near the apex and large orange patches at the base. The hindwing beneath is either heavily mottled or uniformly grayish brown, often with a violet cast. As the snout butterfly sits with folded wings, it closely resembles a dead leaf, the long snout serving as the petiole and adding to the camouflage.

Classification of the snout butterfly is more complex than is its recognition. Our species has long been known by most authors as *Libytheana bachmanii*, and that nomenclature is employed by Ferris and Miller in the checklists that we follow. Two subspecies range through the United States: the nominate eastern *bachmanii*, which occurs in the Houston area, and the western *larvata* of the arid Southwest. The latter ranges into central Texas and is distinguished by being larger and less angular.

Another form, often called the tropical or southern snout, *L. carinenta*, occurs from Mexico southward through Central and South America. It has also been collected in Texas, and on occasion has ranged far north into the midsection of the country. Scott, Opler, Glassberg, and several others regard all of these butterflies as forms of a single American species, in which case they all fall under *L. carinenta*, which has scientific precedence. Opler states emphatically:"It has been shown that our butterfly is the same as that in the American tropics." There is probably considerable merit in this taxonomic stand, but we have chosen to re-

1. Ventral

2. Larvae

tain the traditional name until there is a general consensus. That name honors the Reverend John Bachman, an ardent naturalist and close friend of Audubon, who married one of Bachman's daughters.

Snout butterflies are swift and erratic in their flight. Wary and difficult to approach, they swirl up into the trees when disturbed. However, they nectar at a variety of flowers and also sip moisture from mud puddles and stream banks. They inhabit riparian woodlands, brushy fields, the thorn-scrub of southern Texas, and even city yards and parks, laying their pale green eggs on the tender leaves of native hackberry species. Sugar hackberry and netleaf hackberry serve as larval food plants throughout much of the state. Spiny hackberry, or granjeno, proves popular in South Texas. The caterpillar is dark green with yellow stripes.

Snout butterflies stage massive but sporadic migrations, undoubtedly dispersing from areas of overpopulation. Opler and Krizek cite one such migration in which 1.25 million butterflies moved across a 250-meter front each minute. Another in Tucson, Arizona, in 1966 "obscured the sun and caused the street lights to be turned on at midday." We have also encountered enormous flights across highways in South Texas. So high was the mortality that it was necessary to stop every few miles to clean the windshield and grill of the car.

Neck (1983a) reports on a 1971 migration of snout butterflies in Austin, Texas. Thousands were seen at various locations in July and early August, and they then began moving northward in enormous concentrations, reaching a peak on August 27. It was probably the same massive flight that reached central Kansas about thirty days later. Neck suggests that ample rain caused profuse plant growth and rapid butterfly reproduction. A subsequent drought then sent the unusually high population winging northward.

Neck (1984) also describes a more random and nondirectional mass migration in southern Texas in 1978. During June, July, and September, he observed large flights of butterflies moving in various directions. Such movements were probably in response to scattered rainfall that provided a mosaic of lush plant growth across the region, resulting in isolated concentrations of snout butterflies and local migrations.

SIZE: 1⅝–1⅞ inches.
DESCRIPTION: Long "snout" and angular wings distinctive. Upper forewing with white spots at tip and orange patches at base. Dimorphic, with underside of hindwing either mottled or uniformly grayish brown.
SIMILAR SPECIES: None.
SEASON: Nearly year-round; especially April–November.
LARVA: Green, with yellow stripes.
FOOD PLANTS: Hackberry species.

Longwings
FAMILY HELICONIIDAE

Most recent authors consider the longwings a subfamily or tribe of the Nymphalidae. These colorful and fascinating butterflies, however, have several structural and behavioral characteristics that set them apart from all others. We thus follow the checklists of Ferris and Miller in assigning them to their own family, as much for the convenience of the reader as through any conviction as to the proper taxonomy.

The concepts of family, genus, and species, after all, are artificial human constructions devised for our convenience. They help us indicate relationships among populations, at least as we understand them at the present. The various butterfly populations, however, do not adhere to the strict order we impose. They may seem closely related by some criteria, widely separated by others. Entomologists are constantly combining insect forms and separating others to fit the latest data. For the purposes of this book, we join the "splitters" rather than the "lumpers," seeking to segregate groups of butterflies easily recognizable by the novice. Whether the longwings actually belong to the family Heliconiidae or to the subfamily Heliconiinae remains a matter for debate.

The group is a small one, containing about seventy species. Most inhabit the American tropics, and only one, the gulf fritillary, occurs commonly in our area and through much of the United States. We also include two other species, the Julia and the zebra, that wander sporadically northward to Houston and beyond.

The longwings have elongated wings, slender bodies, large eyes, and long antennae. Only two pairs of legs are functional for walking, as is the case with the Nymphalidae. Larvae of the longwings feed almost exclusively on passionflowers, and both the caterpillars and the adults are distasteful to predators.

The colorful gulf fritillary, Agraulis vanillae, *is abundant throughout the region. Here it feeds at common sunflowers.*

1. Zebra (*photo by Carlos Hernandez*)

The butterflies advertise their unpalatability with bright colors and striking patterns. Such warning colors are called "aposematic colors." All sip nectar from blossoms, but butterflies of the genus *Heliconius* are unique in feeding on pollen as well. They gather the pollen with the proboscis and dissolve nutrients in it with drops of saliva.

The tall, ribbed eggs of the longwings are usually laid singly on leaves, petioles, or tendrils of passion-flower vines; however, some species deposit their eggs in clusters. The caterpillars have rows of long, spurred spines, with another pair of spines or horns on their heads. The hanging chrysalides are distinctly "sway-backed," with wing cases protruding, and are often decorated with bizarre flaps and spines. Male butterflies patrol areas near food plants in search of recently emerged females, or they may select a mature chrysalis and wait nearby, mating with the emerging female before she has even unfurled her wings.

Through their long mutual evolution, the longwings and the host passion-flowers have developed amazing "strategies" and countermeasures in the ongoing battle for survival. Female butterflies usually avoid laying their eggs on plants already containing other eggs, presumably to prevent larvae from consuming all the leaves and subsequently starving. They visit several sites until they find suitable plants. Some passion-flower species, in return, develop tiny growths that resemble eggs, thereby inhibiting oviposition by the female longwing.

It has long been assumed that the longwings gain their acrid, distasteful body juices from their hosts. DeVries notes, however, that there is no hard chemical evidence that this is so. "In fact," says DeVries, "it appears that the defenses are manufactured by the adults by as of yet unknown means." It seems likely that some of the raw materials for such a synthesis may come from the passion-flowers, for the lives of host and butterfly seem inextricably intertwined.

Whatever the source of the longwing's defense, it has created an amazing cycle of protective mimicry. Many otherwise palatable butterflies in several families resemble longwings, presumably gaining a measure of protection by this Batesian mimicry. In addition, forms of the highly variable longwing species resemble each other, often taking the pattern and colors of the most abundant species in a given region. Although all may be distasteful, they reinforce the warning with a common pattern. This is known as Müllerian mimicry.

These cycles of mimicry and individual variation make the study of the Heliconiidae extremely complex. It is enough, writes Klots, to "drive the entomologist crazy." At the same time, it offers great opportunity for research. Longwings are often long-lived, with life spans of as much as six months, and they are relatively easy to breed in captivity. It is clear, says DeVries, that the heliconians will provide "many interesting questions for the next century, as they have for the past."

Gulf Fritillary
Agraulis vanillae

The large, brilliantly marked gulf fritillary is one of our most common and beautiful butterflies. Its wings are not as narrow as those of other Heliconiidae, but they appear noticeably elongated. Bright red-orange above with black markings, the gulf fritillary also has three black-rimmed white spots near the leading edge of the forewing. Females are slightly browner, with heavier dark markings. On the underside, the brown hindwings and tips of the forewings are splashed with elongated silver spots. The true fritillaries of the genus *Speyeria* also have silver spots below, but they are not closely related. The latter range through the northern and western states and do not occur in Texas.

Gulf fritillaries fly virtually throughout the year in the Houston area, appearing even in December and January on warm, sunny days. There are several broods through the spring and summer, and adults seem to reach a peak concentration from August until November. A tropical species that ranges through most of South and Central America and the West Indies, the gulf fritillary inhabits much of the southern United States. It stages periodic northward migrations, however, and sometimes reaches even the northern tier of states. Individual adults may live for several weeks.

The gulf fritillary relies on passionflowers as larval food plants, utilizing both the common purple passion-flower, *Passiflora incarnata*, and the smaller yellow passion-flower, *P. lutea*, in Houston. In addition to these native species, several of the exotic cultivated *Passiflora* serve as potential hosts. According to Scott, the female butterfly is more particular in her choice of hosts than is the larva. The latter will eat several species of passion-flowers in the laboratory that

1. Dorsal

2. Dorsal

3. Ventral

are ignored by the adult while laying her yellow eggs.

The caterpillar is glossy black or slate-gray with red-orange dorsal and lateral stripes. It also has six rows of long, branching black spines. The angular brown chrysalis has several knobby projections and hangs downward from a silken pad, often on the stem of the food plant.

The gulf fritillary inhabits woodland edges, brushy fields, roadsides, and urban gardens, visiting a variety of flowers for nectar throughout the day. Ajilvsgi lists lantana, butterfly bush, zinnia, aster, thistle, and verbena as some of its favorites. The flight is fast and steady, with shallow wingbeats. Males patrol their territories in search of mates.

Rutowski and Schaefer describe the courtship behavior of the gulf fritillary in Arizona. In most successful courtships, the male performs what the authors describe as a "wing clap display," in which he alights beside the female and repeat-

4. Larva

Julia
Dryas iulia
Orange longwing, Iulia

The long, narrow wings of the male Julia are bright orange above, with a narrow black border on the margin of the hindwing. The female is duller orange with more extensive black markings. Both are plain yellow-orange below. This species might conceivably be mistaken for the gulf fritillary, but it is longer winged, has a less extensive dark pattern above, and lacks the silver spots below.

A tropical species that ranges from Brazil through Central America and the West Indies to peninsular Florida and southern Texas, the Julia occurs sporadically in the Houston area. It flies year-round near the Mexican border and wanders northward in summer through the southern plains, occasionally as far as eastern Nebraska. Williams notes that it occurs primarily in the Colorado and Guadalupe river watersheds during its wanderings in Texas, but we have encountered this striking insect in eastern Houston and Baytown in Harris County and at Wallisville in Chambers County. At this writing, however, we have not seen the Julia in the Houston area for several years, perhaps because of severe freezes that would preclude any overwintering and local reproduction. All of our sightings have been from September through November, the best time to see most vagrants from deep South Texas as they wander northward through the summer.

The Julia is fast and agile on the wing, maneuvering adeptly through the dense vegetation of the tropical forests and subtropical woodlands it prefers. It is strongly attracted to flowers and visits a number of species in the clearings and fields near its wooded habitats. Perhaps coincidentally, each individual we have seen in this region has been feeding at lantana, one of the most universally

edly claps his wings together, often catching the female's antennae between his wings. It appears likely that this display transfers chemical signals to the female and clearly announces the species' identity.

We have also watched male gulf fritillaries mating with newly emerged females, sometimes before the latter's wings had fully expanded. In the extreme, mating was initiated just as the female's abdomen emerged from the chrysalis.

SIZE: 2½ – 3 inches.

DESCRIPTION: Elongated orange wings with black markings. Silver spots on hindwing and tip of forewing below.

SIMILAR SPECIES: Silver spots of the true fritillaries are not elongated. Those species do not occur in our region.

SEASON: Virtually year-round; most common from August through November.

LARVA: Black or slate-gray with orange stripes and black spines.

FOOD PLANTS: Passion-flower species.

1. Male, dorsal

2. Male, ventral

popular nectar sources for butterflies. Julias apparently engage in "trap-lining," following a set feeding route each day to take advantage of local flowers. Although they stop at many blossoms, their visits are normally short. Emmel (1991) suggests that this "eat-and-run" behavior may indicate a greater dependence on rapid flight to avoid hungry birds than on the distastefulness attributed to most longwings.

In addition to visiting flowers, the Julia also sips moisture from mud puddles and stream banks. The Preston-Mafhams report that it has been seen sipping liquid from the corner of a cayman's eye in Brazil, and we have seen Julias and other tropical butterflies perch on the heads of basking turtles to probe their eyes in the rainforests of Ecuador.

Males patrol all day in search of mates, and females lay their yellow eggs singly on tender leaves or tendrils of passion-flower vines. Several references suggest that the small yellow passion-flower, *Passiflora lutea*, is used most frequently in Texas. The brown caterpillar has fine, transverse black lines and spots and bears six rows of branching spines. These spines may cause a rash on human hands, perhaps because of a yellow fluid exuded from their tips. The warty, brown chrysalis is ornamented with gold and hangs by the tip of the abdomen from a silken pad. Adults may live for a few weeks, a long life span compared to many small butterflies but shorter than that of some heliconians.

Fabricius first described the Julia as *Papilio iulia* in 1775, according to Brown and Heineman. Eighteen years later he also introduced the name "Julia," but the older classical spelling clearly takes scientific precedence. Both come from the feminine form of "Julius." Many older publications refer to the species as *Dryas julia*, while newer ones use *D. iulia*. Most, however, retain the more familiar "Julia" as the common name. The genus, *Dryas*, takes its name from Greek mythology. Dryas was the father of Lykurgos, King of Thrace. Because the Julia is not highly migratory, local populations in tropical America and on various islands vary in their color and the extent of the dark markings on their wings. Numerous subspecies have been recognized by various authors.

SIZE: 3–3⅝ inches.
DESCRIPTION: Long, narrow wings. Orange above with few dark markings; plain yellow-orange below.
SIMILAR SPECIES: Gulf fritillary is more strongly marked above and has silver spots below.
SEASON: All year in South Texas; strays northward in late summer and fall. Most likely in Houston from September to November.
LARVA: Brown, with black markings and spines.
FOOD PLANTS: Passion-flowers.

Zebra
Heliconius charitonius
Zebra longwing

The beautiful and unmistakable zebra butterfly is unfortunately a rare visitor to Houston from Mexico and the lower Rio Grande Valley. We have seen it occasionally within the city and at several other locations in Harris and Chambers counties, but have encountered it in recent years only at Mercer Arboretum. There a small, free-flying colony has been established on cultivated hybrid passionflowers.

Williams reports that a population at the Houston Arboretum and Nature Center in Memorial Park was apparently killed by extremely cold weather in 1983 and had not been reestablished as of 1990. Vagrants are most likely to appear in late summer or fall, and barring a severe freeze, these wanderers can establish breeding colonies on the passion-

flowers that grow abundantly throughout the area.

A tropical butterfly with many subspecies or races, the zebra ranges from South America northward through Central America and the West Indies to southern Florida and Texas. It occurs in the southern tip of our state at least from April through November and perhaps year-round during mild winters. From this population stronghold, periodic migrants reach as far as South Carolina, Nebraska, and New Mexico during the summer months. The major movement, however, takes place through the drier central portion of Texas, and zebras appear more frequently in the Austin region than they do in Houston or along the coast.

Its long, narrow, black wings crossed by yellow stripes, the zebra heliconian should not be confused with the zebra swallowtail. The latter is black and white, with the slender tails characteristic of

1. Dorsal

2. Ventral

swallowtail species. Indeed, there is no other species in North America that resembles *Heliconius charitonius*, although the poisonous and distasteful compounds in its body make it a model for mimicry complexes throughout the tropics.

The zebra inhabits forests and woodland edges, flying with a slow, fluttering wingbeat. If disturbed, however, it darts into the woods with surprising agility and can be difficult to approach. A "trapliner," the zebra follows a selected route each day, visiting the same flowers to feed on pollen. The pollen collected on its modified proboscis is broken down by enzymes into amino acids and other nutrients and absorbed by the butterfly. Lantana appears to be a favorite source of both nectar and pollen, and it is on this plant that we have most frequently seen the zebra in our area.

Males patrol their routes in search of females, sometimes mating with those fresh from their chrysalides. Scott, in fact, describes matings in which the male is attracted to a female pupa, landing on it and resting head downward, sometimes in company with one or two other males. The male recognizes female pupae and is not attracted to those of other males. When the female is about to emerge, Scott writes, the male breaks through the pupal shell with his abdomen and mates with her even before she has emerged.

The female lays a few eggs each day over a period of several weeks or months. During that time, she may deposit a total of a thousand eggs, provided she has an ample diet of nectar and pollen. Consequently, there are no synchronized broods as there are in many other butterfly species that lay all their eggs within a few days. In the laboratory, zebras survived for four and one-half months on a pollen diet; they failed to live more than one month without the pollen.

3. Larva

Eggs are deposited singly or in small groups on various species of passionflowers, the only larval food plants. The caterpillar is creamy white with dark bands and spots and bears six rows of branching black spines. The ornate brown chrysalis has paler wing cases and is ornamented with metallic silver or gold spots, flanges on the abdomen, and numerous short spines.

Adult zebra butterflies usually remain within a few hundred yards of their home territories, assembling in late afternoon to roost communally through the night. Most hang upside down from twigs and leaves, their disruptive pattern making them hard to see as they rest in the dappled woodland shade. In studying communal roosts in Mexico, Waller and Gilbert found that fresh butterflies first associated with established members at pollen plants during the day. Later in the afternoon, the new recruits followed the older butterflies to their roosting sites.

The zebra owes its scientific name to Greek mythology. The genus is derived from Helicon, a mountain in the Greek province of Boeotia frequented by the Muses. The Charites were the three Graces, or goddesses of beauty, constant attendants of Aphrodite. The beautiful *Heliconius charitonius* is no myth, but it appears in the parks and gardens of Houston and southeastern Texas much less frequently than we would like.

SIZE: 3–3½ inches.

DESCRIPTION: Long, narrow black wings with yellow stripes.

SIMILAR SPECIES: None.

SEASON: Most of the year in deep South Texas; wanders northward to Houston on rare occasions. Usually seen in late summer or fall.

LARVA: White, with dark spots and black spines.

FOOD PLANTS: Passion-flowers.

Nymphalids or Brush-Footed Butterflies

FAMILY NYMPHALIDAE

Adult nymphalids of both sexes have the front pair of legs dramatically reduced in size and covered with long, hairlike scales, resulting in the name "brush-footed butterflies." Although useless for walking, these tiny forelegs function as chemoreceptors. Family members share a common wing venation and have finely scaled antennae; however, there are no easily observed generalizations that characterize all of the diverse species. Quite simply, if a North American butterfly seems to fit in no other family, it is probably one of the Nymphalidae.

Some authors include the snout butterflies (Libytheidae), longwings (Heliconiidae), satyrs or browns (Satyridae), and milkweed butterflies (Danaiidae) as subfamilies of the Nymphalidae. Although there may be some degree of taxonomic merit to this system, we have chosen to follow Ferris in placing each of these easily recognizable groups in its own family. Such an arrangement clearly aids in the field in separating unknown butterflies into manageable categories.

Nymphalids range greatly in size, but many of our species are colorful medium to large butterflies that occur in a wide variety of habitats. Some have irregular wing margins or tail-like projections, but there is no characteristic common shape. Most are strong, fast fliers, and many are attracted to flowers. Others, however, do not visit flowers at all, feeding instead on tree sap, rotting fruit, dung, or carrion.

Brown and Heineman note that the Nymphalidae are well represented among the known fossil butterflies, indicating their ancient lineage. As a result, those authors suggest, "the present members of the family represent many twigs on the evolutionary tree."

The eggs frequently have a ribbed pattern and are laid singly or in clusters

Blooming goldenrod provides nectar for many butterflies including this pearl crescent, Phyciodes tharos, *during the autumn months.*

 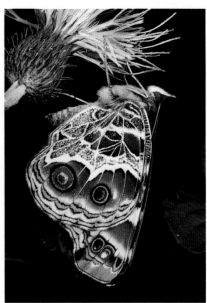

1. Phaon crescent   2. American painted lady

or strings. Hatching from groups of eggs, the larvae often remain together during their early instars, feeding communally. Many conceal themselves in shelters of webbed or folded leaves, emerging to feed at night. Nymphalid caterpillars typically are covered with rows of branching spines or bristly tubercles and often have a pair of "horns" on the head. Pupae hang head downward from silken mats by the hooks of their cremasters and may be ornamented with tubercles and metallic spots.

The Nymphalidae overwinter both as larvae and adults. Hibernating butterflies frequently appear on warm winter days, although this population will not breed until food plants become available in the spring.

Variegated Fritillary
Euptoieta claudia

The variegated fritillary inhabits open, sunny fields, prairies, and roadsides throughout the Houston area. Although it is relatively common and occurs virtually all year, it is seldom found in large numbers. Its low, erratic flight and wary nature make it difficult to approach except when it nectars at flowers. The genus name, according to Opler and Krizek, reflects this elusive behavior. It is derived from the Greek *euptoietos*, meaning "easily scared." The species name comes from Claudius, the name of several Roman emperors.

The wings above are tawny, brownish orange marked with a complex, variegated pattern of black spots. Beneath, the wings have a mottled, cryptic blend of dark spots and light patches, resembling somewhat a dead leaf. *Euptoieta claudia* lacks the prominent silver spots on the hindwings below that characterize the gulf fritillary and the true fritillaries of the genus *Speyeria*. The latter are northern butterflies that do not occur within our area. The similar Mexican fritillary, *E. hegesia*, ranges through the tropics and occurs in the Rio Grande Valley. Although it wanders sparingly northward in Texas, it should not be expected in Houston. *Hegesia* differs from *claudia* in having the wings above a brighter orange and the inner portion of the hindwings unmarked.

The variegated fritillary reveals its close relationships with the gulf fritillary and with the true fritillaries by its choice of larval food plants. It uses both passionflowers like the former and violets and pansies like the latter. In addition, it lays its eggs on a number of other plants in a variety of families. Ajilvsgi notes that it apparently prefers species of flax in Texas, but we have found it most commonly on both purple and yellow passion-flowers in the Houston area, often in company with larvae of the gulf fritillary.

1. Dorsal

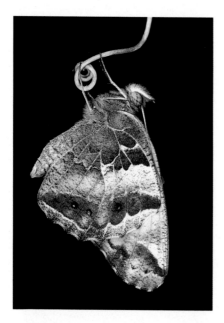

2. Ventral

3. Larva

The pale greenish or cream-colored eggs are laid singly on the leaves or stems of an appropriate food plant, and both the larvae and the pupae are fully as beautiful as the adult butterflies. The shiny, red-orange caterpillar has dorsal and lateral black stripes enclosing white patches, and six rows of branching black spines adorn its body. The pearly white or pale blue-green, gemlike chrysalis bears black or dark brown spots, yellow antenna cases, and shimmering golden tubercles.

The variegated fritillary ranges from the southern United States through the higher elevations of tropical America to Argentina. None of its stages can withstand extremely cold weather, but adults move northward in the spring and summer to colonize most of the U.S. and southern Canada. Those populations then die out in winter. In the Houston area, however, *E. claudia* occurs virtually throughout the year. It hibernates as an adult, and these butterflies may appear on warm days even in midwinter.

SIZE: 1¾–2½ inches, occasionally larger. Size varies greatly.
DESCRIPTION: Brownish orange above with black markings. Lacks silver spots below.
SIMILAR SPECIES: Gulf fritillary is longer-winged, brighter orange, has silver spots below. True fritillaries (*Speyeria*) have silver spots below, do not occur in our area. Mexican fritillary unmarked on inner portions of hindwings above.
SEASON: Late February through December; occasional in midwinter.
LARVA: Red-orange, with black stripes containing white spots, branching black spines.
FOOD PLANTS: Passion-flower, violets, pansies, flax, mayapple, purslane, stonecrop, others.

Bordered Patch
Chlosyne lacinia
Sunflower patch, Scudder's patched
butterfly, Patch butterfly, Adjutrix patch,
Lacinia checkerspot

This colorful insect is not a regular member of Houston's butterfly fauna. A tropical species that ranges from southern Arizona and Texas through Central and South America to Argentina, it wanders northward during the warm summer months, sometimes reaching Kansas and Nebraska. Houston lies on the extreme eastern edge of this range, and the bordered patch occasionally occurs in dry, open areas of western Harris County. So bright and colorful is this striking butterfly, however, that it is likely to be noticed when present in any number.

Howe notes that the bordered patch "is probably our most variable butterfly, for there seems to be almost endless polymorphism of wing color and pattern." The typical Texas form, named *Chlosyne lacinia adjutrix* by Scudder in 1875, is black above with small white spots and a wide orange-yellow band across the wings. The underside mirrors this contrasting pattern. No other butterfly in our area has similar markings, although there are related patch species in South and West Texas.

In other populations, the broad transverse band varies from white to yellow or almost red. In some forms, it is reduced or absent entirely. Neck (1980) reported an aberrant male from Austin, Texas, in which the median band was absent except for a few tiny spots, closely resembling the tropical form. It was courting a normal, orange-banded female.

The female bordered patch lays her greenish yellow eggs in clusters on the underside of the leaves of sunflowers, ragweeds, crownbeard, cocklebur, and various other members of the family Asteraceae. Scott documents an average of

1. Dorsal

2. Ventral

3. Young larvae, on communal web

139 eggs per cluster. The hatchling larvae then remain together through their third instar, feeding communally and sometimes webbing leaves together into silken shelters. They later wander off to complete their development alone. As winter approaches, third-instar larvae enter hibernation in response to the short photoperiod; there is also evidence that they may go into an inactive diapause during unusually hot, dry periods in summer. Several broods appear each year in South Texas.

Caterpillars of the bordered patch vary dramatically in color. Some are orange-red; others, black. Still others are striped. All are heavily armored with black spines. Neck, now with the Houston Museum of Natural Science, carried out his Ph.D. research on the genetics of larval color polymorphism. He found that the orange-red "rufa" form is caused by a dominant gene that prevents the other

4. Mature larva

two forms from appearing. Presence of a recessive gene produces the striped "bicolor" form, which is dominant to the recessive black "nigra." Pupae are also variable, ranging from white to black.

In spite of their high degree of geographic variability, most adult bordered patch butterflies that appear in Houston will be easily recognizable from the accompanying photographs. They nectar primarily at white and yellow flowers, while males also sip fluids from mud puddles, dung, and carrion.

SIZE: 1¾–2¼ inches.
DESCRIPTION: Black, with broad orange band.
SIMILAR SPECIES: None in our area.
SEASON: All year in South Texas; wanders northward in summer and fall.
LARVA: Orange, black, or striped; with black spines.
FOOD PLANTS: Sunflowers, ragweeds, crownbeard, cocklebur, other composites.

Texan Crescent
Anthanassa texana
Texas crescent, Texan crescentspot

The Texan crescent was first described from New Braunfels, Texas, in 1863. Some authors place it in the genus *Anthanassa*; others assign it to *Phyciodes* with the other crescents. The outer margin of the forewing is uniquely concave, and the wings are dark brownish black with white spots. Most specimens have at least some reddish brown at the wing bases. The underwings are more strongly buffy orange at the base, with black markings and whitish spotbands. No other small butterfly in our area is similarly marked.

A year-round resident of the southern U.S., from the southeastern states through Texas to California, the Texan crescent ranges through Mexico to Guatemala. The Texas population tends to wander northward in the summer, occa-

sionally reaching North Dakota and Minnesota. The southeastern population, however, seems less inclined to migrate. Known as the Seminole crescent, *A. texana seminole*, the latter is considered a distinct species by some authors.

An inhabitant of stream beds, dry arroyos, thorn-scrub woodlands, and city parks and gardens, *A. texana* occurs frequently in Houston throughout much of the year. It sips nectar from a variety of flowers. Males perch on exposed twigs and dart out to inspect all intruders, chasing off potential rivals. Encountering a receptive female, the male begins an elaborate courtship "dance," flying loops around his prospective mate.

Most references list the early stages of the Texan crescent as "not reported" or "poorly known," but Ajilvsgi describes them in some detail. Hatching from clusters of eggs laid on the undersides of leaves, young larvae are greenish brown with pale, flattened tubercles. The ma-

1. Dorsal

2. Ventral

3. Larva

ture larva is yellow-brown with black and white stripes along the sides. Spines on the lower body are greenish white; the others are brown. Documented food plants include members of the acanthus family.

SIZE: 1–1¾ inches; female larger than male.
DESCRIPTION: Black with white spots, some red at base of wings above. Buffy orange at base of wings below, with black and white markings. Wing margin strongly concave.
SIMILAR SPECIES: Other crescents orange with black pattern.
SEASON: March–November.
LARVA: Yellow-brown, spiny.
FOOD PLANTS: Flame acanthus, ruellia, water-willow, dicliptera, tube-tongue, shrimp plant, and other members of the Acanthaceae.

Phaon Crescent
Phyciodes phaon
Phaon crescentspot, Mat-plant crescent

This southern crescent is a common resident of the Houston area throughout much of the year. It inhabits open fields, marshes, dunes, roadsides, and even city lawns wherever its widespread food plant, frog-fruit, occurs. It takes nectar from frog-fruit blossoms and from a wide variety of flowers, although it seems particularly fond of asters and other small composites in the fall. It also sips moisture at mud puddles and damp patches of earth.

The phaon crescent looks much like the pearl crescent, with which it often shares its habitats; however, it can be identified by the pale cream band across the forewing. The pearl crescent is orange above with black markings. The phaon crescent has a broad black band across the middle of the forewing above, followed outwardly by the cream-colored band and then an orange one. That pattern is also reflected on the underside. A winter form is darker below, a variation caused by the shorter photoperiod during development.

A resident from the southeastern states to West Texas and southern California, *Phyciodes phaon* ranges southward to Cuba, Mexico, and Guatemala. In summer it strays northward through the midsection of the country, where it establishes short-lived colonies that fail to survive the winter. In general, the phaon crescent prefers prairies and the coastal plains.

According to Opler and Krizek, males spend most of the warm daylight hours patrolling in search of prospective mates, usually near colonies of the host plants. Mating occurs from late morning through midday, and the female is the carrier during mated flights.

Females lay their eggs in clusters on the underside of frog-fruit leaves. Also

1. Dorsal

2. Ventral

140 / Nymphalids or Brush-Footed Butterflies

called fog-fruit, mat-plant, and mat-grass, frog-fruit is placed in the genus *Lippia* in most current butterfly books. However, the several species have recently been moved to the genus *Phyla*. *Phyla (Lippia) lanceolata* and *P. nodiflora* are most often cited as the hosts of the phaon crescent, but *P. incisa*, the Texas frog-fruit, probably serves as well. It appears to be the most common of the genus in the immediate Houston area, but we have not as yet been able to find the butterfly larvae.

The variable caterpillars are reported to be olive-brown with both lighter and darker lines. They are also adorned with numerous spines. The brown pupae are mottled with black and cream. Pyle (1981) reports that only about 5 percent of crescent eggs survive to the adult stage, a mortality rate typical of most butterflies. Predators and parasitic wasps and flies take a heavy toll at every stage of the metamorphosis.

The phaon crescent takes its name from classical mythology. Phaon received from Aphrodite a small box of ointment that made him the most beautiful of men. Sappho then fell in love with Phaon and wrote her most passionate love songs to him. When Phaon tired of her, Sappho threw herself into the sea.

SIZE: ⅞–1¼ inches.
DESCRIPTION: Orange and black, with pale cream-colored band across forewing.
SIMILAR SPECIES: Pearl crescent lacks pale forewing band.
SEASON: Virtually throughout the year.
LARVA: Olive-brown, with light and dark lines, numerous spines.
FOOD PLANTS: Frog-fruit.

Pearl Crescent
Phyciodes tharos
Pearly crescentspot

The little pearl crescent inhabits open, weedy fields, roadsides, and even city lots throughout the Houston area. It is orange above with black borders and an intricate pattern of black scrawls and spots, the female more heavily marked than the male. The hindwing beneath is buffy or yellowish, with a brown marginal patch containing a light crescent. Early spring and late fall broods are darker and more heavily marked below. This form is given the name "marcia" in some references.

One of the most abundant and widespread of the butterflies in eastern North America, the pearl crescent was first described in 1773. For two hundred years, however, it has been the source of much confusion within the entomological community. Numerous names have been assigned to geographical and seasonal varieties, all of which were regarded as forms of a single species. In the last few years, populations across much of Canada and through the western states have been designated as a distinct species, the northern pearl crescent. Some authors assign it the name *Phyciodes selenis*; some use *P. pascoensis*. Others, including Miller, still relegate the northern form to subspecies status under *P. tharos*.

The nominal species as presently described ranges from the northern states southward through the eastern two-thirds of the U.S. to southern Mexico. The northern pearl crescent occupies most of Canada and the Rocky Mountains, with isolated communities in the northern and northeastern states. The zone of overlap in the North is further confused by the presence of still another species, the tawny crescent, *P. batesii*. Fortunately for the beginner, Houston hosts only *P. tharos* among these similar butterflies. The only other crescent likely to occur in our area is the phaon cres-

1. Dorsal

2. Summer form, ventral

cent, *P. phaon*, and the latter is easily separated from the pearl crescent by the presence of a cream-colored band across the forewing.

An active, pugnacious butterfly, the pearl crescent darts out to investigate intruders ranging from other butterflies to humans. It feeds avidly at a wide variety of flowers and swarms around mud puddles and wet patches of soil, sometimes in large numbers. Unlike many butterflies that normally sit with wings pressed together tightly over their backs, pearl crescents routinely open their wings widely when feeding or when basking in the sun. Their flight is low, often just above the grass tops, and they escape pursuit by darting in among the grasses and weed stems.

The female deposits her eggs in clusters on the underside of aster leaves and may lay up to seven hundred eggs during her short lifetime. The young larvae are gregarious but do not spin a sheltering web; later they disperse to develop separately. Those hatching late in the fall may interrupt their development to hibernate and then resume feeding in the spring.

The pearl crescent has probably profited from the cutting of woodlands and the introduction of agriculture, allowing it to expand its range into the open fields it prefers. Williams suggests that the pearl crescent is outnumbered in the immediate Houston area by the phaon crescent, but we find both of them abundant in many areas around the city. They breed almost continuously through the year, disappearing only during the coldest midwinter weather.

3. Spring and fall form, ventral

SIZE: 1–1½ inches.
DESCRIPTION: Orange above, with black markings. Hindwing below tawny, with brown marginal patch containing light crescent.
SIMILAR SPECIES: Phaon crescent has cream-colored band across forewing.
SEASON: At least March–December.
LARVA: Dark brown, with brown spines and yellow lines. Dark head with white patches.
FOOD PLANTS: Asters.

Question Mark
Polygonia interrogationis

This common butterfly takes its name from the silver mark on the underside of the hindwing. Consisting of a curved line and a dot, it does indeed look like a stylized question mark. This is one of several "anglewing" butterflies that share a similar wing shape, with irregular margins and short tail-like projections. Orange above, with dark markings, they are cryptically patterned below and resemble dead leaves when they perch with closed wings. All of the other anglewings in the same genus, sometimes collectively called "commas," are smaller than the question mark and have only a single silver comma mark, without the dot below it. The scientific name of the question mark comes from the Greek *polygonos*, "many angled," and the Latin *interrogatio*, "question."

Polygonia interrogationis ranges throughout most of eastern North America, from southern Canada to central Mexico. It inhabits moist woodlands, wooded swamps, and even city parks and yards, wherever its larval food plants can be found. Various species of elms and hackberries serve as primary host plants, and most references also list nettle, false nettle, and hops. Heitzman and Heitzman, however, suggest that the latter plants "need to be confirmed." We have found many larvae on both elm and hackberry in the Houston area.

The adult question mark is seasonally dimorphic. The summer form, sometimes called "umbrosa," has the upperside of the hindwings largely black. The winter form, which emerges in the fall and hibernates until the following spring, has orange hindwings with dark spots. The latter also has longer tails tipped with violet. In addition, there are two different underwing patterns. One form is plain brown below; the other is heavily streaked and mottled, often with blue and purple. These are not sexual differences, for the sexes are similar.

Question marks do not normally visit flowers for nectar. Instead, they take nourishment from tree sap, rotting fruit, and even animal dung. The male is aggressively territorial, perching on a tree trunk or limb and flying out to challenge any intruder. He seeks a mate during the late afternoon hours.

The pale green, ribbed eggs are barrel-shaped and are laid singly or stacked one on top of another, forming chains of up to eight eggs. When ovipositing, the female flies along and alights on leaves of the proper shape, seeking an appropriate food plant. When she finds one, however, she often "bounces off" that leaf and alights nearby, sometimes laying her eggs on an adjacent plant. The hatchling caterpillars must then find their way to the proper host before they can feed.

The larvae are highly variable, ranging from yellow to reddish brown to almost black. Strongly patterned with colorful spots and bands, they bear a fierce-looking array of branching spines. Pupae range from yellowish to greenish brown, with two short horns on the head and a series of metallic silver or gold spots. They hang head downward from a silken pad, often on fences or beneath the eaves or window ledges of buildings.

Question marks fly throughout most of the year in Houston. Winter adults hibernate during the coldest weather, seeking shelter in tree cavities, beneath loose bark, or even under old boards. They emerge on warm, sunny days, basking with spread wings on tree trunks and other exposed perches. Some authors suggest that the summer form estivates during hot, dry periods, much as its winter counterpart hibernates to escape the cold. Longer lived than many of our butterflies, these two broods thus sustain the population throughout the year. Glassberg also notes that question marks stage dramatic southward migrations along the

1. Summer form, dorsal

2. Winter form, dorsal

3. Pair mating, ventral

4. Larva

eastern seaboard in the fall, the same individuals moving back north in the spring to repopulate the northeastern states.

In our area there appear to be several almost continuous broods, for we have found actively feeding larvae throughout the months the trees hold their leaves. It is possible that some adults estivate during unusually hot periods, and others hibernate in midwinter. Even then, however, the pretty question mark may appear in your backyard on a sunny day, fanning its angled wings and darting about in rapid, erratic flight.

The eastern comma, or hop merchant, *Polygonia comma*, occurs throughout most of the eastern U.S. and ranges into northeastern Texas. We have not encountered it as far south as Houston, nor has Williams reported it; however, it might be overlooked should strays appear in our area. Somewhat smaller than the question mark, it has similar color forms and a silver "comma" on the hindwing below.

SIZE: 2¼–3 inches.
DESCRIPTION: Orange above with dark markings; mottled brown beneath. Angled, short-tailed wings with silver "question mark" on underside of hindwing.
SIMILAR SPECIES: Eastern comma is smaller, has single curved silver mark below.
SEASON: February–December; irregular on warm winter days.
LARVA: Highly variable, ranging from yellow to black. Marked with colored spots and bands, bears branching spines.
FOOD PLANTS: Elm and hackberry species. Nettle, false nettle, and hops also reported.

Mourning Cloak
Nymphalis antiopa

Although its name seems to imply a drab, somber butterfly, the unmistakable mourning cloak is extremely attractive when seen in good light. Wings that first appear black are really deep maroon, reflecting purple highlights as they shimmer in the sun. Their ragged, irregular margins are bordered with creamy yellow. Just inside the border is a row of gleaming, iridescent blue spots. Flying up from cover, the mourning cloak fairly glows as it darts rapidly about. Dropping back to the ground or alighting on a tree trunk, however, it closes its wings to reveal a cryptic, camouflage pattern of grayish black bordered by the mottled, cream-colored band.

Widely distributed, the well-known mourning cloak occurs throughout most of North America. It ranges from the tundra line in Alaska and Canada southward through the U.S. to central Mexico, occasionally reaching South America. Other populations inhabit northern Eurasia, and the species wanders sporadically to England, where it is has been given the more charming name of "Camberwell beauty." The scientific name stems from Greek mythology; Antiope was the leader of the Amazons.

Shapiro notes that in spite of its enormous range, the mourning cloak remains remarkably stable in its form. It looks much the same throughout the world, and seasonal variations seem to be nonexistent. Shapiro demonstrated that occasional aberrations result from temperature shock to the pupae. Sudden chilling, for example, may result in a form with unusually wide creamy borders.

Unfortunately for Houstonians, the mourning cloak is relatively rare in our area. The extensive U.S. range does not normally include peninsular Florida, southern Louisiana, and southern Texas. Indeed, Opler's range map shows it skirting the entire Texas Coast, and Williams writes that "this species does not occur near the Gulf or on the Coastal Plains." The latter author states that there are barely enough records to include it in his annotated checklist of Southeast Texas. To a large extent, this is true, but we have encountered adult mourning cloaks several times in various parts of Houston. We also discovered a brood of two dozen mature larvae descending a cedar elm in our backyard in Baytown to pupate beneath the eaves of our house. While never abundant within our area, the mourning cloak does occur sporadically, and its large size and unique pattern make it easy to identify.

Adults seldom feed at flowers. Instead, they take nourishment from tree sap and rotting fruit, as do several other nymphalids. Holes chiseled by sapsuckers provide abundant feeding stations for the butterflies. They land on the tree trunk above the sap flow and walk down to it,

perching head downward to sip the sweet liquid. Bitzer and Shaw investigated the territorial behavior of male mourning cloaks and found that they defend large areas averaging more than three hundred square meters, darting out to chase off other butterflies and even birds. They fly short patrols from different perches, changing perches from time to time to cover the entire territory.

The female deposits her eggs in clusters, forming rings around the twigs of appropriate food plants. Willow, cottonwood, birch, elm, and hackberry all serve as primary hosts, while some references mention mulberry, rose, and several others. The gregarious caterpillars are black with a fierce array of long black spines. Tiny white flecks cover the body, which also has a dorsal row of brick-red spots. The pupae are brown or gray, with numerous pink-tipped tubercles. When clustered together, both larvae and pupae twitch in unison if disturbed, a de-

1. Dorsal

2. Ventral

3. Larva

fense mechanism that may serve to frighten away potential predators.

The mourning cloak is perhaps our longest-lived butterfly. Adults may survive for ten or eleven months, and a single brood sustains northern populations throughout the year. Scott quotes a European experiment in which hundreds of mourning cloaks were marked and released. After emerging in June and July, they flew up to seventy kilometers and then entered estivation, remaining dormant until fall. Emerging to feed and replace fat supplies, they then hibernated through the winter. They did not mate until the following spring. Scott notes that this pattern may also occur in Canada and the northern states.

Farther south, however, there are probably two or more overlapping broods. Fall adults hibernate through the winter, seeking sheltered niches and protecting themselves with chemicals in their bodies that serve as natural antifreeze. They occasionally emerge on warm, sunny days to fly around and take nourishment from tree sap or decaying fruit. Mourning cloaks are among the first butterflies to appear again in the spring, sometimes before the snow has melted.

This long life, combined with hibernation in winter and estivation in summer, makes it difficult to determine the dynamics of a mourning cloak population. To further complicate matters, some adults apparently migrate southward each fall while others remain behind. The larvae we encountered in the Houston area were mature in early April, and the adults emerged from pupae later the same month. The exact timing of the breeding cycle, however, remains in question.

SIZE: 3–3½ inches.
DESCRIPTION: Wings above dark maroon, with row of blue spots; irregular margins creamy yellow. Grayish black below, with pale margins.
SIMILAR SPECIES: None.
SEASON: Uncommon and irregular throughout the year.
LARVA: Black, with white flecks and row of red spots on back; black spines.
FOOD PLANTS: Willow, cottonwood, birch, elm, hackberry, others.

Red Admiral
Vanessa atalanta
Alderman, Nettle butterfly

The red admiral can be confused with no other North American butterfly. Its velvety black forewing has white spots at the tip and a median band of bright red-orange. That color also borders the black hindwing, appearing to connect with the forewing band when the butterfly perches with wings spread wide. After flashing its bright colors as it darts rapidly about, the red admiral seems almost to vanish when it perches again and folds its wings. The dark hindwing below is cryptically mottled with brown and blue, while the forewing pattern is muted and less distinct. Sitting head downward on a tree trunk, this common backyard butterfly exhibits near-perfect camouflage.

The red admiral occurs throughout most of North America south of the high Arctic. It ranges from Alaska and Canada south through the U.S. and the highlands of Mexico to Guatemala. Other populations inhabit northern Africa, Europe, and western Asia, and introductions have established it in Hawaii and New Zealand. First described from Europe by Linnaeus in 1758, this beautiful butterfly takes its scientific name from classical mythology. Atalanta of Boeotia was the daughter of King Schoeneus. Her great beauty gained her many admirers, but she killed those she conquered in races. She was finally defeated by Hippomenes, whom she married.

Red admirals are territorial and highly aggressive, darting out to challenge passing birds and mammals as well as other butterflies. They frequently alight on humans, apparently taking salts from perspiration. Regular visitors to a variety of flowers, they also feed at tree sap, ripe fruit, and animal dung and sip moisture at mud puddles.

The female deposits her pale green,

1. Dorsal

2. Ventral

3. Larva

barrel-shaped eggs singly on leaves of host plants, but she may lay several eggs on the same plant. Nettles serve as the primary larval host, but false nettle and pellitory are also used. All are in the family Urticaceae. One would expect that the red admiral's bright pattern provides a warning of toxicity, but Emmel (1991) reports that larvae and adults are not known to assimilate poisonous compounds from the stinging nettles.

The highly variable larvae range in color from yellow-green to black. They are heavily mottled with lighter spots and covered with short spines. The caterpillar further conceals itself by constructing a tube of leaves in which it lives, eating away at its temporary shelter. When it has eaten one refuge, it moves on to construct another. The hanging chrysalis is brown or gray, faintly marked with black and ornamented with golden tubercles.

Red admirals apparently hibernate as both pupae and adults. They also stage long migrations, leaving the coldest regions of their range and recolonizing them the next year. Glassberg reports that "tens of thousands streamed north through the New York area in the spring and summer of 1990," and Opler and Krizek cite massive migrations of thousands of red admirals in Florida during April and May of 1953 and 1955 and in Maine during June 1957. They have also been reported from ships far out at sea.

Red admirals inhabit shrubby fields, marshes, woodland clearings, and city parks and yards throughout the Houston area. They may even appear on warm winter days, perching upside down on tree trunks in the rays of the warming sun. We encounter them in our own backyard throughout much of the year, but we have yet to locate the larvae and their food plants. Their fresh condition suggests they have recently emerged, but red admirals are strong fliers that wander far from colonies of their host.

SIZE: 1¾–2½ inches.

DESCRIPTION: Velvety black above, with white spots on tip of forewing. Red-orange band crosses forewing and borders hindwing.

SIMILAR SPECIES: None.

SEASON: March–November. Hibernating adults also appear on warm winter days.

LARVA: Highly variable; yellow-green to black; mottled with light spots; numerous short, stout spines.

FOOD PLANTS: Nettle, false nettle, pellitory.

American Painted Lady
Vanessa virginiensis
American lady, Virginia lady, Hunter's butterfly

The beautiful American painted lady, *Vanessa virginiensis*, looks much like the painted lady, *V. cardui*. Both are orange above with black markings, a few white spots ornamenting the black tips of the forewings. Their hindwings above have a series of small submarginal spots. This species, the American painted lady, however, has two large eyespots outside the intricate cobweb pattern on the underside of the hindwing; the painted lady has a row of four or five smaller eyespots.

The American painted lady was described and named in 1773 by Drury from a series of specimens taken from the middle Atlantic states: New York, Maryland, and Virginia. From the latter location he coined the scientific name, *V. virginiensis*. In 1775, however, Fabricius named the same species *V. huntera*, and it was long known by the common name of "Hunter's butterfly," although Drury's description clearly has scientific precedence. A checklist committee of the North American Butterfly Association has recently suggested using simply "American lady" as the common name.

V. virginiensis occurs from coast to coast across southern Canada and the United States, ranging through Mexico and the highlands of Central America to Columbia. It is also a migrant and temporary colonist in the West Indies and Europe. Although less migratory than the widely distributed *V. cardui*, it is probably not capable of surviving severe winter conditions and may recolonize the northern portion of its range each year.

The wide-ranging American painted lady seldom occurs in large numbers in any area. Williams suggests, however, that the Edwards Plateau of Central

1. Dorsal

2. Ventral, emerging from pupa

3. Larvae, young and mature

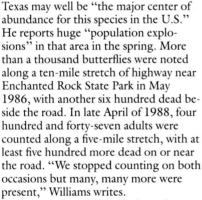

Texas may well be "the major center of abundance for this species in the U.S." He reports huge "population explosions" in that area in the spring. More than a thousand butterflies were noted along a ten-mile stretch of highway near Enchanted Rock State Park in May 1986, with another six hundred dead beside the road. In late April of 1988, four hundred and forty-seven adults were counted along a five-mile stretch, with at least five hundred more dead on or near the road. "We stopped counting on both occasions but many, many more were present," Williams writes.

The American painted lady prefers open areas with low vegetation, inhabiting weedy fields, woodland clearings, and vacant lots within the city. There it visits a wide variety of flowers for nectar and also feeds on tree sap and decaying fruit. When startled, it darts off in erratic flight but often returns to the same place a few moments later, sitting with wings spread wide as it sips nectar from a flower or basks in a patch of sunlight on the ground.

The female lays her pale yellow-green, barrel-shaped eggs singly on the upper leaf surface of the host plant, and the caterpillars build individual shelters by webbing together the leaves with silk. Small larvae incorporate plant hairs in their tents; larger ones often include the flower heads. The group of plants variously called everlasting, cudweed, pussytoes, evax, and rabbit-tobacco in the genera *Antennaria, Gnaphalium, Anaphalis*, and *Evax* usually serves as larval food plants; however, other members of the family Asteraceae are sometimes utilized as well.

The caterpillars are nearly as colorful and intricately marked as the adults. Velvety black, they have a series of narrow transverse yellow bands and a pair of silver-white spots on each abdominal segment. There are four rows of branching black spines, each spine arising from a broad red base. Some mature larvae pupate within their shelter; others transform into hanging pupae on a nearby twig or stem. The chrysalis may be either pale gray with greenish brown markings or golden green marked with purplish brown.

The adult American painted lady flies nearly year-round in Houston but seems most abundant in spring and fall. A hardy species, it hibernates as an adult and may appear on warm winter days to bask in the sun. The spring and summer form is larger and more brightly colored; the fall and winter form is smaller and paler.

SIZE: 1¾–2½ inches.

DESCRIPTION: Orange above with black pattern, white spots on tip of forewing. Two large eyespots on hindwing beneath.

SIMILAR SPECIES: Painted lady similar above, but has four or five smaller eyespots on hindwing beneath.

SEASON: April–November; occasional throughout the winter.

LARVA: Black, with transverse yellow bands and white spots. Black spines have broad red base.

FOOD PLANTS: Everlasting, cudweed, pussytoes, evax, other Asteraceae.

Painted Lady
Vanessa cardui
Thistle butterfly, Cosmopolite, Cosmopolitan

The painted lady is the most widely distributed butterfly in the world, occurring on all of the continents except Antarctica and Australia. A population in Australia and New Zealand was formerly regarded as a subspecies of *Vanessa cardui*; however, most authors now consider it to be a separate species. The painted lady was first described from Sweden by Linnaeus in 1758, taking its name from the Latin *carduus*, "thistle," after one of its favorite larval food plants. "Thistle butterfly" has long served as an alternate common name, as have "cosmopolite" and "cosmopolitan," the latter two reflecting its extensive range.

Next to the monarch, the painted lady is also our most conspicuous butterfly migrant. Unable to withstand extremely cold weather, the North American population resides year-round primarily in Mexico and the Desert Southwest. Early each spring it begins moving north and east to quickly recolonize most of the U.S. and Canada.

Ferris and Brown describe a 1973 migration that began in Mexico and southern California in March. "By April," they report, "thousands and perhaps millions of butterflies had reached Colorado and Wyoming, where they presented a hazard to driving along some roads by obscuring vision." By early June, the painted ladies arrived on the shores of Hudson Bay. Knowlton cites records of similar migrations in Utah.

Painted ladies do not fly strict migration routes as do the better-known monarchs. Their massive flights apparently arise from population explosions in favorable years. Return migrations in the fall are much less extensive, and most of the northern broods produced through the summer probably perish with the

1. Dorsal

2. Ventral

156 / Nymphalids or Brush-Footed Butterflies

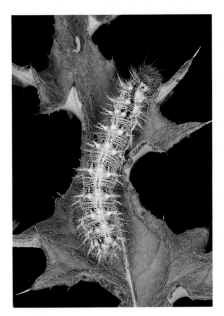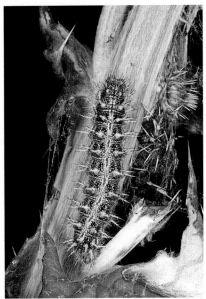

3. Larva

4. Larva

cold. The next spring, however, others move northward to start the cycle once again, undoubtedly aided by their acceptance of a wide spectrum of larval food plants.

More than one hundred host plants have been documented for the painted lady, and both Scott and Ajilvsgi list many of them. Most are in the composite, mallow, and pea families, but many others are utilized on occasion. Here in Southeast Texas, we find most painted lady larvae on thistles; in Trans-Pecos Texas, we find them on globe-mallows.

Females lay their pale green eggs on the upper side of the leaves, and the larvae make individual nests by folding leaves together with silk. The spiny caterpillars are highly variable in color, ranging from lilac or yellow-green to almost black. They have black heads and are heavily mottled with contrasting colors.

The adult painted lady bears a close resemblance to the American painted lady.

Its wings above are orange, often with a rosy pink blush, and they are patterned with black. Small white spots dot the dark tip of the forewing, and a row of dark spots borders the hindwing. The underside of the hindwing provides the key to separating the two similar species. The painted lady has four or five small eyespots; the American painted lady has only two much larger eyespots.

The painted lady is enormously adaptable in its habitat choices. Bailowitz and Brock, in their book on Arizona butterflies, note that it occurs from above timberline on the San Francisco Peaks to near sea level at Yuma. In Texas, it seems to prefer open fields and marshes, but it seems at home, too, in arid thorn-scrub brushlands and urban gardens. It occurs most abundantly in Houston in the spring and fall, but some remain through the summer and others appear on sunny days even in midwinter.

According to Williams (1990), the

painted lady was common throughout the spring and summer months of 1983 until August 17, when Hurricane Alicia hit the upper Texas coast. After that, Williams writes, "this species has been quite uncommon in the Checklist Area." As noted previously, however, populations rebound quickly when conditions are favorable, and the painted lady is one of our most adaptable and resilient butterflies. Numbers fluctuate from year to year, but this beautiful nymphalid can usually be found in Houston wherever flowers are in bloom.

SIZE: 2–2½ inches.
DESCRIPTION: Pinkish orange above with dark pattern, white spots on tip of forewing. Four or five small eyespots on hindwing beneath.
SIMILAR SPECIES: American painted lady similar above, but has only two large eyespots on hindwing beneath.
SEASON: March–November; occasional throughout the winter.
LARVA: Variable. Usually lilac to yellow-green, with dark mottling, branching spines.
FOOD PLANTS: Thistles, mallows, many others.

Buckeye
Junonia coenia
Common buckeye

The beautiful and strikingly marked buckeye is on the wing throughout much of the year in Houston, but it is particularly abundant during the autumn months. Then it ranks as one of the most common of all our butterflies. Large numbers sip nectar from stands of flowers or bask in the warm sun, spreading their wings to reveal the prominent eyespots and then darting off again in rapid, swirling flight when approached.

Considerable confusion attends the classification of the buckeye and its relatives. Older references place them in the genus *Precis*, but present taxonomists reserve that name for Old World species, using the genus *Junonia* for the New World complex. The specific epithet *lavinia* was also used for the buckeye; that has now been replaced by *coenia*. Thus, our common North American species will be found under *Junonia coenia* in recent publications.

Adding to the confusion, however, are a number of tropical forms that range northward into southern Florida and deep South Texas. Some authors treat them as distinct species; others, as subspecies or varieties. They appear under such names as the mangrove buckeye, *J. evarete*; tropical buckeye, *J. genoveva*; and dark buckeye, *J. nigrosuffusa*. DeVries comments that the genus is distributed throughout North, Central, and South America and the West Indies. "It is unknown exactly how many species there are," he writes, "and much remains to be done in unraveling the puzzle of what constitutes a species."

To simplify matters, only one of these butterflies occurs normally in Houston. The North American Butterfly Association committee on nomenclature has recently suggested calling *J. coenia* the "common buckeye" to distinguish it

1. Dorsal

from all others. It has a wide white bar across the forewing tip, partially enclosing an eyespot, and the uppermost of the two eyespots on the hindwing above is much larger than the other. In contrast, the tropical species have an orange suffusion in the forewing bar, and the upper hindwing eyespot is smaller.

The buckeye is a common resident through the southern states and into Mexico. It cannot survive freezing temperatures in any stage of its life cycle, but it moves quickly northward each spring to colonize most of the U.S. and southern Canada. There it may produce two or three more generations before the fall adults begin a southward migration, sometimes in enormous numbers. It is these returning buckeyes, in addition to those produced through the long Texas breeding season, that contribute to the large autumn population throughout Houston. Adults emerging during the shorter photoperiod in the fall are rose-

red on the hindwing beneath, a form sometimes called "rosa." Spring and summer adults are tan or light brown beneath, either with or without two small eyespots.

Buckeyes prefer open, sunny locations, congregating in fields, dunes, and woodland clearings, as well as along roadsides. The pugnacious males patrol from territorial perches in search of mates and dart out to challenge anything that passes by, no matter how large it might be. They often sit with open wings while nectaring at flowers or when basking in the sunlight, and they congregate frequently at mud puddles to sip moisture. Nervous and wary, they seem able to detect the slightest movement and fly quickly when disturbed. The large eyespots may aid in scaring away some predators, particularly young and inexperienced birds.

The female buckeye lays her dark green eggs singly on the leaves of a variety of larval food plants. Snapdragon,

2. Ventral

3. Larva

toadflax, false foxglove, plantain, and ruellia prove particularly popular, and gerardia is utilized heavily in Houston in late summer and fall. Most hosts are in the snapdragon (Scrophulariaceae) and acanthus (Acanthaceae) families.

The caterpillar is black, with dorsal and lateral stripes made up of white and yellow spots. There are four rows of iridescent blue-black spines, the lower ones on each segment rising from broad orange bases. Unlike many of the related nymphalids, buckeye larvae do not make protective nests by webbing together leaves of their host.

The source of the buckeye's scientific name apparently remains in question. Opler and Krizek suggest that the genus *Junonia* may owe its origin to Juno, wife of Jupiter in Roman mythology. *Coenia* could have come from either Jan Henri de Coene or Constantinus Fidelio Coene. Both were important French painters, and either, certainly, would have been honored by so beautiful a namesake.

SIZE: 2–2½ inches.
DESCRIPTION: Brown above, with eyespot and white bar on forewing; upper eyespot on hindwing above much larger than lower. Tan or rose-red hindwing below.
SIMILAR SPECIES: Tropical buckeyes have upper eyespot on hindwing scarcely larger than the others. They do not normally occur in the Houston area.
SEASON: February–November; occasional in midwinter. Most abundant in fall.
LARVA: Black, with stripes of white and yellow spots. Iridescent blue-black spines, lower ones from orange bases.
FOOD PLANTS: Gerardia, snapdragon, toadflax, false foxglove, plantain, ruellia, others.

Red-Spotted Purple
Limenitis arthemis astyanax

Two very different butterflies compose the species *Limenitis arthemis* in eastern North America. They were formerly considered separate species, but recent evidence clearly shows them to be more closely linked. The red-spotted purple, subspecies *astyanax*, is black above with iridescent blue or blue-green scaling, particularly on the outer portion of the hindwing. Bright orange-red marks cluster near the base of the wings below, and the underside of the hindwing has a submarginal row of orange-red spots. Occurring throughout the southern states, the red-spotted purple is thought to be a Batesian mimic of the pipe-vine swallowtail, deriving some protection from predators by its resemblance to that distasteful butterfly.

The white admiral, also called the banded purple, is the nominate subspecies, *arthemis*. It ranges from Alaska and subarctic Canada to the northern tier of states. Wildly different in appearance, the white admiral has broad white bands crossing both wings above, the band on the hindwing bordered outwardly by a row of red spots. Where these two forms meet in a belt across New England and the Great Lakes states, however, a wide range of hybrids can be found, and those hybrids are healthy and fertile. According to Lederhouse, females in the zone of overlap breed at random with males without regard to the amount of white banding on their wings, and nearly complete genetic mixing of the two subspecies occurs. Scott reports that the white band is the result of a recessive gene, while several other genes produce the blue shading and the red spots on the upperside of the hindwing. There are no structural differences between the two forms.

The genus contains several species collectively called "admirals," but only the red-spotted purple and the viceroy occur

1. Dorsal

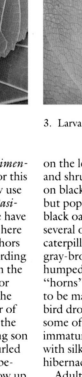

2. Ventral, emerging from pupa

3. Larva

in our area. Both *Basilarchia* and *Limenitis* have been employed as names for this genus, but most recent authors now use the latter. Ferris and Miller retain *Basilarchia* in their checklists, which we have elected to follow in most cases, but here we defer to the majority of new authors and use *Limenitis*. That name, according to Opler and Krizek, is derived from the Latin *limen*, meaning "threshold" or "entrance of the house." Artemis, the daughter of Zeus and the twin sister of Apollo, was the moon goddess and the goddess of hunting. Astyanax, young son of Hector and Andromache, was hurled to his death from the walls of Troy because Odysseus feared he would grow up with the virtues of Hector. Together, these two characters from classical mythology survive in the scientific name of the red-spotted purple.

Females lay their pale green eggs singly on the leaves of a wide variety of trees and shrubs. We have found them only on black cherry in the Houston area, but poplar, aspen, cottonwood, the black oaks, hornbeam, hawthorn, and several others have been reported. The caterpillar is cryptically patterned with gray-brown, green, and white, with a humped thorax and two long, knobby "horns" just behind the head. It appears to be masquerading as an unpalatable bird dropping, perhaps fooling at least some of its predators. In the fall, the immature larva rolls a leaf and secures it with silk, spending the winter in this hibernaculum.

Adults can be found sparingly from March until November in deciduous and mixed woodlands and along wooded streams and marshes throughout our region. This is not one of our more abundant species, however, and finding it may require some effort. Although it takes nectar from a variety of flowers, it seems to prefer feeding on tree sap, decaying fruit, insect honeydew, dung, and carrion. It often perches high in the trees but descends to the ground to feed and to sip at mud puddles and moist stream banks.

Ritland reports finding seven hybrids between red-spotted purples and viceroys in northern Florida and southern Georgia within a period of thirteen months. He also recorded two mixed mating pairs. He attributes this profligate behavior, in part, to habitat overlap in which both species utilize a common larval food plant. In addition, Ritland notes, red-spotted purples are greatly outnumbered by viceroys and may not have much choice in mates. Finally, the viceroys in that region already represent intraspecific "hybrids" between two geographic races and may not have evolved effective isolation mechanisms for mating.

SIZE: 3–3½ inches.
DESCRIPTION: Black above, with iridescent blue or blue-green. Orange-red spots at base of wings and bordering hindwing beneath.
SIMILAR SPECIES: Pipe-vine swallowtail has tailed hindwings, lacks red spots at base of wings below.
SEASON: March–November.
LARVA: "Bird-dropping" pattern of gray-brown, green, and white; two long horns behind head.
FOOD PLANTS: Black cherry, poplar, aspen, cottonwood, others.

Viceroy
Limenitis archippus

The viceroy is perhaps best known as a mimic of the more famous monarch and takes its name from that relationship. A viceroy is a governor who rules an area as the representative of the sovereign. Most recent authors use the genus *Limenitis* for the viceroy and its admiral relatives; however, some employ the name *Basilarchia*. This species is the namesake of Archippus, a Greek poet.

The wings of *Limenitis archippus* are orange or orange-brown above with strongly marked black veins. There is a black line across the hindwing, a mark that serves to distinguish the viceroy from the larger monarch, *Danaus plexippus*, and the queen, *D. gilippus*. There are white spots in the dark forewing tip and a row of small white spots in the black margins of the wings. The wings beneath are lighter orange but reflect the same pattern, and the distinctive black hindwing line is easily seen.

Several subspecies or races of the viceroy occur across the continent, ranging from southern Canada through most of the U.S. to central Mexico. They vary in ground color from bright orange to rich chestnut and in the width of the hindwing line. The darker forms inhabit Florida and the Southwest and are presumed to mimic the queen, which is more common as a permanent resident in those regions than is the migratory monarch.

Viceroys prefer moist habitats along stream courses, lake shores, swamps, and wet meadows, wherever willows grow. The various species of willows serve as preferred larval hosts throughout most of the viceroy's range, but aspen, poplar, cottonwood, apple, plum, cherry, and a number of other trees serve as alternate hosts. Adults visit flowers for nectar but are more often seen feeding at tree sap, insect honeydew, or ripe fruit. They also

1. Dorsal

2. Ventral, emerging from pupa

3. Larva

164 / Nymphalids or Brush-Footed Butterflies

land at mud puddles and stream banks to sip moisture and bask in the sun.

Males patrol all day near the host plants in search of receptive females, often returning to the same perch day after day. According to Opler and Krizek, the requirements for perches and territories may be highly specific, for males of successive generations sometimes occupy the same perch year after year. When males encounter each other, they abruptly soar high into the air in stylized combat, the winner returning to his territory. Mating occurs mainly in the afternoon, with the female as the carrier during flight, and egg-laying takes place in midafternoon.

The female deposits her pale green or yellow eggs singly on the tips of young leaves, usually no more than two or three per tree. The larva looks much like that of the red-spotted purple and closely resembles a fresh bird dropping. Mottled with patches of green, brown, and white, it has a humped thorax that bears two rough "horns." The strangely shaped pupa is brown and white with a flattened protuberance extending from the abdomen. Scott describes it as like "a finless dolphin with a western saddle."

The viceroy can be seen throughout the Houston area from April to November, but it is seldom present in large numbers. There are several broods a year, and the third-stage larva hibernates through the winter. In response to the decreasing photoperiod in the fall, the half-grown caterpillar chews away a portion of a leaf blade, leaving a segment hanging by the midrib. It then rolls that remaining section into a tube and ties it with silk. Fastening the leaf petiole securely to the twig with silk to keep it from falling, the larva then retreats into its hibernaculum for the winter. It will emerge again in spring when new leaves and flower catkins begin to unfurl.

The adult viceroy has long been considered a Batesian mimic of the monarch and queen, obtaining protection from predators by its resemblance to those distasteful butterflies. Recent work in Florida, however, suggests that the viceroy may also be distasteful to birds. In that case, all are part of a complex involving Müllerian mimicry. A greater number of similar-looking unpalatable butterflies enables birds to learn more quickly to avoid them, thus sparing more members of the complex.

Further complicating the picture, Williams has even suggested that some of the viceroys in Southeast Texas mimic the very common gulf fritillary, *Agraulis vanillae*. He reports some specimens with longer, brighter orange forewings that seem more to resemble the latter species. Viceroys across the Houston area do seem to vary considerably in color, and all probably receive some protection by adopting the stereotypical orange-and-black pattern that advertises unpalatability in nature.

SIZE: 2⅝–3 inches.
DESCRIPTION: Orange or orange-brown, with black veins; black line across middle of hindwing; black wing margins contain a row of white spots.
SIMILAR SPECIES: Larger monarch and queen lack black line across hindwing.
SEASON: April–November.
LARVA: Blotched with green, brown, and white; thorax with pair of knobby horns.
FOOD PLANTS: Mainly willow; also poplar, aspen, cottonwood, cherry, apple, plum, others.

Amymone

Mestra amymone
Common mestra, Noseburn wanderer,
Texas bagvein, Texas bag-wing

This small, delicate butterfly bears little resemblance to most of its nymphalid relatives. Its wings above are pearly white with darker gray bases and margins; a pale orange band borders the trailing edge of the hindwing. Below, the amymone is pale brownish orange with bands of creamy white. The fragile wings become quickly rubbed and tattered, and the amymone flies slowly and haltingly, sailing with few wing beats just above the ground.

Mestra amymone occurs throughout the year in the Rio Grande Valley and south through Mexico to Costa Rica. According to Ajilvsgi, it breeds as far north in Texas as Austin and possibly Waco. Williams writes that it can be common in Bastrop and Buescher state parks in Bastrop County, although it decreased markedly after the cold spell in December 1989. In spite of its seemingly weak flight, the amymone occasionally stages massive migrations, moving northward through the Great Plains in large swarms. At times it even reaches South Dakota and Minnesota.

Houston, however, is on the eastern edge of the migration zone, and the amymone occurs in our area only as a rare visitor. It should be looked for on the inland prairies of western Harris and neighboring counties. With its pale wings, it might be confused with the white pierids rather than being recognized as a member of the Nymphalidae.

The amymone prefers weedy fields, roadsides, and woodland edges, where it visits a variety of flowers. Several species of *Tragia* serve as larval food plants. Commonly called "noseburn," they are nettlelike, with stiff, stinging hairs. The caterpillar is described as brown with a row of green diamonds on its back and

eight rows of spines. The red-and-black head also carries two prominent spines, each terminating in a knob.

Mestra amymone is the only member of its genus to occur regularly in Texas and the U.S.; several others inhabit the West Indies and tropical America. The origin of the genus name is apparently unknown, although Opler and Krizek suggest it may come from Mestria, a Roman surname. Amymone, in Greek mythology, was one of the fifty daughters of Danaus; her mother was Europa. Amymone married Enceladus, but murdered him on their wedding night.

Some authors use "noseburn wanderer" and "Texas bagvein" or "Texas bag-wing" as common names of the amymone. The first comes from the larval food plant and the adult's propensity to migrate long distances; the latter two apparently stem from the fact that the base of the costal vein on the butterfly's forewing is greatly swollen. The North American Butterfly Association recently adopted "common mestra," noting pronunciation difficulties with the traditional name.

SIZE: 1½–1¾ inches.
DESCRIPTION: Gray and pearly white above, with orange hindwing border. Pale brownish orange below, with white bands.
SIMILAR SPECIES: None.
SEASON: All year in South Texas; wanders northward June–November. Rare visitor to Houston area.
LARVA: Brown, with row of green diamonds; spiny; pair of knobbed spines on head.
FOOD PLANTS: Noseburn.

1. Dorsal (*photo by Geyata Ajilvsgi*)

Goatweed Leafwing
Anaea andria
Goatweed butterfly

The goatweed leafwing takes its name from the larval food plants, various species of *Croton* that are usually called goatweeds. It appears under the name "goatweed butterfly" in most current guidebooks, but the nomenclature committee of the North American Butterfly Association has recently adopted "goatweed leafwing" as a more descriptive term. We concur with that decision. Some authors place *Anaea andria* and related leafwings in the family Apaturidae with the emperors; others assign both groups to the Nymphalidae, a course we follow here.

A. andria is both sexually and seasonally dimorphic, and the various forms can be somewhat confusing. The male is bright red-orange above, with sparse black markings along the wing margins. The female has a lighter orange ground color with a more extensive dark pattern. Both have falcate forewings and short hindwing tails, and both are cryptically patterned with gray and brown below. A winter form is more heavily marked above, with longer tails and more dramatically sickle-shaped forewings.

Several related species range northward from the tropics to Florida and deep South Texas. They differ primarily in having more sinuous, scalloped wing margins, but the distinctions are not easy to make. While *andria* is common throughout the Houston area, however, other *Anaea* species would occur only as extremely rare strays.

Goatweed leafwings inhabit fields, stream banks, and woodland edges wherever the abundant crotons grow. Large, robust insects, they usually perch on the ground or on tree limbs and trunks, where their cryptic, leaflike underwings make them very difficult to detect. When approached, they take off in darting, erratic flight, flashing the bright color that undoubtedly helps to startle potential predators. Adults seldom visit flowers, preferring to sip rich liquids from tree sap, rotting fruit, and dung.

The female lays her eggs singly on the underside of goatweed leaves, and the resulting larvae live in protective tubes made by pulling together the edges of a leaf and fastening them with silk. The stout, gray-green bodies of the caterpillars are covered with tiny tubercles. The greenish pupae, too, are unusually short and stout.

The goatweed leafwing ranges through the south-central and southeastern U.S. and parts of Mexico, wandering northward occasionally to Michigan and Minnesota. In the South, it occurs throughout much of the year, hibernating in winter as an adult.

Riley (1980) showed that larvae reared in the laboratory under long photoperiods (sixteen hours of daylight) produced summer-form adults, while those getting a shorter photoperiod (twelve hours of light) produced winter-form adults. The appropriate form is apparently determined during the fifth-instar larval stage. Riley (1988) also found that summer-form females mated within two days of emerging from the pupa, while winter females did not mate and produced no mature eggs for at least twenty days. Field studies confirm these laboratory data. Adults emerging as the daylight period becomes shorter enter reproductive diapause and hibernate without mating; they will then reproduce the following spring.

Williams notes that the goatweed leafwing is most abundant in the Houston area from midsummer through early fall: "One day there may be none, and on the next day a great many." On September 4, 1989, he recorded ninety-four adults in less than three hours in western

1. Male, dorsal

2. Female, dorsal

3. Female, ventral

Harris and eastern Waller counties; about the same number was seen in one hour in early October 1983.

SIZE: 2¼–3 inches.

DESCRIPTION: Red-orange above, with black pattern; females more heavily marked than males. Falcate forewing tip; short hindwing tail. Leaflike gray-and-brown pattern below.

SIMILAR SPECIES: Tropical leafwing species similar, but do not normally occur in the Houston area.

SEASON: Throughout most of the year; more common in late summer and fall.

LARVA: Stout-bodied; gray-green, covered with small tubercles.

FOOD PLANTS: Various goatweed species.

4. Larva

Hackberry Emperor
Asterocampa celtis
Hackberry butterfly

The hackberry emperor is one of two common emperors found throughout the Houston area. It is also the most widespread of the North American *Asterocampa* species, ranging from extreme southern Canada through most of the eastern U.S. and the central plains to the Desert Southwest and Mexico. In our area of Texas, however, it is not as abundant as the tawny emperor, *A. clyton*.

A resident of open woodlands and stream corridors, *A. celtis* also wanders into cities and suburbs wherever hackberry trees are found. The various hackberry species in the genus *Celtis* serve as the only larval food plants and give this pretty, active butterfly its scientific name. The genus *Asterocampa* stems from the Latin *aster*, "star," and *campa*, "caterpillar," according to Opler and Krizek. Those authors do not suggest the reason for this choice, but one might speculate that the name was coined because of the radiating, starburst spines on the larva's head.

The hackberry emperor is olive-brown or grayish brown with a complex pattern of dark markings. A series of white spots ornaments the outer portion of the forewing, and the hindwing bears a row of rounded eyespots. A single round, black eyespot marks the outer margin of the forewing above. The similar tawny emperor lacks the forewing eyespots, both above and below, and is a richer orange-brown. Males of both species have triangular hindwings; the hindwings of the larger females are broadly rounded.

Both the hackberry emperor and the tawny emperor are highly variable geographically, and a number of named forms exist across the country. Some authors have granted them species status, but most now recognize only *A. celtis*, *A. clyton*, and a third species known as the Empress Leilia, *A. leilia*, that ranges into southern and western Texas from Mexico. Timothy Friedlander, in his doctoral dissertation at Texas A&M University, clarified the relationships of the many *Asterocampa* forms.

The hackberry emperor often perches high in the trees, sailing out to challenge other butterflies, animals, or even people. It has a peculiar flap-and-glide flight and when alarmed is difficult to approach. However, it may also dart down to land on an intruder's head, perhaps out of curiosity, perhaps in search of salts from perspiration. More than one gardener has been the subject of such close attention. Male emperors are particularly active from early afternoon until dusk, patrolling for females or diving at them as they pass by a carefully selected perch.

Hackberry emperors seldom visit flowers, instead feeding at sap flows, overripe fruit, animal dung, and carrion. Neck (1983b) describes repeated visits to the flowers of snakewood, *Colubrina texensis*, while ignoring other nearby nectar plants. Most of those visitors proved to be females, and Neck suggests they are seeking a nitrogen source rather than the carbohydrate-rich nectar.

The female lays her eggs singly or in small groups on the leaves of hackberry trees. The yellow-green caterpillar has a pair of branching, spiny horns on its head, appendages appropriately called "antlers" by one author. Yellowish dots and stripes ornament the body, the last segment of which is forked. There are probably several broods a year in Houston, with adults appearing from at least March through October. In the fall, the third-instar caterpillar of the last brood turns brown and hibernates, emerging the next spring to regain its green color and continue its growth before transforming into a yellowish to bluish green chrysalis.

1. Male, ventral

SIZE: 2–2½ inches; female larger than male.

DESCRIPTION: Olive-brown or gray-brown, with dark pattern. Whitish spots on outer forewing and row of eyespots on hindwing above. Round, dark eyespot near outer margin of forewing both above and below.

SIMILAR SPECIES: Tawny emperor is richer orange-brown; lacks eyespot on forewing above and below.

SEASON: Through much of the year; at least March–October.

LARVA: Yellow-green, with yellowish pattern. Rear segment forked; head with two branching, spiny horns.

FOOD PLANTS: Hackberry species.

Tawny Emperor
Asterocampa clyton

The tawny emperor ranges through most of the eastern United States to northeastern Mexico. Isolated populations also occupy portions of Arizona and New Mexico. It is highly variable geographically, and several of the forms were once considered to be distinct species. Although not as common as the hackberry emperor throughout much of its range, the tawny emperor is the more abundant species in Houston. Two different subspecies may occur in our region, the nominate *Asterocampa clyton clyton* of the eastern states and *A. c. texana*. The latter, common in the central portion of the state, has been called the "Texas emperor" or "pale emperor."

Warmer orange-brown above than the olive-brown hackberry emperor, these forms of the tawny emperor also lack the round, dark eyespots on both the upper and lower surfaces of the forewings that characterize *Asterocampa celtis*. Males have triangular hindwings, while those of the larger females are broader and rounded. In some individuals, the hindwings are heavily scaled with dark chocolate-brown.

Like *A. celtis, clyton* utilizes only hackberries as larval food plants. Ajilvsgi states that it is known to use all of the species in the state except spiny hackberry, *Celtis pallida*. According to Brown and Heineman, the extensive planting of hackberry windbreaks on the prairies, a practice inaugurated in the mid 1930s, contributed greatly to the range expansion of *Asterocampa* species. By the 1950s, they had moved into shelter belts far to the west of their former range.

Scott notes that female tawny emperors seem to prefer groves of mature hackberry trees lining streams and rivers, while Pyle (1981) suggests the species is more of a specialist than the hackberry emperor and does not adapt to city habi-

1. Male, dorsal

2. Female, dorsal

3. Male, ventral

4. Female, ventral

tats as successfully. However, when we planted a hackberry seedling in our backyard in Baytown, we were rewarded almost immediately. Many large broods of tawny emperor larvae have magically appeared on what is still a small tree, and the adults swirl about our yard throughout most of the year.

Tawny emperors visit flowers infrequently, preferring to feed on tree sap, insect honeydew, animal droppings, and carrion. Pyle (1981) notes they are "passionately fond of the juices of rotting fruit," and are lured by overripe figs, pears, peaches, and persimmons. The butterflies also gather at mud puddles and damp patches of sand to sip water with its dissolved salts and amino acids.

Tawny emperors are most active from late morning through midafternoon, perching in the sunlight and darting out to investigate potential mates as well as intruders to their territories. They fly earlier in the day than hackberry emperors,

an adaptation that probably enables the two species to share the same habitat. The larvae of *A. clyton* also consume mainly mature leaves, while the feeding of *A. celtis* caterpillars is confined to younger, more tender leaves.

The tawny emperor lays her creamy, ridged eggs in large clusters on the underside of hackberry leaves, or less frequently on the bark. As many as two hundred to five hundred eggs may be included in a single batch, forming a flat-topped, truncated pyramid of several layers. Upon emerging, the larvae stay together and feed communally in their early stages. Stamp (1984) reports that after feeding in one location, the caterpillars may move to another site as much as three meters away. She suggests this may reduce predation by birds that learn to recognize extensive leaf damage caused by the large number of larvae. During such movements, the larvae walk along the branches, and leadership of the procession continually changes. They follow trails of silk laid down by the leaders and reassemble at the new feeding site.

These caterpillars are greenish with yellow markings varying from dorsal chevrons to stripes. The rear segment is forked; the head bears a pair of branching horns. Several broods occur each year, and adults frequently overwinter and appear on warm sunny days. Young larvae may also hibernate. Stamp (1983) describes groups of tawny emperor larvae in Florida that moved to the ends of hackberry branches and made secure tents by tying the sides of the leaves together. They secured each leaf to the twig with silk and hibernated inside, slowly turning from green to pinkish brown to blend with the dead leaves.

In a detailed study of the parasites and predators of *Asterocampa* species, Friedlander (1984) found that tiny scelionid wasps frequently parasitize the eggs, while stinkbugs are the most common insect predators of the larvae. Tachinid flies and braconid, eulophid, ichneumonid, chalcid, and vespid wasps all take a heavy toll, as do birds and other vertebrates.

In spite of the many threats to the tawny emperor at all stages in its life, it remains a common butterfly throughout our region. Williams counted more than eleven hundred adults in the woods of Stephen F. Austin State Park near Sealy in Austin County in June 1989, while Israel writes of an enormous outbreak in Louisiana in 1980. High local concentrations may be partly the result of the female's habit of laying her eggs in very large clusters. In contrast, the hackberry emperor deposits her eggs singly or in small groups, dispersing her progeny more widely.

SIZE: 2–2¾ inches; female larger than male.

DESCRIPTION: Tawny orange-brown, with dark pattern; row of eyespots on hindwing only. No round, submarginal eyespots on either surface of forewing.

SIMILAR SPECIES: Hackberry emperor more olive-brown or grayish brown; has round eyespot on forewing above and below.

SEASON: Throughout most of the year; especially March–November.

LARVA: Greenish, with yellow pattern of chevrons or stripes. Rear segment forked; head with pair of branching horns.

FOOD PLANTS: Hackberry species.

5. Larvae

Satyrs, Wood Nymphs, and Browns

FAMILY SATYRIDAE

Many authors include these common butterflies as a subfamily, Satyrinae, of the Nymphalidae. There are, however, several unique features of this easily recognizable group, and it seems convenient to separate them here. Brown and Heineman state: "It is our belief that the Satyridae are of ancient lineage and represent an early branching of the nymphaloid stem." Ferris and Miller also grant them family status in their checklists.

A worldwide group of medium-sized butterflies, the Satyridae contains nearly three thousand species. Most are brown with marginal eyespots on the wings, particularly on the underside. A few in other regions are more highly colored, and butterflies in one tropical group, the "ghost satyrs," have transparent wings. The forelegs of both sexes are poorly developed and useless for walking, while one or more forewing veins have greatly swollen bases. These swollen veins contain hearing organs that may allow the butterflies to detect predators. The clubs of the antennae are thin and inconspicuous, and many males have patches of scent glands on their wings.

The early stages of the satyrs also differ from those of most nymphalids. The larvae are generally green or brown, with the rear abdominal segment strongly forked. They lack the fleshy filaments and spines that ornament many nymphalid caterpillars, but are covered with minute tubercles, each set with a short hair. The head often bears two small conelike horns. The chrysalis is smoother in outline than most nymphalid pupae and usually hangs by the cremaster from a silken pad; a few satyrs pupate on the ground beneath debris.

Larvae of most satyrid species feed on grasses or sedges, including bamboo and sugarcane, although some tropical ones utilize palms or club mosses. According to DeVries, "As far as is known there are no satyrines anywhere in the world that feed on dicotyledonous plants." These monocotyledons are not

The little Carolina satyr, Hermeuptychia sosybius, does not frequent flowers. Instead, it sips at sap flows and puddles.

known to contain secondary chemicals for protection, and DeVries thus speculates that the larvae and resulting adults are universally palatable to vertebrate predators. The high silica content of many grasses, however, may reduce digestibility and contribute to the slow growth of most satyr caterpillars. Many species have but a single brood each year, while others take two years for development.

Some satyrs inhabit marshes and meadows; others are denizens of shady woodlands and river bottoms. The arctics, *Oeneis*, and alpines, *Erebia*, as their names imply, occur even on high mountain tops and in the Far North; these genera, however, do not range into Texas. All have an erratic bouncing, dancing flight, remaining close to the ground and seeking shelter among the grasses when disturbed. They usually perch with wings tightly closed, camouflaged by their dull colors, but may open their wings widely to bask in patches of sunlight. Populations tend to be localized and do not migrate or wander far from their specific habitats.

At first glance, these rather drab butterflies may seem dull and uninteresting when compared with the flashy swallowtails and nymphalids. On closer study, however, their delicately detailed eyespots and intricate patterns make them a fascinating group for study. Because of their highly local nature, and because the caterpillars tend to hide by day and feed at night, the life histories and behavior of many species are poorly known. For ardent lepidopterists, the gemlike Satyridae constitute a fascinating group of butterflies.

1. Georgia satyr

Southern Pearly Eye
Enodia portlandia
Pearly eye

The southern pearly eye should not be expected in central Houston, but it inhabits the woodlands and stream corridors to the north where stands of giant cane occur. We have encountered it sparingly in Montgomery and Liberty counties and have investigated larger colonies in the Sam Houston National Forest in San Jacinto County.

Called simply "pearly eye" by many authors, *Enodia portlandia* is one of three confusing sibling species. It thus seems better to designate this butterfly as the "southern pearly eye" to distinguish it from the northern pearly eye, *E. anthedon*, and the Creole pearly eye, *E. creola*. The former was only recently recognized as a separate species and does not occur in Texas except, perhaps, in the extreme northeastern corner of the state. The latter ranges into eastern Texas and may share the same habitats as the more common southern pearly eye. All were formerly included in the genus *Lethe*.

Much larger than other satyrids found in Houston, *E. portlandia* is brown above with a row of black eyespots bordering each wing. The underside is purplish brown, but with much the same pattern. The curved row of forewing eyespots below contains only four spots, and the dark brown line across the middle of the forewing is relatively straight or slightly sinuous. In contrast, *E. creola* has five spots in the forewing band below, and the dark line is strongly arched. The male *creola* also has elongated forewings bearing raised scent patches between the veins, a feature lacking in the female. These differences are difficult to see in the field without collecting the butterflies, and more work is required to determine the relative abundances of the southern and Creole pearly eyes in the canebrakes of the Big Thicket. Both range through the southeastern states, from the southern Atlantic Coast to the forests of East Texas.

Pearly eyes seldom visit flowers, feeding instead on tree sap, decaying fruit, animal droppings, and carrion. They also imbibe moisture at mud puddles. Males perch on tree trunks to wait for passing females and apparently do not patrol regular territories as do many other butterflies. They fly late in the day and are active until dusk, with courtship occurring at nightfall.

Most authors report three broods of the southern pearly eye each season, and adults appear from March through October. The female lays her eggs singly on the leaves of giant cane, but the breeding biology has apparently not been thoroughly investigated. The mature caterpillar is lime-green with a yellow stripe on each side just below the spiracles. Four fainter yellow lines mark the back, and the entire body and head are profusely dotted with tiny whitish tubercles, each tipped by a short hair. The head bears a pair of short, pink-tipped horns, while the last abdominal segment is also pink and strongly forked. The greenish chrysalis usually hangs from the underside of an arching cane leaf.

Parasites take a heavy toll of southern pearly eyes in the area we investigated in San Jacinto County. Forty empty pupal cases were found on the giant cane along a stream bank, but only two of those pupae had developed fully. All others bore the small, round hole through which a parasite had emerged. Five additional pupae were also collected in seemingly good condition, but each of those, too, proved to be parasitized, yielding one or more medium-sized tachinid flies. Of the two caterpillars found, one developed into an adult butterfly, while the other again produced a parasitic fly.

1. Dorsal

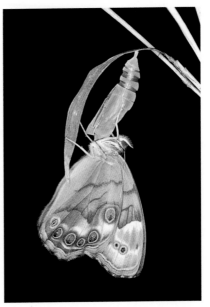

2. Ventral, emerging from pupa

3. Larva

SIZE: 1¾–2¼ inches.

DESCRIPTION: Warm brown above and purplish brown below; both sides with a marginal row of rounded eyespots. Four eyespots on underside of forewing.

SIMILAR SPECIES: Creole pearly eye has five eyespots in marginal row on underside of forewing; dark line across forewing more strongly arched. Other more common satyrids in Houston are much smaller.

SEASON: March–October.

LARVA: Lime-green, with yellow stripes and tiny whitish tubercles. Head and last abdominal segment each with pair of pinkish horns.

FOOD PLANTS: Giant cane. Switch cane also reported in southeastern states.

Gemmed Satyr
Cyllopsis gemma
Jeweled satyr, Gemmed brown

Plain brown above, the gemmed satyr lacks the eyespots on the underside of the hindwing that characterize our other small satyrs. Instead, it has a marginal purple-gray patch containing a smaller iridescent black area with silver highlights, the "gem" from which the species takes its name.

Cyllopsis gemma ranges from the mid-Atlantic Coast westward through the southeastern states to Kansas and Texas and thence southward into Mexico. It inhabits much of eastern Texas and the coastal plain but seldom occurs in large numbers. We find it sparingly in the Houston area, and Williams reports that the most he found in one place was nine at Stephen F. Austin State Park in June 1989. Small and somewhat secretive, it can easily be overlooked.

The gemmed satyr seems to prefer wet, grassy woodlands, where it apparently feeds on tree sap and overripe fruit. It does not visit flowers. Most authors list the larval food plants as "various grasses," documenting especially Bermuda grass. There are several broods each year, and the fourth-instar larvae of the last fall brood hibernate through the winter.

The caterpillar is reported to be yellow-green with green stripes in the summer; tan or brown with darker brown stripes in the fall. A pair of horns adorns the head, and the end of the abdomen is strongly forked. The pupa also varies from green to brown. Scott notes that the gemmed satyr is "one of only a few butterflies known to have seasonal forms in both larvae and pupae," and Pyle (1981) suggests this change may allow them to blend with the seasonally changing colors of the grasses.

The only larva we have encountered in our region was found on giant cane on March 5, 1993. It pupated almost imme-

1. Ventral, emerging from pupa

diately, however, and the cane may simply have been a convenient site for pupation rather than an actual food plant. Because the caterpillar was tan with brown stripes, the color typical of the fall brood, we assume it had recently emerged from hibernation.

SIZE: 1¼–1⅜ inches.
DESCRIPTION: Brown above; light brown below, with darker striations. Purplish gray patch on underside of hindwing contains reflective black scales.
SIMILAR SPECIES: Other small brown satyrs have eyespots on hindwing below.
SEASON: March–October.
LARVA: Yellow-green with green stripes in summer; tan with brown stripes in fall. Abdomen forked; head with pair of horns.
FOOD PLANTS: Bermuda grass; other grasses likely.

Carolina Satyr
Hermeuptychia sosybius
Southern satyr, Carolinian satyr

This smallest of the satyrs is also the most abundant in the Houston area. It inhabits grassy woodlands, stream corridors, and even urban parks and yards, flying virtually throughout the year. Dark, unmarked mouse-brown above, it has a series of small yellow-rimmed eyespots bordering both wings below.

The nomenclature of the Carolina satyr presents a problem best left to specialists. Once listed as *Euptychia hermes*, it was later moved to a new genus and classified as *Hermeuptychia hermes* subspecies *sosybius*. Subsequent taxonomists split the complex into two distinct species, listing both the Carolina satyr, *H. sosybius*, and the Hermes satyr, *H. hermes*. The former ranges throughout the southeastern states westward to Texas,

while the latter occurs from South Texas into Mexico. Pyle (1981) notes, however, that where the ranges overlap in our state, "Carolina and Hermes satyrs cannot be distinguished in the field."

The checklists of Ferris (1989) and Miller (1992) still include both forms as full species, but Opler's field guide (1992) combines the two as *H. sosybius*, which ranges from the southeastern U.S. southward throughout mainland tropical America. Glassberg (1993), on the other hand, returns to *H. hermes sosybius*. We adopt Opler's stand and list the Carolina satyr as *H. sosybius*; the butterfly remains unaffected by the confusion in taxonomy.

The Carolina satyr occurs widely in our region, fluttering weakly through open woodlands and yards and alighting frequently to rest and hide among the grasses. Males patrol all day in search of receptive females, but are most active in

1. Dorsal

1. Dorsal

2. Ventral

white. There is apparently a single brood in the North, two or more in the South, and the larvae hibernate through the winter.

Although the little wood satyr is the most widespread of the satyrids in the eastern U.S., and at times the most abundant, much remains to be learned about its biology. A butterfly once regarded as a form of *Megisto cymela* has recently been separated as a distinct species, Viola's wood satyr, *M. viola*. It occurs along the southeastern Atlantic Coast and wanders occasionally westward to Louisiana and Arkansas. Where the two similar species overlap, they do not seem to interbreed.

In addition, Opler suggests that *M. cymela*, as we now know it, may actually consist of two reproductively isolated species that cannot be separated by external appearance. In much of the East, Opler writes, there are two successive broods that appear so close together that the second could not possibly be the off-spring of the first. There is evidence that each group has differently colored larvae and that they overwinter in different stages.

Another small satyr, *M. rubricata*, inhabits the arid Southwest and ranges into western and central Texas. Called the red satyr, it differs in having a single eyespot and a bright, reddish central area on the forewing above and below. Fairly common in the Texas Hill Country, it is reported from Washington and Fayette counties by Williams and could conceivably stray into the immediate Houston area. We have not found it here. (See photo below.)

SIZE: 1⅝–1⅞ inches.
DESCRIPTION: Brown, with two large eyespots on each wing, both above and below. Upper spot may be reduced on hindwing above; smaller spots often present below.
SIMILAR SPECIES: All except red satyr lack eyespots on upper surface of wings. Carolina satyr has more, smaller spots below.
SEASON: April–September.
LARVA: Pale brown, with dark dorsal stripe. Head and forked "tail" whitish.
FOOD PLANTS: Grasses, including orchard grass and centipede grass.

Red Satyr

Common Wood Nymph
Cercyonis pegala
Wood nymph, Large wood nymph, Southern wood nymph, Blue-eyed grayling, Goggle eye

The common wood nymph does not normally occur in Houston. We include it here because of its interesting biology and because it may occasionally stray into the region. We have seen it at least twice in nearby Waller and Austin counties, and Orr considers it "rare" on his checklist of the Houston area. The local subspecies, *Cercyonis pegala texana*, is relatively common in the Texas Hill Country and was originally described by W.H. Edwards from Bastrop in 1880.

The largest of our satyrids, the common wood nymph also ranks as one of North America's most variable butterflies. Miller lists twelve distinct subspecies, and scores of other forms have been described and named across the continent. Many were once considered to be separate species. Collectively, they range across most of southern Canada and the United States, skirting only peninsular Florida, southern Louisiana, and much of eastern and southern Texas.

The Texas subspecies has a rectangular yellow patch on the rich cocoa-brown forewing, enclosing two large black eyespots that have white or blue pupils. The wings beneath are paler and mottled with brown striations, the forewing mirroring the pattern above, the hindwing bearing a series of yellow-rimmed eyespots. Females are larger and paler than males and have larger forewing spots. *Texana* is typical of the coastal and southern populations; those occurring in northern inland areas are smaller, with the yellow forewing patches reduced or absent entirely.

The common wood nymph inhabits prairies, overgrown fields, open woodlands, and roadsides. Its flight is slow and erratic. When disturbed, it often dives

1. Ventral

ever, emerge a few days after the males and are capable of living for several months. These authors suggest this female longevity may be an adaptation for deferring egg-laying as long as possible after mating.

The female deposits her eggs singly on a variety of grasses, producing as many as three hundred eggs and dispersing them widely across the fields. Caterpillars hatch in fourteen to twenty-five days and enter hibernation almost immediately. Only after emerging the next spring will they begin to feed on the leaves of the grasses, going through six instar stages before pupating. Thus, summer is well on its way before the year's crop of adult wood nymphs emerges once again.

SIZE: 2–3 inches.
DESCRIPTION: Brown above, with yellow patch on forewing enclosing two large eyespots. Mottled brown below, with similar pattern on forewing and series of spots on hindwing.
SIMILAR SPECIES: Southern pearly eye lacks yellow patch, has more eyespots on upper surface of wings. Other satyrs much smaller.
SEASON: May–October.
LARVA: Green, with paler stripes; anal fork reddish.
FOOD PLANTS: Grasses, including purpletop, wild oats, and several bluestem species.

into the grasses or nearby thickets, sitting with tightly closed wings on a stem or twig where its cryptic pattern provides near-perfect camouflage. In spite of its large size, it can be very difficult to relocate. Males patrol open, grassy areas all day in search of females, which land to mate if they are receptive to the males' advances. Some authors state that adults visit flowers only rarely, relying mainly on sap and overripe fruit for sustenance. Others contend wood nymphs nectar voraciously at a variety of flowers. Indeed, the habits undoubtedly vary with individual populations and with the resources available.

The common wood nymph has but a single brood each year. Adults appear in May in the South, as late as June or July farther north. Some remain on the wing until September or October. According to Opler and Krizek, males live no more than two or three weeks. Females, how-

unusually rubbery bodies and tough, leathery wings capable of withstanding the attack of a predator that has yet to learn of their unpalatability.

The larvae of our danaids are smooth-skinned, lacking the spines of many nymphalids, but have soft, fleshy tentacles at each end. They are vividly banded with black, yellow or orange, and white, a sequence of colors that serves in nature as a warning to potential predators. Consequently, they feed fully exposed rather than constructing tents of leaves and silk or seeking concealment, as do many other caterpillars. Humans have, in a sense, adopted this same warning system in the signs and barriers we erect to caution motorists of roadway construction and other hazards. Adults, too, have orange-and-black wings and white-spotted black bodies, and they serve as models for such well-known mimics as the viceroy.

1. Queen, female

Monarch
Danaus plexippus

The familiar monarch undoubtedly ranks as the most famous and widely loved butterfly in North America. It is a summer resident across southern Canada and the contiguous states and stages a massive southward migration to spend the winter in more hospitable climates. During these long flights, individuals often wander off course, and vagrants show up even in Europe. Others have colonized Australia and a number of oceanic islands, including Hawaii. Additional populations range throughout most of lowland Central and South America, where they have no need for such migrations and are more sedentary.

The male monarch is bright burnt orange above, with black veins and white-spotted black borders. There is a black scent patch on a vein across the middle of the hindwing. The female is usually a duller orange than her mate, with more thickly scaled black veins. She lacks the hindwing scent patch. Both sexes are slightly paler below, but with the same easily recognizable pattern. The closely related queen, *Danaus gilippus*, is somewhat smaller and more brownish orange. It also lacks the strongly marked black veins on the upper surface of the wings.

Monarchs inhabit open fields, marshes, pastures, and roadsides, visiting a wide variety of flowers for nectar. They serve as major pollinators of the milkweeds used as larval food plants, but they also seem particularly attracted to verbena, lantana, asters, goldenrods, thistles, and mist-flower. Males patrol over open areas through much of the day, seeking receptive females. The mated pairs often remain coupled for more than an hour, the male carrying the female if they fly.

The female lays her creamy, cone-shaped eggs singly on the underside of milkweed leaves. Milkvines and dogbanes serve less frequently as larval hosts. The caterpillar is colorfully ringed with yellow, black, and white bands. A pair of long, fleshy tentacles adorns the thorax; a shorter pair arises near the end of the abdomen. The short, stout pupa that hangs by its cremaster from a silken pad is green with spots of black and metallic gold. No artist ever carved from precious jade and gold a more beautiful ornament than the chrysalis of the monarch butterfly.

As they feed, monarch larvae assimilate poisonous cardiac glycosides from the milky juices of their food plants. As a result, they and the subsequent adults are distasteful to birds, a fact they advertise with their bright warning colors. Different milkweed species contain different amounts of the chemicals, however, and some monarchs are better protected than others, depending on which hosts they utilized. Malcolm and Brower, working in Florida, demonstrated that when female monarchs have a choice of milkweed species with either high or very low glycoside concentrations, they select the more toxic one on which to lay their eggs. Van Hook and Zalucki also found, however, that when presented with an array of milkweeds of varying glycoside levels, female butterflies preferentially oviposited on those of intermediate strength. It seems reasonable to assume this selection provides good protection without unduly taxing the larva's own digestive system.

As fall approaches, the northern monarch populations begin to stream southward. In the West, they flock to locations along the California coast; in the East, they may seek refuge in peninsular Florida or the Keys. Adults raised across the broad midsection of the continent, however, funnel down along the Gulf of Mexico and through Texas, heading for the recently discovered wintering grounds in the mountains of central Mexico. They come by the hundreds, by

1. Fall migration along Galveston Bay

2. Tagged monarch

3. Larva

the thousands, and by the tens of thousands. Their slow, gliding flight may carry them two thousand miles from Canada to Mexico. They stream along the Texas beaches and across the plains, stopping to feed at autumn flowers and roosting communally through the night in trees along their route.

Millions of the large orange-and-black butterflies eventually reach their traditional winter home. There they hang like fluttering draperies from the trees, remaining inert during the coldest weather, drinking at stream banks and feeding sparingly on warmer days. They gradually lose their toxicity and suffer some predation by birds. The larger the colony, the better the protection, for predators tend to hunt along the edges, leaving the center of the masses undisturbed. These colonies have become major tourist attractions, an important factor in their preservation. Timber cutting and loss of these age-old refuges would

seriously cripple North America's monarch population.

The butterflies emerge from reproductive diapause and mate before they leave Mexico in the spring, moving northward across the Rio Grande. They fly now as individuals, a steady flow rather than a rushing stream, the females intent on finding stands of milkweed on which to lay their eggs. They arrive in Houston in early March to discover the green milkweed already in bloom, and they stop to produce another monarch brood. A few weeks later, newly emerged butterflies, too, take up the northward journey. Slowly the monarchs move on, until the "grandchildren" or "great-grandchildren" of the overwintering population reach the northern states and Canada. It is getting well into summer, and the season is short in northern latitudes, but they find time to raise yet another brood before it's time to leave.

Abundant in the Houston area in

spring, monarchs then decrease in numbers as most depart in their northward migration. A few remain through the summer, and the numbers begin to build again in fall. Now they find shore milkweed and other species, which they seem to prefer to the coarser green milkweed used in spring. They are also fond of the red-and-yellow Mexican milkweed that is widely planted in wildflower gardens across the region. High in toxic glycosides, it serves as a prime larval food plant in its native tropics. One or two last broods of eggs develop into winged adults, and they, too, join the migrating throng.

Some will have flown all the way from Canada, an incomparable feat proved by tagging and recapturing individual butterflies. Pioneered by Fred and Norah Urquhart, who have carried out considerable monarch research, tagging projects are now being used in Texas and are widespread across the country.

No individual butterfly will make the round-trip journey from Mexico northward to the breeding grounds and back. It is the descendants of previous populations that return to the same mountain valleys and the same roosting trees year after year. Guided by a map etched in their genes, they find their way to a winter refuge they have never seen. It is one of the most remarkable feats in nature, this instinctive migration of the monarch butterfly.

SIZE: 3½–4 inches.

DESCRIPTION: Orange, with black veins and white-spotted black borders. Male has scent patch on hindwing.

SIMILAR SPECIES: Queen is smaller, browner, and lacks heavy black veins above. Mimic viceroy is smaller, has strong black line across hindwing both above and below.

SEASON: March–December; most abundant in spring and fall.

LARVA: Ringed with yellow, black, and white bands. Pair of fleshy tentacles in front and back.

FOOD PLANTS: Milkweed species; less frequently milkvine and dogbane.

Queen
Danaus gilippus

Slightly smaller than the more familiar monarch, the queen is a darker chestnut or orange-brown, with white spots across the outer portion of the forewing and in the marginal black borders. The male has a black androconial scent patch on the upperside of the hindwing, as does its monarch counterpart.

Two different subspecies of the queen occur in the United States. Houston's form, *Danaus gilippus strigosus*, ranges northward from Mexico through Texas and the Desert Southwest and occasionally wanders into the Great Plains. Sometimes called the "striated queen," it has white scaling bordering the narrow black veins of the hindwing. The southeastern subspecies, *D. g. berenice*, ranges from Florida around the Gulf to the Mississippi Valley and sparingly northward along the Atlantic Coast. Other forms occupy the lowlands throughout most of tropical America.

The queen frequents open fields, dunes, deserts, and stream corridors, and its habits are much like those of the monarch. It does not stage dramatic migrations, however, and occurs primarily in the southern states. Vagrants that wander northward may briefly colonize an area, but they cannot survive the freezing winter.

Most courtship and mating activity takes place in the afternoon. The male flies around the female, extending the "hair pencil" scale tufts on his abdomen to waft pheromones around her head. The scent stimulates the female to land, and the male continues his fragrant offerings until she closes her wings, exposing her abdomen for mating. If they fly during copulation, the male carries his mate with him as he sails along.

The female lays her eggs on milkweeds and less frequently on twinevines, or climbing milkweeds, which are members of the same family, Asclepiadaceae. The larva is brownish white with red-brown and yellow transverse bands and a yellow-

1. Male, dorsal

2. Male, ventral

ish stripe along each side. It has three pairs of long, fleshy tentacles; the larval monarch has only two. The short, rounded chrysalides of both danaids are green with golden spots.

Like the monarch, the queen sequesters toxic compounds from the milkweeds and is distasteful and emetic to birds and other vertebrate predators. Across much of the continent, the viceroy mimics the monarch and presumably gains a measure of protection. In Florida and the Southwest, however, the monarch is primarily a migrant, seldom remaining through the summer to breed. In those regions, the viceroy mimics the more abundant queen, assuming a darker russet color to further the charade.

In the Houston area, queens appear to be common in some years, more elusive in others. We find larvae primarily on shore milkweed in late summer and early fall, sometimes sharing plants with the caterpillars of the monarch.

3. Larva

SIZE: 3–3½ inches.

DESCRIPTION: Orange-brown, with scattered white spots on tip of forewing and in black borders. Male has black scent patch on hindwing. Local subspecies, *strigosus*, has white scaling along veins on hindwing above.

SIMILAR SPECIES: Monarch is larger; veins more heavily marked with black on upperside. Soldier, or tropic queen, *D. eresimus*, has stronger black viens on hindwing above; confined to deep South Texas. Viceroy has black line across hindwing above and below.

SEASON: March—December; erratic from year to year.

LARVA: Brownish white, with transverse bands of red-brown and yellow. Has three pairs of soft, fleshy tentacles.

FOOD PLANTS: Chiefly milkweed species; also other members of family Asclepiadaceae.

Skippers

FAMILY HESPERIIDAE

The skippers take their name from their fast, erratic, darting flight. Most are small to medium-sized insects with stout, hairy bodies and relatively small wings. Although temperate species tend to be drab, some tropical skippers are resplendent in iridescent hues. Authors occasionally suggest that skippers are intermediate between butterflies and moths, but they are clearly more closely allied with the former. Taxonomists classify skippers in the superfamily Hesperioidea, while they place the "true butterflies" in a second superfamily, Papilionoidea. These are categories established for our convenience, of course, but they serve well in demonstrating the division of the butterflies into two large and distinct groups.

The skippers, with more than three thousand species, have a worldwide distribution. They are poorly represented in the Arctic and Subarctic and at high elevations, however, and appear much more abundantly in tropical regions. Nearly three hundred species occur in North America, many of them as rare vagrants into deep South Texas from Mexico.

Both skipper sexes have three pairs of fully developed and functional walking legs. Their heads and eyes are unusually large, and the antennae are short and set far apart, protruding toward the sides rather than forward. The unique antennal clubs narrow at the tip and are bent back into distinct hooks. Most skippers have a very long proboscis and nectar avidly at a wide variety of flowers. They also collect at mud puddles to sip fluids rich in salts and nutrients.

Skippers lay their spherical eggs singly on the leaves of their larval hosts. The caterpillars lack spines and are usually smooth-skinned, having at most a sparse covering of short hairs. Their large heads attach to slender "necks," making them immediately recognizable as skipper larvae. They roll leaves or build silken leaf nests, living and pupating within these shelters, at least

A little tropical checkered skipper, Pyrgus oileus, *is dwarfed by the large flower head of a sunflower at which it feeds.*

1. Tropical checkered skipper, female   2. Clouded skipper, female

partially protected from predators and parasites. They often emerge at night to feed.

With the exception of a single tropical species that strays into Arizona and West Texas, North American skippers fall into three distinct subfamilies. Only two occur in the immediate Houston area. Members of each group differ in their structure and habits and in their larval food plants.

The Pyrginae are usually called the spread-winged, or open-winged, skippers. Most wear somber shades of brown, black, or black-and-white, and they perch with wings spread wide. A few species, two of which we illustrate in this book, have long tails on their hindwings. Almost all use broad-leaved plants as larval foods, principally oaks, mallows, and legumes.

The Hesperiinae comprise the closed-wing skippers, also called the branded skippers. Males of many species have a distinctive brand, or stigma, of specialized scent scales on the forewing. Mainly brown or orange-and-brown, the Hesperiinae perch with wings tightly folded or with the hindwings opened more widely than the forewings, an attitude quite different from that of any other butterfly. Almost without exception, the larvae feed on grasses and sedges; in the tropics they may use palms and related monocotyledons.

A third subfamily, Megathyminae, contains the giant yucca skippers, a small group whose larvae burrow into the leaves and stems of yuccas and agaves. Large and rather strikingly marked butterflies, they are accorded full family status by some lepidopterists. None occurs regularly in the Houston area, but the yucca giant skipper, *Megathymus yuccae*, inhabits western and central Texas and ranges into the Big Thicket, wherever native yuccas grow.

With their small size, rapid flight, and generally drab colors, the skippers are the most difficult group of butterflies to identify. Many look disturbingly alike, and their classification is based partially on microscopic dissection and inspection of the genitalia. In addition, the Hesperiinae seldom display fully the upper surfaces of their wings. Without collecting and close examination, many will fly off as simply "skippers." By careful examination of the photographs included here, however, the amateur should be able to identify most of the common species. Many are characterized more easily by the underside of the wings than by the upperside.

We do not include every species that might occur in Houston. A number have ranges that border our region, and they may appear as strays from time to time. Other rare skippers wander northward from the Rio Grande Valley. Although they are not usually migratory, these little butterflies are strong fliers capable of erratic movements. A thorough study of the fascinating skippers requires collecting and systematic documentation; the casual butterfly enthusiast will do well to learn the common species and enjoy their lively, darting antics.

Silver-Spotted Skipper
Epargyreus clarus

The handsome silver-spotted skipper is one of the largest and best-known skippers in North America. The long, dark brown forewing is crossed by a broad band of translucent golden orange spots above and below, while the hindwing below bears a large silvery white patch. The scientific name apparently stems from the Greek *argyros*, "silver," and the Latin *clarus*, meaning "clear" or "bright."

The silver-spotted skipper ranges across the continent, from extreme southern Canada to northern Mexico, avoiding only the more arid regions of western Texas and the Great Basin. It frequents brushy fields, roadsides, and open woodlands, nectaring at a wide variety of flowers and sipping moisture from mud puddles. Opler and Krizek write that it prefers blue, red, pink, and purple flowers, although it sometimes visits white ones as well. In general, it avoids plants with yellow blooms.

Active mainly during the morning and early afternoon, adults hang upside down from leaves in the late afternoon and at night. Males perch on foliage and dart out at other butterflies, engaging them in swirling battles and chasing them from the area. Mating occurs near midday, the female carrying the male as they fly together in copulation.

The mated female lays her spherical green eggs singly on plant leaves. Flying along with a characteristic slow, bobbing flight, she touches a host to determine its species and then lands nearby to lay an egg. Her landing site, however, might be the leaf of another plant, and it is left to the hatchling caterpillar to find the proper food nearby.

Most references list black locust as the major host, including also wisteria and a wide variety of legumes. In eastern Harris and western Chambers counties, how-

1. Dorsal

2. Ventral

3. Egg and young larva

4. Mature larva

ever, we have found caterpillars primarily on false indigo, *Amorpha fruticosa*.

The young larva hides beneath a folded flap of leaf, but as it grows it builds a tent by tying several leaflets or leaves together with silk. Greenish yellow with darker crossbands, the caterpillar has a red-brown head with two large orange spots at the front. In raising larvae in captivity, we found that when disturbed they usually turned abruptly to face their "attacker," flashing their orange false eyes in an apparent attempt to dissuade potential predators.

The silver-spotted skipper is not as abundant as some of the smaller skippers in Houston, but it occurs widely through much of the year. There are probably at least three or four broods, with the last one overwintering as hibernating pupae.

SIZE: 1¾–2½ inches.

DESCRIPTION: Large, dark brown; golden orange spots across forewing above and below; silvery white spot on center of hindwing below.

SIMILAR SPECIES: Hoary edge, *Achalarus lyciades*, similar but with diffuse white patch on outer edge of hindwing below; occurs north of Houston area.

SEASON: February–December.

LARVA: Greenish yellow, with darker crossbands; brown head with two orange eyespots.

FOOD PLANTS: False indigo, black locust, wisteria, many other legumes.

Long-Tailed Skipper
Urbanus proteus
Bean-leaf roller

A number of skippers with long hind-wing tails occur in tropical America, and several range northward at least occasionally to Texas' Rio Grande Valley. *Urbanus proteus*, the long-tailed skipper, is the most abundant and widely distributed of these species in the United States. Dark brown above with light spots on the forewing, it is paler below with darker hindwing bands. The robust, hairy body and wing bases above are iridescent green, a distinctive feature separating this species from other tailed skippers.

Proteus ranges throughout most of South and Central America and the West Indies. It is a year-round resident of southern Texas and Florida, where the winter generation survives as adults but remains somewhat inactive. In the spring these butterflies begin to wander gradually northward, producing two or three more broods. The long-tailed skipper may stray up the Mississippi Valley as far as Illinois and along the Atlantic Coast to New York, but these wanderers cannot survive prolonged freezing temperatures. Trapping experiments indicate an extensive southward migration in the fall.

An uncommon but regular visitor to the Houston area, *U. proteus* is most often seen on warm, sunny days in late summer and early fall. Newly emerged individuals are distinctive and easily recognized, but perfect specimens are difficult to find. The tails are fragile and quickly broken. Brown and Heineman note that in Jamaica, where it is widely distributed, "lizards and birds play havoc with the tails of this skipper."

The long-tailed skipper frequents brushy fields, woodland edges, coastal dunes, and even suburban gardens, taking nectar at a wide variety of flowers.

1. Dorsal

2. Ventral

Males perch on foliage a few feet above the ground to await passing females; at night they roost upside down under leaves and branches, a trait common to many of the tropical skippers.

Females lay their eggs in small clusters beneath the leaves of a variety of viny legumes, and the larvae sometimes become pests in the South on cultivated beans. This leads to the common name "bean-leaf roller." The caterpillars live in nests of rolled leaves tied with silk. A variety of other plant families, including the crucifers and monocotyledons such as the canna, have been claimed as larval hosts, but Opler and Krizek comment that these records "are probably erroneous."

The genus of the long-tailed skipper owes its scientific name to the Latin word *urbanus*, meaning "citizen of a city." Proteus was a sea deity of Greek mythology. Poseidon, god of the sea, gave to Proteus the gift of prophecy and the power to assume a variety of different shapes.

SIZE: 1½–2 inches.

DESCRIPTION: Long hindwing tails; iridescent green on body and wing bases above.

SIMILAR SPECIES: Dorantes longtail lacks green iridescence; has more broadly rounded hindwings that join the tails almost at right angles. White-striped longtail, *Chioides catillus*, has long silver band on hindwing below; occurs infrequently as stray from South Texas. (See photo p. 213.)

SEASON: Occasional through much of the year; most often occurs July–October.

LARVA: Yellow-green, with black dorsal line; yellow to red stripe and two green lines along each side. Dark head with two large yellow spots on front.

FOOD PLANTS: Beans, other viny legumes.

Dorantes Longtail
Urbanus dorantes
Dorantes skipper, Lilac-banded longtail, Brown tailed skipper

Although the dorantes longtail is not as common as the similar long-tailed skipper, *Urbanus proteus*, it wanders northward occasionally to the Houston area from deep South Texas. We encounter it mainly in September and October as it takes nectar from a variety of flowers. It seems particularly attracted to lantana and mist-flower.

The dorantes longtail resembles the long-tailed skipper but lacks the green iridescence on the body and wing bases above, the distinction cited in all current butterfly manuals. The green color of *U. proteus*, however, is not readily visible in poor light or when the wings are closed. It is thus a difficult mark to use in the field. More reliable for the butterfly watcher is the fact that the hindwing of *proteus* is narrowly triangular, its outer margin flowing into the tail at an oblique angle. In contrast, the hindwing of *U. dorantes* is broadly rounded, and its margin joins the tail almost at right angles. This difference in wing shape and tail attachment can be seen under most conditions.

A tropical species that ranges throughout much of South and Central America and the West Indies, the dorantes longtail appears from at least June through October in the southern portions of Texas and may occur throughout the year. It strays northward through the eastern portions of the state, sometimes reaching Kansas and Missouri. Established in Florida in 1969 from Central American stock, it is now a year-round resident in that state. A long-lived winter brood does not become reproductive until spring; there are two or three other broods through the warmer months.

The dorantes longtail frequents road-

1. Dorsal

sides, brushy fields, and woodland edges and clearings, feeding at flowers and hanging upside down under leaves while roosting. The female lays her lustrous, iridescent green eggs on cultivated and wild beans as well as on a variety of other viny legumes.

This species is listed in references under a variety of common names. Most authors call it the dorantes skipper, but the North American Butterfly Association recently adopted the name dorantes longtail as being more descriptive.

SIZE: 1½–2 inches.

DESCRIPTION: Brown, with long tails; conspicuous transparent spots on forewing, dark bands on hindwing below. Hindwing broadly rounded; margin meets tail at right angle.

SIMILAR SPECIES: Long-tailed skipper has green iridescence on body and wing bases above. Hindwing is narrower, triangular; margin flows into tail at oblique angle. White-striped longtail, *Chioides catillus*, has long silver band on underside of hindwing. (See photo right, below.)

SEASON: June–November; most frequently September–October.

LARVA: Green to pinkish orange, brown at rear, with dark dorsal line. Head brown or black, covered with many lighter hairs.

FOOD PLANTS: Beans, other viny legumes.

2. Ventral

White-striped Longtail

Northern Cloudywing

Thorybes pylades
Northern cloudy wing, Cloudy wing

Three very similar species of cloudywings inhabit eastern North America; several others occur in the West. The northern cloudywing, *Thorybes pylades*, is the most common and widely distributed of the genus, ranging across most of the continent from Canada to northern Mexico. We find it regularly throughout the Houston area, while the other two eastern species occur less frequently. Precise identification of the three requires careful examination and is not always possible in the field. Without collecting, most *Thorybes* are best considered generic "cloudywings."

T. pylades is dark chocolate-brown above and below, with a series of small, triangular, translucent spots across the forewing. The male has a costal fold, a flap containing scent scales along the leading edge of the forewing. It is the only member of the genus with this feature.

The southern cloudywing, *T. bathyllus*, and the confused cloudywing, *T. confusis*, reach the limits of their ranges in our area, and both occur occasionally. The former has larger forewing spots aligned in a broad band; the latter has a much narrower forewing band. Each of these two species has been called the "eastern cloudywing" by one or more authors, indicating the problems in identification and nomenclature that exist within the genus.

The more common northern cloudywing favors woodland clearings and brushy fields. It readily visits flowers for nectar and congregates at mud puddles and stream banks. Males perch on the ground or on low vegetation to wait for passing mates. Most courtship occurs in late morning; mating takes place in early afternoon. Females lay their eggs on beg-

gar's ticks, bush clovers, and a number of other legumes. There are apparently several broods each year in Southeast Texas, with adults appearing from early March until November.

SIZE: 1¼–1¾ inches.

DESCRIPTION: Dark brown; with small, triangular, translucent spots on forewing. Male has costal fold.

SIMILAR SPECIES: Southern cloudywing with larger spots in distinct forewing band. Confused cloudywing has narrow band. Males of both species lack costal fold.

SEASON: March–November.

LARVA: Green, with dark dorsal line; two pink lines on each side; head black or dark brown.

FOOD PLANTS: Beggar's ticks, bush clovers; many other legumes reported.

1. Dorsal

2. Ventral

Sickle-Winged Skipper
Achlyodes mithridates
Bat skipper

This large and unusually shaped skipper can scarcely be mistaken for any other species. Many authors list it as *Achlyodes thraso*, but Miller, Opler, and others have more recently called it *A. mithridates*. The confusion stems from what Brown and Heineman, in their book *Jamaica and Its Butterflies*, term "Fabricius's brief and noncommittal description" in 1793. It was not until much later that closer examination of the manuscript illustrations of Fabrician species revealed the true nature of *mithridates*. Until then, it was believed to be an Indian butterfly. The nominate subspecies occurs in Jamaica; ours is subspecies *tamenund*, described by Edwards from near Waco, Texas, in 1871.

The broad, rounded wings are dark brown, glossed with an iridescent sheen of lavender and copper and crossed by bands of bluish gray spots. The female is lighter and more mottled than the male. Both sexes, however, have sickle-shaped forewings, a distinctive feature formed by an indentation in the outer margin just below the hooked tip.

A. mithridates ranges widely through South and Central America and the West Indies to southern Texas. It is a year-round resident in the southern tip of our state. While not a common Houston butterfly, it does wander northward along the coast and through the central portions of Texas, particularly from August through November. Strays have been found as far north as Arkansas and Kansas. Williams lists records for Brazoria, Waller, and western Harris counties, and he discovered it "laying eggs in September near the western city limits of Houston."

At home in the tropical thorn-scrub forest or in city gardens, the sickle-winged skipper flies with an unusual jerky flight.

It perches with wings spread widely and often seeks shade and shelter on the underside of leaves. A variety of different flowers serve as nectar sources.

Larvae feed primarily on lime prickly-ash, *Zanthoxylum fagara*, in Texas, but citrus is also used throughout the wide range of the species. The mature caterpillar has a bright yellow stripe along each side. Below the stripes, it is green; dorsally, it is a more bluish green with numerous tiny yellow dots. The head capsule is brown and roughly textured. The larva constructs a leafy tent by sewing several leaflets together with silk, living and pupating within its refuge. The green pupa is covered with a powdery white bloom and secured by a silken girdle.

SIZE: 1½–1⅞ inches.
DESCRIPTION: Dark brown, with purplish iridescence and bands of bluish gray spots. Notch below tip of forewing gives it a sickle-shaped appearance.
SIMILAR SPECIES: No large skipper has a similar wing shape.
SEASON: All year in South Texas; wanders northward primarily August–November.
LARVA: Green, with yellow lateral stripes; more bluish green on back, with yellow dots; head dark.
FOOD PLANTS: Lime prickly-ash, citrus.

1. Dorsal

2. Larva

Juvenal's Duskywing

Erynnis juvenalis
Juvenal's dusky wing,
Eastern oak dusky wing

This large, dark skipper is common across much of eastern North America in the spring, ranging from southern Canada to central Texas and the Gulf Coast. It reaches its southern limit in the Houston area, however, and is less abundant here than the following species, Horace's duskywing, *Erynnis horatius*. Juvenal's duskywing is apparently single-brooded throughout most of its range, and it appears in Texas with our earliest butterflies, flying from February until May.

Blackish brown above, *E. juvenalis* has several glassy white spots near the tip of the forewing, which is also mottled with black and bluish gray. The female is lighter than her mate, making her contrasting markings more distinct. Both are paler beneath, with much the same pattern. The key to identification of Juvenal's duskywing is the presence of two round, light spots on the hindwing below, a characteristic lacking in the similar Horace's duskywing. Otherwise, the two species look very much alike and probably cannot be safely separated in the field.

Juvenal's duskywing inhabits oak woodlands and adjacent fields, visiting flowers readily and sipping moisture from wet earth. It often basks in the sun on a bare patch of ground, its wings open widely, but it roosts with wings folded rooflike over its back like a moth.

The male patrols its territory from a low perch, sailing out in pursuit of passing butterflies, constantly searching for a receptive female of his species. Mating occurs from midday through the afternoon, the female carrying her mate as they fly.

Eggs are laid singly on a wide variety of oaks, the larvae forming nests by fold-

1. Ventral

2. Larva

ing leaves and tying them with silk. The mature caterpillar is green and covered with tiny yellow tubercles; its tan head is broadly heart-shaped, with three orange patches along each side.

The last-instar larvae hibernate through the winter before pupating, the adults emerging early the following spring. When we raised them in captivity, however, they pupated quickly because of the longer photoperiod. The adults then emerged late in the fall.

Erynnis, the genus of the duskywings, was named for one of the evening spirits in Greek mythology, according to Opler and Krizek. Juvenal, whom this species honors, was a satirical poet of ancient Rome.

SIZE: 1¼–1¾ inches.

DESCRIPTION: Blackish brown, with glassy white spots on forewing. Two round, light spots on hindwing beneath. Female paler and with more contrasting pattern than male.

SIMILAR SPECIES: More abundant Horace's duskywing nearly identical; lacks two light spots on hindwing beneath.

SEASON: Spring; usually February–May.

LARVA: Green, with yellow dots; head tan, with orange patches.

FOOD PLANTS: Wide variety of oaks.

Horace's Duskywing
Erynnis horatius
Brown dusky wing, Horace's dusky wing

Horace's duskywing, *Erynnis horatius*, looks much like Juvenal's duskywing, *E. juvenalis*. The latter species, however, is apparently single-brooded throughout its range and appears only in the spring. *Horatius* has three different broods in Texas, flying from very early spring until late fall. It is by far the most common duskywing in Houston and the surrounding area.

Horace's duskywing is dark brown above, the male more uniformly colored than his mate and with very little pattern contrast. The female displays a much more dramatic array of large translucent spots and dark markings. Both sexes lack the two round, pale spots on the underside of the hindwing that distinguish Juvenal's duskywing.

E. horatius ranges from the northern states to the Gulf of Mexico and westward through the eastern half of Texas. Other populations inhabit the western states but are largely absent from the Great Plains. The species prefers oak woodlands and nearby clearings, but wanders widely to brushy fields and roadsides in search of flowers at which to nectar. It also congregates at mud puddles.

Females lay their eggs singly on the tender growth of a variety of oaks, although Heitzman also reared the larvae on wisteria. Caterpillars we found on water oak in June were pale jade-green with numerous yellowish white tubercles, each tubercle giving rise to a short hair. The broadly heart-shaped heads of the early instars were dark brown; those of the mature larvae were tan with three orange patches on each side. Each caterpillar fashioned a tight refuge by folding leaves together and stitching them with silk. Pupation occurred within the leaf shelter and the resulting chrysalis was green. Larvae of the autumn brood hibernate

1. Male, dorsal

2. Female, dorsal

3. Ventral

220 / Skippers

4. Larva

through the winter; those hatching earlier in the year develop immediately.

The origin of this species' name is apparently in question. Opler and Krizek
note that there were two ancient Romans
named Horatius. One was a legendary
hero; the other, known as Horace, was
a poet.

SIZE: 1¼–1¾ inches.
DESCRIPTION: Dark brown. Male has
    little pattern contrast; female has large
    translucent spots and contrasting dark
    patches on forewing.
SIMILAR SPECIES: Juvenal's duskywing
    has two round, light spots on hind-
    wing beneath.
SEASON: February–November; three
    broods.
LARVA: Green with tiny, pale tubercles;
    head capsule tan, with six orange
    patches.
FOOD PLANTS: Various oak species; wis-
    teria also reported.

Funereal Duskywing

Erynnis funeralis
Funereal dusky wing,
Streamlined dusky wing

Black wings and white hindwing fringes immediately distinguish the funereal duskywing from all other *Erynnis* species in the Houston area. It takes its name from its somber coloring. The forewing is narrow and pointed, with a brown patch near the center; the hindwing is broadly triangular. The sexes look much alike, without the dimorphism exhibited by Horace's duskywing.

Scott considers the funereal duskywing to be a subspecies of *E. zarucco*, a butterfly of the southeastern states. He calls them collectively the "streamlined dusky wing." Although *E. zarucco*, the "zarucco duskywing" of most authors, has brown hindwing fringes instead of white, intermediates between the two occur in Louisiana and Florida. The breeding biology of the two forms is much the same, and Scott's points have some merit. For now, however, other references continue to list both as full species. Only *E. funeralis* occurs in the Houston area.

The funereal duskywing ranges from Texas and the Southwest through tropical America to Argentina. It also strays northward through the plains and along the Mississippi Valley to Nebraska and Illinois. The larvae feed on a variety of widely distributed legumes, including vetches, indigos, and alfalfa. Thus, there are few habitats unsuited to this dark duskywing, and it appears in brushy fields, woodland edges, roadsides, and even deserts.

The common rattlebush, *Sesbania drummondii*, appears to be a major food plant throughout our region. We find larvae webbing together the leaflets to form shelters from early spring until mid December. Many, however, are parasitized by small wasps, evidence that their protective measures do not always prove successful.

SIZE: 1¼–1¾ inches.

DESCRIPTION: Black, with white hindwing fringes. Forewing narrow, with brown patch; hindwing broadly triangular.

SIMILAR SPECIES: Other local duskywings browner, lack white fringe on hindwing.

SEASON: February–December; several broods.

LARVA: Pale green, with yellow line on each side; covered with pale tubercles, each with a short hair; head light brown, with paler orange-brown patches.

FOOD PLANTS: Rattlebush, vetch, indigo, alfalfa, wide variety of other legumes.

1. Dorsal

2. Ventral

3. Larva

Wild Indigo Duskywing
Erynnis baptisiae
Indigo dusky wing, Baptisia dusky wing

Wild indigos, *Baptisia* species, are the most frequent native hosts of the wild indigo duskywing, giving it both its common and scientific names. Widespread introduction of crown vetch as a ground cover along interstates and other highways and along railroad beds, however, has greatly increased the abundance and range of this large, dark skipper. It occurs from southern New England to the Gulf Coast and west to Nebraska and south-central Texas.

Williams lists *Erynnis baptisiae* as "rare and irregular" in Southeast Texas, noting that it has been recorded along the northern fringes of the region and "possibly in the Piney Woods." Opler's range map shows it skirting the Texas coastal plain. However, we have found larvae on wild indigo plants in several locations along the coast from Padre Island to the Bolivar Peninsula, raising them successfully to adults. Rickard also reports the species from southwestern Harris County and lists rattlebush, *Sesbania*, as an alternate host.

The wild indigo duskywing is a darker blackish brown than Juvenal's and Horace's duskywings and lacks the white hindwing fringe of the funereal duskywing. The outer portion of the forewing is lighter than the base, with a central brown patch, a few glassy spots near the tip, and a pattern of dark and light bands. Other closely related duskywings with similar patterns do not occur in Texas.

An inhabitant of open fields, dunes, and woodland edges, *E. baptisiae* sips nectar from a variety of flowers. Freshly emerged males also gather at mud puddles to drink. The males perch atop low shrubs during much of the day, but patrol continuously during late afternoon. According to Opler and Krizek,

1. Dorsal

they fly low, oval routes up to thirty meters long, constantly searching for mates.

Females lay their eggs singly on wild indigos and other legumes, and the heavy-bodied larvae look much like those of other duskywings. Greenish with pale tubercles, each sprouting a short hair, they have brown, heart-shaped heads with lighter markings.

2. Larva

SIZE: 1⅛ – 1⅝ inches.
DESCRIPTION: Dark blackish brown;
  forewing with brown central patch and
  pattern of dark and light bands on
  outer half; hindwing fringes brown.
SIMILAR SPECIES: Black funereal duskywing has white hindwing fringes.
  Other local duskywings lighter brown.
SEASON: April–November; several
  broods.
LARVA: Light green, with faint yellow
  stripe on each side; heavily dotted with
  pale tubercles, each with a short hair;
  head brown, with pale pattern.
FOOD PLANTS: Wild indigos, lupines,
  crown vetch, rattlebush, several other
  legumes.

Common Checkered Skipper
Pyrgus communis
Checkered skipper

Pyrgus communis may well be North America's most abundant skipper, a status reflected in its scientific name. *Communis* is Latin for "common." Most books call it simply the "checkered skipper," but many recent authors prefer "common checkered skipper," distinguishing it from other closely related species. The tropical checkered skipper, for example, also occurs in our area.

The male *P. communis* is dark gray above, with long blue-gray, hairlike scales on the body and wing bases. Numerous white spots checker the wings above, while the fringes of the wings are also checkered. The female is usually somewhat darker, her wings checkered black-and-white. She also lacks most of the long basal hairs. Both sexes are whitish below, with bands of dark gray or olive-gray spots across the hindwings.

The common checkered skipper occurs as a permanent resident from the central states through much of tropical America. In summer it strays northward as far as Canada, establishing short-lived colonies that do not survive the winter. Because the larvae feed on a wide variety of plants in the mallow family, including both wild species and such cultivars as hollyhocks and hibiscus, this charming skipper can occupy almost any open, sunny habitat. It moves readily into yards and gardens as well as fields and weedy roadsides.

One of our first butterflies to appear in spring, *P. communis* occurs in Houston from late February or early March through November. In warm winters without a freeze, it may be on the wing in smaller numbers throughout the year. It visits a wide variety of flowers for nectar and also flocks to mud puddles and damp places to drink, often perching with wings spread. Males are extremely pugnacious, darting out at anything that invades their territories. Active through most of the day, they patrol extensively for females from midday until midafternoon.

Females lay their greenish eggs singly on buds or young leaves of plants in the family Malvaceae. The larvae live in nests of rolled leaves. We find them primarily on globe-mallows in West Texas, on *Sida* species in the East. This species and the following, the tropical checkered skipper, frequently share the same arrowleaf sida plants that spring up as weeds in our flower beds, causing some initial confusion in our field notes.

SIZE: ¾–1¼ inches.
DESCRIPTION: Checkered dark gray and white, male with long blue-gray hairs on body and wing bases; female usually darker than male. White below, with bands of gray or olive-gray spots.
SIMILAR SPECIES: Tropical checkered skipper has three dark blotches on leading edge of hindwing below.
SEASON: February–November; occasionally throughout the year.
LARVA: Tan or greenish brown, with dark and light stripes; covered with tiny white tubercles, each with a short hair; head and collar black; head covered with yellow-brown hairs.
FOOD PLANTS: Sidas, globe-mallows, many other mallows.

1. Dorsal

2. Ventral

3. Larva

Tropical Checkered Skipper
Pyrgus oileus
Blue-gray skipper

Pyrgus oileus looks much like the previous species, *P. communis*, and often flies with it. Without capturing the butterflies or examining them closely, it is difficult to distinguish between the two. Williams, in his annotated checklist for Southeast Texas, states that *oileus* is "rather uncommon" in our area. We find it almost as abundant as *communis*, however, at least in eastern Harris County.

The male tropical checkered skipper is dark gray above with white spots. An extensive mat of blue-gray hairs covers the bases of the wings. The female is usually darker, with the long hairs confined primarily to a small area of the hindwing. Both sexes have a strong infusion of brown on the hindwing beneath, thus producing less contrast between the pale ground color and the darker bands of spots.

The white spots along the edge of the hindwing above are larger in *P. oileus* than they are in *P. communis*. In the former, these marginal spots are almost as large as those in the inner, submarginal row. This and the brownish underwings of *oileus* are listed by most authors as the distinguishing features between the two species. Few references, however, cite the best distinction, especially in the field. The tropical checkered skipper, *P. oileus*, has three dark blotches along the leading edge of the hindwing below; these marks are not present on the common checkered skipper.

As its name suggests, the tropical checkered skipper occurs only along the extreme southern edge of the United States. It ranges from Florida around the Gulf of Mexico to southeastern and southern Texas, then south through the West Indies and mainland tropical America to Argentina. A few individuals stray northward from the Gulf Coast into the southern states.

1. Larva

The habits of *oileus* are presumably much like those of the better-known *communis*. It frequents brushy fields, roadsides, woodland clearings, and yards and gardens, where the larvae feed on a variety of mallows. In the Houston area, the caterpillars utilize arrowleaf sida, also called axocatzin, webbing together leaves to build shelters.

The species takes its scientific name from Oileus, King of the Locrians, mentioned in the *Aeneid* and the *Iliad*. One of the Argonauts, Oileus sailed with Jason in search of the golden fleece.

SIZE: 1–1⅜ inches.
DESCRIPTION: Dark gray, with checkered pattern of white spots. Male lighter, with thick mat of blue-gray hairs on body and wing bases above. Underside of hindwing suffused with brown and bearing three dark blotches along the leading edge.
SIMILAR SPECIES: Common checkered skipper lacks three dark blotches on leading edge of hindwing below.
SEASON: March–November; several broods.
LARVA: Green, with faint dorsal line; covered with small white tubercles; head black.
FOOD PLANTS: Sida, other mallows.

2. Dorsal

3. Ventral

Swarthy Skipper
Nastra lherminier
Fuscous skipper

The genus *Nastra* contains a dozen species of small skippers that range through the American tropics. The swarthy skipper, the neamathla skipper, and Julia's skipper are the only three species occurring within the United States. They were once placed in the genus *Lerodea*. They are extremely difficult to separate in the field, and even collected specimens prove troublesome. The ranges of the three overlap in the Houston area.

The swarthy skipper is plain dark brown above, sometimes with a trace of two light spots on the forewing. The forewing beneath is yellow-brown on the leading edge and at the tip, while a larger rear portion is a contrasting dark brown. Distinctive pale veins mark the yellow-brown hindwing below.

Nastra lherminier ranges through the eastern states, from the Atlantic Coast westward to Kansas and East Texas. It reaches its western limits near Dallas and

Houston. An inhabitant of grassy fields and clearings, it flies low to the ground and visits a variety of flowers for nectar.

Little bluestem grass is the only larval host listed by most authors, but Johnson grass has been accepted by young larvae in the laboratory. The breeding biology and early stages of the swarthy skipper, however, have not been fully described.

SIZE: ⅞–1 inch.
DESCRIPTION: Dark brown above, rarely with two light spots on forewing. Yellow-brown below; hindwing with lighter veins, forewing with large dark area at rear.
SIMILAR SPECIES: Neamathla skipper lacks pale veins on hindwing below; has smaller dark area on underside of forewing. Julia's skipper has two to five light spots on forewing; also lacks pale veins on hindwing below.
SEASON: March–October; probably two broods, March–June and August–October.
LARVA: Not fully described.
FOOD PLANTS: Little bluestem grass.

1. Dorsal

2. Ventral

Neamathla Skipper
Nastra neamathla
Southern swarthy skipper

This small, drab skipper closely resembles the swarthy and Julia's skippers that also occur in the Houston area. It is brown above, sometimes with minute light spots on the forewing. Yellow-brown below, it lacks the paler scaling that outlines the hindwing veins of the swarthy skipper. The yellow-brown area on the underside of the forewing is also larger, covering more than the outer half. Only a small portion of that forewing is dark brown.

According to Opler and Scott, the neamathla skipper resides in Southeast Texas, peninsular Florida, and the Keys, ranging southward as far as Costa Rica. Scott states that it reaches its western limits in Harris and Galveston counties. Other authors, however, describe populations from western Texas as well as from southern Arizona and California. These discrepancies may arise because of the similarity of the three *Nastra* species; dissection and microscopic examination of the genitalia provide the best proof of identity.

Rickard reports extensive collecting and rearing of the *neamathla/julia* complex. Male genitalia of specimens from Hardin County in Southeast Texas appeared to be "pure" *N. neamathla*, while those from areas west of Houston, beginning near Sealy in Austin County, were typical of *N. julia*. Specimens from Harris County were intermediate, indicating a clinal species. Rickard could not distinguish the larvae of the two forms, but he notes that they commonly utilized Johnson and Dallis grasses in urban vacant lots.

The neamathla skipper also frequents moist, open fields and marsh edges from March through October. There are apparently at least three broods each year, but the early stages have not been fully described.

1. Ventral

SIZE: ⅞–1 inch.

DESCRIPTION: Brown above, occasionally with minute spots on forewing. Yellow-brown below; lacks pale scaling on hindwing veins.

SIMILAR SPECIES: Swarthy skipper has pale hindwing veins below; larger dark area contrasting with yellow-brown forewing below. Julia's skipper has more prominent light spots on forewing above.

SEASON: March–October; three or more broods.

LARVA: Not fully described.

FOOD PLANTS: Johnson grass, Dallis grass.

Julia's Skipper
Nastra julia
Julia skipper, Western swarthy skipper

While the swarthy and neamathla skippers reach the western edge of their ranges in Southeast Texas, Julia's skipper moves northward from a year-round stronghold in the southern tip of the state. It occurs from April until October throughout much of southern and central Texas, ranging northward to Dallas and along the coast to Galveston Bay.

The ranges of all three *Nastra* species overlap in the Houston area, and they can be extremely difficult to separate. Indeed, Scott suggests *N. julia* and *N. neamathla* may hybridize in Galveston County, and Rickard's studies in Harris and surrounding counties support that hypothesis. It thus appears that the neamathla and Julia's skippers might best be considered forms of a single clinal species. Identification of these forms can be almost impossible in the field, and the only certain way of separating the *Nastra* complex is by examination of the genitalia.

Julia's skipper is brown above, with two to five yellowish spots on the forewing; the others have at most a hint of tiny pale spots. The underside of the hindwing lacks the paler veins of the swarthy skipper.

Julia's skipper occurs from Texas through central Mexico, with other populations in western Arizona and California. It has also been called the "western swarthy skipper." It frequents open, grassy areas in scrubby woodlands, stream banks, roadside ditches, and even flower gardens, but little is known about its breeding biology or life history. Larvae apparently feed on Bermuda, Johnson, and Dallis grasses and in captivity have also taken St. Augustine grass.

1. Ventral

SIZE: $^{15}/_{16}$–1⅛ inches.
DESCRIPTION: Brown above, with two to five pale spots. Yellow-brown below, without light hindwing veins.
SIMILAR SPECIES: Swarthy skipper has pale hindwing veins. Neamathla skipper has, at most, tiny forewing spots.
SEASON: April–October.
LARVA: Not fully described.
FOOD PLANTS: Bermuda, Johnson, Dallis, and St. Augustine grasses.

Clouded Skipper
Lerema accius

Our only representative of a tropical American genus, *Lerema accius* is the most abundant blackish-brown skipper in the Houston area. It can be found regularly from February through November in grassy fields, woodland clearings, roadsides, and urban gardens. Its low, swirling flight is difficult to follow, but the clouded skipper readily visits a wide variety of flowers, sitting passively to feed and allowing close examination.

Both sexes have a band of three white dots in a straight line near the tip of the forewing. The male usually has one or two other small white spots; the female has several larger ones. This pattern is visible on both forewing surfaces. A strong black stigma marks the male's forewing above, but this scent patch is inconspicuous against the dark ground color. The hindwings of both sexes are beautifully shaded and mottled with violet-blue, especially on freshly emerged butterflies.

The clouded skipper ranges across the southeastern coastal plain and through Texas to South America. It also wanders northward as far as New England, Illinois, and Kansas, sometimes producing another brood before succumbing to freezing weather. Recent experiments in northern Florida also suggest there may be a return fall migration, for directional malaise traps have captured numerous adults flying south.

Several grasses, including St. Augustine, have been reported as larval food plants, the female laying her eggs singly on the leaf blades. Shortly after hatching, the larva folds the leaf and stitches it with silk, living and feeding within this shelter. When it consumes that leaf, it moves to another and quickly builds a new refuge. The caterpillar is white or pale greenish, finely mottled and stippled with dark green. The white head is bor-

1. Female, dorsal

2. Female, ventral

dered and striped with black. Pupation occurs within the leaf shelter, and the chrysalis is pale green and dusted with a powdery white bloom. The long, free proboscis extends to the tip of the abdomen; the head is tipped with a sharp horn.

We find larvae of the clouded skipper most commonly on the rustyseed paspalum, *Paspalum langei*, that springs up as a persistent weed in our flower beds. Because we leave a few clumps of this grass for the butterflies, we are blessed throughout most of the year with these pretty skippers that swirl around our yard and sip nectar from our flowers.

3. Larva

SIZE: 1–1½ inches.

DESCRIPTION: Dark blackish brown. Forewing with small white dots; hindwing below shaded with violet-blue.

SIMILAR SPECIES: No other dark skipper has violet-blue shading on hindwing below. Compare also forewing spot pattern.

SEASON: February–November.

LARVA: Pale greenish white, finely marbled with dark green; head white, with black border and stripes.

FOOD PLANTS: Rustyseed paspalum, St. Augustine, several other grasses.

Least Skipper
Ancyloxypha numitor
Least skipperling

This pretty little skipper occurs commonly throughout most of the year in Southeast Texas. It prefers wet, open areas and inhabits freshwater marshes, roadside ditches, and rice fields, wandering as well into lawns and gardens within the city. Its small size and flashing orange-and-black pattern make it relatively easy to identify.

The forewing above is largely black or dark blackish brown, usually with a suffusion of orange near the leading edge. The orange hindwing is broadly bordered with black. The hindwing below is entirely yellow-orange, and the forewing below is bordered by the same orange color. Its black base is often concealed while perching, and the undersides of the wings then appear completely orange. The black is easily visible in flight, however, for the least skipper flies with weak, fluttering movements.

A common species throughout most of eastern North America, the least skipper ranges from southern Canada to Florida, the Gulf Coast, and South Texas. Strays occasionally turn up as far west as Colorado.

The least skipper prefers low-growing flowers and sips nectar from a variety of species. The male patrols for a mate by flying low over grassy areas through most of the day. The female lays her eggs on a variety of grasses, including marsh millet, bluegrass, and cultivated rice, and the larva makes a protective shelter by drawing together with silk the opposite sides of the leaf blade.

The rather formidable genus name, according to Opler and Krizek, stems from the Greek *ankylos*, meaning "curved" or "hooked," and *xiphos*, "sword." This species is the namesake of Numitor, King of Alba, as mentioned in the *Aeneid*. The

1. Dorsal

2. Ventral

grandfather of Romulus and Remus,
Numitor was dispossessed of his crown
by his brother Amulius. The grandsons
later killed Amulius and restored Numitor to the throne.

SIZE: ¾–1 inch.
DESCRIPTION: Small; with weak, fluttering flight. Forewing largely black
above, with orange suffusion. Orange
hindwing bordered with black above,
entirely orange below. Black base of
forewing below often hidden while
skipper is perched.
SIMILAR SPECIES: Southern skipperling
is even smaller; orange wings above
have only narrow black border; orange
hindwing below has distinct white ray.
SEASON: February–December.
LARVA: Grass-green; head dark brown,
ringed with white line.
FOOD PLANTS: Marsh millet, bluegrass,
rice, other grasses.

Southern Skipperling

Copaeodes minimus
Tiny skipper, Minimus skipperling

This tiny orange butterfly ranks as North America's smallest skipper. It is abundant throughout the Houston area from at least March into November, frequenting open, sunny fields and roadsides as well as urban lots and gardens. It often flies with the least skipper, but is easily recognized by its smaller size and the lack of extensive dark areas above and below. Formerly listed as *Copaeodes minima*, the scientific name has recently been changed to *C. minimus* to conform to the standards of biological nomenclature.

The southern skipperling is bright orange above. Some specimens have narrow black borders or dark veins, and the male has a tiny black stigma on the forewing. Beneath, both wings are orange, with a distinct light ray running across the hindwing from base to outer margin.

This white ray can easily be seen as the butterfly perches with folded wings or sips nectar from a flower, and it is diagnostic of the species.

C. minimus ranges from the southeastern states along the coastal plain through Texas to Costa Rica or Panama. In summer, it wanders slightly northward, but it is not a long-distance traveler with its weak, erratic flight. Roy Kendall has reported egg-laying on Bermuda grass and has raised the larvae in captivity. No other larval hosts have been reported, and the life history of the southern skipperling remains poorly known.

The related orange skipperling, *C. aurantiacus*, occurs in western and central Texas. Williams notes that it is the most common of the skipperlings in Austin, and he collected it once in the Sharpstown area of southwestern Houston during the dry summer of 1985. We have not, as yet, found the orange skip-

1. Ventral

perling within our area. Slightly larger than the southern skipperling, it lacks the white ray across the underside of the hindwing.

SIZE: ½-¾ inch.

DESCRIPTION: Orange above and below, with distinct light ray across hindwing below.

SIMILAR SPECIES: Least skipper is larger, with extensive black areas. Orange skipperling lacks white hindwing ray.

SEASON: March–November.

LARVA: Not fully described.

FOOD PLANTS: Bermuda grass; perhaps other grasses.

Fiery Skipper
Hylephila phyleus
Fiery branded skipper

The fiery skipper is the most abundant of several orange-and-brown skippers that swirl across the fields and lawns throughout the Houston area. It is the only North American member of its genus; most others occur in South America. The genus name comes from the Greek words *hyle*, "forest," and *philos*, "loving." In spite of this, *Hylephila phyleus* is a butterfly of open, sunny areas and perfectly at home along our roadsides and in our yards and gardens.

The fiery skipper exhibits strong sexual dimorphism. The smaller male is bright orange above, with a black stigma and dark, sawtooth margins edging both wings. He is paler orange below, the hindwing bearing scattered black spots. The female is larger and dark brown above, with an irregular band of orange spots across her wings. Orange-yellow or brownish yellow below, she has scattered dark spots and an irregular pale band. The antennae of both sexes are much shorter than those of related skippers, barely exceeding the width of the head.

The dark spots on the underside of the hindwing provide the best means of identifying the fiery skipper in the field, since it frequently sits with wings tightly closed. They are diagnostic of the species, but they vary considerably in size and clarity. In our experience, the spring and fall broods have larger, distinct spots, while adults flying in midsummer have almost clear orange hindwings with only a few tiny dots.

A resident across the southern states, from the Atlantic to the Pacific, the fiery skipper ranges southward through the West Indies and mainland tropical America to Argentina. It strays northward to the northern tier of states, particularly in the East, but cannot withstand harsh winters. It may succeed in

1. Male, dorsal

2. Male (top) and female, lightly marked, ventral

3. Female, heavily marked, ventral

raising as many as two or three other broods, however, before the summer ends. In Southeast Texas, it appears from at least March through November and frequently longer, breeding almost continuously.

Fiery skippers visit a variety of flowers, utilizing both wild and cultivated species. Males perch close to the ground among the grasses to await potential mates. Pursuing a female in fast, darting flight, the male coaxes her to land and walks around her, fluttering his wings. Most mating is with virgin females, and the coupling may last for forty minutes or more. If the pair is disturbed, the female carries her mate as they fly. Unreceptive females flutter their wings or raise their abdomens to prevent mating, or they may simply ignore the advances and fly away.

A variety of grasses serve as larval hosts. These include especially Bermuda grass and crabgrass, but St. Augustine, bluegrass, bent grass, and sugarcane have also been documented. The caterpillar constructs a shelter by rolling and tying leaf blades with silk, and in mowed lawns, it builds this refuge horizontally amid the roots. The fiery skipper is one of the few butterflies that adapt to the disturbance of a regular mowing program. It amply rewards this sacrifice of a few grass blades in your lawn by its cheerful, charming presence at your flowers.

SIZE: 1–1⅜ inches; female larger than male.

DESCRIPTION: Male orange above, with sawtooth dark borders. Female brown, with band of scattered orange spots. Both lighter below, with scattered small dark spots on hindwing.

SIMILAR SPECIES: Other small orange skippers lack dark dots on hindwing. See also whirlabout and sachem.

SEASON: March–November; often longer.

LARVA: Gray-brown to yellow-brown, with three dark stripes; head black, with red-brown stripes.

FOOD PLANTS: Several grasses, including lawn grasses.

Whirlabout
Polites vibex

"Whirlabout" aptly describes this fast-flying little skipper and its darting, swirling flight. The same name would apply as well to many of our other hesperids. *Polites vibex* is sexually dimorphic; the male and female appear dramatically different, especially on the upper wing surfaces.

The male resembles the male fiery skipper, its orange wings above bordered with black. The hindwing border is smoothly edged, however, not sawtoothed as in the fiery skipper. The orange-yellow hindwing below bears larger dark, paired blotches, rather than small black spots. The female whirlabout is dark brown above, with a few whitish or yellowish spots on the forewing. Her hindwing below is dusky yellow, with diffuse dark patches similar to those of her mate.

The whirlabout ranges across the

1. Female, dorsal

2. Male, ventral

3. Female, ventral

southeastern states and southward through the West Indies and much of Central and South America. It occurs throughout southeastern and southern Texas, particularly along the coastal plain. Although not as common as the fiery skipper, it appears in the Houston area through much of the year, inhabiting open fields, coastal dunes, roadsides, and vacant lots.

Adults readily visit flowers, and males perch on low twigs and grasses during the afternoon to watch for passing females. The mated females lay their eggs on grasses, and the larvae live in tubes made by rolling leaves and tying them with silk. The caterpillars may feed primarily at night.

SIZE: 1–1¼ inches.
DESCRIPTION: Male orange above, with smooth-margined black hindwing border; orange-yellow hindwing below with paired dark blotches. Female dark brown above, with light forewing spots; dusky yellow below, with diffuse hindwing blotches.
SIMILAR SPECIES: Male fiery skipper has black sawtooth border on hindwing above; smaller black spots on hindwing below. Females do not look alike.
SEASON: March–November.
LARVA: Pale green, with faint lateral stripes; head black, marked with creamy stripes and spots.
FOOD PLANTS: Grasses, including St. Augustine, Bermuda grass, and paspalums.

Southern Broken Dash
Wallengrenia otho
Broken dash, Red broken dash

Called simply "broken dash" by most authors, *Wallengrenia otho* is probably best named the southern broken dash to distinguish it from the sibling northern broken dash, *W. egeremet*. Until recently, both were considered subspecies or color forms of a single species. The unusual stigma, or scent patch, on the forewing of each is broken into two parts, resulting in the common name.

Otho occurs sparingly throughout much of Southeast Texas, although it seems to prefer open areas near wooded swamps and stream bottoms. Its range extends from the southern Atlantic Coast around the Gulf to Texas, then southward through tropical America. It wanders sparingly northward to the midsection of the country. *Egeremet*, as its common name indicates, is more northern in its distribution, ranging through the eastern states from the Canadian border to the Gulf of Mexico. The two species fly together in the Piney Woods of East Texas, but *egeremet* appears to reach its southern limit just north of Houston. The southern broken dash, *W. otho*, is the species to be expected here, although Rickard reports both from Lake Houston.

Dark brown above, the male has an orange or red-orange area along the leading edge of the forewing and a small orange spot on the wing just outside the stigma. The female looks much like her mate, but with two pale orange spots in the midsection of the forewing. Both also have a small line of three light spots near the tip of the wing.

It is the underside of the hindwing that is most distinctive in both sexes. Reddish orange or rust-red, it contains a faint, curved band of pale spots. No other skipper has quite the same color and pattern, and the southern broken

1. Orange form, ventral

2. Red form, ventral

dash can be identified as it perches with closed wings or stops to sip nectar from a flower. The hindwings of its northern counterpart are dark brown or purplish brown with a similar band of spots.

W. otho is on the wing from March to at least October in our region, but much remains to be learned about its habits and biology. Until recently it has been confused with *egeremet* throughout the Southeast. The caterpillar feeds on weedy grasses and builds the webbed-leaf shelter typical of most skipper larvae. Pyle (1981) notes that it thrives in a wide array of habitats throughout its range, and therefore must utilize a variety of grasses. Kendall reared this species on St. Augustine grass in Texas.

SIZE: 1–1¼ inches.
DESCRIPTION: Brown above, with orange area along leading edge of forewing, small orange spots. Hindwing below red-orange to rust-red, with faint curving band of pale spots.
SIMILAR SPECIES: Northern broken dash less likely in Houston area; has brown or purple-brown hindwing below.
SEASON: March–October; year-round in South Texas.
LARVA: Green, mottled with white and red-brown; orange lateral spots; head dark, marked with white.
FOOD PLANTS: Grasses.

Little Glassywing
Pompeius verna

Dark blackish brown both above and below, the little glassywing has a series of distinct, translucent white spots on both surfaces of the forewing. The largest central spot just below the stigma of the male is elongated; the corresponding spot on the female is square. The hindwing beneath often has a faint purplish or rusty gloss, and there is usually an indistinct band of pale spots.

The genus takes its name from the ruler Pompeius, who formed the Roman triumvirate with Caesar and Crassus. It is closely related to *Polites*, and *verna* was placed in that genus before becoming *Pompeius verna*. The female is known as one of the "three black witches," along with the female dun skipper and northern broken dash, because of its somber coloring. The female dun skipper may also have a few diffuse white spots on the forewing, and Opler states that the females and some males must be captured to be reliably identified. Glassberg, however, points out that the little glassywing has a white area on the antenna just below the club, a feature not shared by the other "witches." The accompanying photos clearly show that distinctive mark.

The little glassywing occurs from southeastern Canada through the eastern half of the United States to the Gulf Coast. Opler's range map shows a disjunct Southeast Texas population centered near Houston. More collecting records are needed to determine the extent of the Texas range.

Moist areas near shaded woodlands are apparently the little glassywing's preferred habitats. There it visits a variety of flowers, and males also sip moisture at mud puddles. Perching on low vegetation in sunlit clearings, the males wait for passing females, darting out in hopes of stimulating them to mate. Purpletop is the only larval food plant listed by most

1. Male, ventral

2. Female, ventral

authors, but other grasses probably serve as well. There are apparently at least two broods in Texas, with adults on the wing from April until September.

SIZE: 1–1¼ inches.

DESCRIPTION: Dark blackish brown, with white spots on both surfaces of forewing. Hindwing below with faint row of pale spots. White area on antenna below the club.

SIMILAR SPECIES: Female dun skipper may also have small white spots on forewing, but lacks white on antenna. Clouded skipper has distinct, mottled pattern on hindwing below.

SEASON: April–September; possibly longer.

LARVA: Yellow-green to brown, with dark lines and small dark bumps; head red-brown, rimmed with black.

FOOD PLANTS: Purpletop; probably other grasses.

Sachem
Atalopedes campestris
Satchem, Field skipper,
Campestris skipper

As its scientific name indicates, the sachem is a butterfly of open, sunny places; the Latin *campestris* means "of the fields." This active skipper frequents not only fields and pastures, however, but a wide variety of disturbed areas, including roadsides, powerline and railroad corridors, and city lawns and gardens. It perches on low vegetation or on the ground, visiting a wide array of flowers but darting off in typical erratic skipper fashion if disturbed.

The male is orange above, bordered irregularly with brown. It has an extremely large, rectangular black stigma on the forewing. These specialized scent scales of male skippers produce pheromones used in courtship and mating. The female is larger and highly variable, ranging from light orange-brown to dark brown above. A square, glassy spot near the middle of the forewing provides a distinctive mark. Dingy brown below, the female has an irregular, sharply angled band of square cream-colored spots on the hindwing. A similar pattern on the hindwing of the male is less distinct because of the lighter, dingy yellow ground color.

The sachem ranges widely across the southern United States and southward through the tropics to Brazil. It is a regular summer stray and temporary colonist to the northern tier of states, particularly in the East, but it cannot survive a severe winter freeze. In Houston, the sachem occurs widely across the area, but in varying numbers. At times it may be abundant; at other times, it can be difficult to find.

Females lay their eggs singly on grasses. Bermuda grass is usually cited as the primary host, but references list a variety of species, including St. Augustine,

1. Female, ventral

crabgrass, goosegrass, and salt grass. The caterpillar builds a tent of webbed leaves at the base of the plant, emerging to clip grass blades and returning with them to its refuge to feed. Adults are on the wing from March into December, with four or five broods in Texas.

SIZE: 1–1½ inches; female larger than male.
DESCRIPTION: Male orange, with brown borders; large rectangular black stigma on forewing above. Female brown, with square glassy spot near center of forewing; brownish below, with angled band of square pale spots.
SIMILAR SPECIES: Female fiery skipper lacks translucent spot on forewing; has black spots on hindwing below. Male fiery skipper has smaller stigma and sawtooth dark borders above.
SEASON: March–December.
LARVA: Olive-green, with dark raised dots; head black.
FOOD PLANTS: Bermuda grass, other grasses.

Broad-Winged Skipper
Poanes viator
Broad marsh skipper

The broad-winged skipper, as its name suggests, is larger than most of the similar orange-and-brown skippers, with broad, rounded wings. This difference in wing shape can appear quite striking when the butterfly feeds at flowers with other species.

The curiously disjunct range of the broad-winged skipper involves two subspecies that inhabit both freshwater and saline marshes across the eastern half of the United States. The inland *Poanes viator viator* ranges from the Dakotas eastward to New York, while our coastal subspecies, *P. v. zizaniae*, occurs from Massachusetts southward along the Atlantic shore to Florida and then westward around the Gulf to central Texas. There are large areas across the country from which the species has not been

recorded, yet various authors report that it can be "incredibly abundant" where it occurs. Presumably, this indicates a close adherence to specific habitat requirements.

The adult's broad, rounded forewings are dark brown above with a few scattered pale spots. These are usually bright orange on the male, paler cream on the female. The hindwing of both sexes is orange with a dark border. The hindwing below is orange-brown with a brighter orange streak running outward from the base through a band of squarish orange spots.

Williams lists records of the broad-winged skipper from Chambers and Galveston counties; however, we have also found it occasionally in eastern Harris county. Although the species breeds primarily in marshy environments, individuals wander into suburban gardens to feed at a variety of flowers. They are especially fond of lantana and mist-flower.

1. Male, ventral

Common reed, wild rice, marsh millet, and other wetland grasses appear to be the larval food plants of our coastal subspecies, but sedges also serve as hosts in inland marshes. The larva lives between a leaf and the stem without building the typical tent, but it reinforces the area with silk. Little is known about the breeding biology and early stages of the broad-winged skipper.

The Yehl skipper, *Poanes yehl*, occurs less frequently in swampy woodlands across the northern portion of our area. Williams reports it from along Spring Creek and the San Jacinto River in northern Harris and Montgomery counties; Rickard, from Lake Houston. Somewhat smaller than the broad-winged skipper, the male has a strong black stigma on the forewing. The hindwing below has a row of three to five bright yellowish spots that contrast more with the longer orange streak than do the diffuse orange spots of *P. viator*.

SIZE: 1¼–1¾ inches.

DESCRIPTION: Large with broad, rounded wings. Forewing above dark brown with orange spots on male, cream spots on female. Brownish hindwing below with long orange streak through row of orange spots.

SIMILAR SPECIES: Smaller Yehl skipper has row of brighter yellowish spots on hindwing below; male has black stigma on forewing above.

SEASON: April–November.

LARVA: Not fully described.

FOOD PLANTS: Common reed, wild rice, marsh millet, sedges.

Dun Skipper
Euphyes vestris
Sedge witch, Dun sedge skipper

The scientific name of the dun skipper has undergone several changes in recent years. First listed as *Euphyes vestris*, it was then changed to *E. ruricola*, a name employed in many volumes still widely used. More recently, however, taxonomists have reinstated *vestris*. Ferris writes in his 1989 supplement to the Lepidopterists' Society checklist: "Because of the confusion surrounding the use of the name *ruricola*, one cannot consider that the Principle of Priority applies here. Therefore *vestris* Boisduval should be restored as the specific epithet."

The local subspecies of the dun skipper is *E. v. metacomet*, named for the Wampanoag Indian chief who led a bloody uprising against New England colonists in the 1670s. This form ranges throughout the eastern portions of North America, from southern Canada to Mexico. Other populations occur in the Rocky Mountains and on the Pacific Coast.

Also called the "sedge witch," the dun skipper is one of the "three black witches" that include the little glassy-wing and the northern broken dash. Both sexes are dark brownish black above and below, the female with two small, diffuse white spots on the forewing. These are in addition to a short line of three tiny pale dots near the wingtip that appear on many skippers. The hindwing below carries a curved row of indistinct pale spots. The male has a well-formed black stigma on the forewing, but it is not easily seen against the dark ground color. In our population, orange scales adorn the butterfly's head and palps.

Dun skippers prefer wet areas near deciduous woods and stream courses, but they wander widely onto the prairies and through suburban lawns and parks, feeding at flowers and sipping from mud

1. Male, ventral

2. Female, ventral

3. Larva

puddles. Males perch close to the ground in open areas to await potential mates.

The female lays her pale green eggs on a variety of sedges. Several authors report the use of grasses as larval hosts, but these apparently remain in question. We found several caterpillars on *Carex brevior*, a low, slender sedge that springs up as a weed in our flower beds. The mature larva was green with numerous short, longitudinal white lines. Its caramel-brown head was striped with creamy yellow and ornamented with an oval black patch outlined in yellow.

Each caterpillar bound together several leaf blades, edge-to-edge, to form a cylinder in which it lived, matting the inside of the refuge heavily with silk. Pupation occurred within the cylinder, its opening capped with a half-inch-long plug of powdery white froth.

SIZE: 1–1¼ inches.

DESCRIPTION: Brownish black; female with two diffuse pale spots on forewing; hindwing below with curved row of indistinct pale spots; orange scales on head.

SIMILAR SPECIES: Little glassywing has larger, more distinct white spot on forewing; white area on antenna at base of club.

SEASON: March–October; perhaps longer.

LARVA: Green, with white lines; head brown and creamy yellow, with black oval spot.

FOOD PLANTS: Sedges.

Lace-Winged Roadside Skipper

Amblyscirtes aesculapius
Cobweb roadside skipper, Cobweb little
skipper, Canebreak roadside skipper,
Textor skipper

About two dozen "roadside skippers" in
the United States and Mexico compose
the genus *Amblyscirtes*. They can be difficult to identify and are separated primarily by the patterns on the underside of
the hindwings. Most are dark butterflies
with rounded wings and small, light
spots above; the antennae and wing
fringes are usually checkered.

The lace-winged roadside skipper is
much more distinctive than its close relatives. Dark blackish brown, it has an irregular line of diffuse pale spots across
the upper surface of each wing. The veins
of the hindwing below are outlined with
buff or white, and they intersect with
two irregular bands of pale spots to give
an unmistakable cobweb effect. It is this
dramatic pattern that gives rise to such
terms as "lace-winged" and "cobweb."

The scientific name of this prettiest of
our roadside skippers, *aesculapius*, is the
Latin form of the Greek Asclepius, the
god of healing and medicine. The son
of Apollo, he was also physician to the
Argonauts. The species was once called
A. textor, a name now long out of date.

The lace-winged roadside skipper visits
a variety of flowers and sips from mud
puddles and stream banks, but it seldom
wanders far from dense bottomland forests or thickets where giant cane grows.
The tall, semi-woody member of the
grass family, *Arundinaria gigantea*, has
been assumed to be the larval host, but
most authors state that the early stages of
this roadside skipper are "not reported"
or "incompletely known."

The species ranges through the southeastern states, from Delaware to Florida
and westward to eastern Oklahoma and
Texas. It reaches the southwestern limits
of that range near Houston. According

1. Ventral

to Williams, "Mike Rickard first discov-
ered this cane-dwelling species in the San
Jacinto bottomlands of eastern Harris
Co. in the early 1970s."

We have not seen the lace-winged
roadside skipper in Harris County, but
we have located sizable colonies north of
Cleveland, Texas, in San Jacinto County.
It should also be expected in the wooded
areas of Liberty and Montgomery counties north and east of Houston. We report our experience with the life history
here, because it does not appear in other
readily available references.

A dozen caterpillars ranging from
three to twenty-six millimeters (one
inch) long were found by carefully
searching stands of giant cane along a
woodland stream. Each was well separated from other larvae, and each was
concealed within a folded leaf. The
smallest larva makes a fold near the tip of
the leaf blade and along one edge; the
mature larva makes a tube by tying to-

2. Larva

gether the opposite edges of the blade. The caterpillar feeds at the end of its shelter, finally leaving only a short tube hanging from a long section of the bare midrib. It then crawls quickly to another leaf and rolls it tightly.

The first larval stages are pale gray-green, with no obvious body markings beyond small transverse wrinkles in the skin. Under a microscope, however, the entire surface is covered with tiny pores, each bearing an extremely short hair. These pores and setae are not visible to the naked eye. The head is an unmarked rusty brown and covered with very short hairs.

In its last instar, the larva has a black collar at the rear of the first thoracic segment. A black line outlines the rusty tan head, with another forked black line down the center. The gray-green body resembles that of the earlier instars.

Before pupation, the caterpillar iso-

lated a segment of leaf slightly more than an inch long by chewing away the blade both above and below, leaving the section hanging by the midrib. It then folded this section along the rib, stitching the edges tightly together. The caterpillar then pupated within this secure shelter suspended in the air.

The pupa was tan in color, with bulging eye cases and a long proboscis reaching nearly to the tip of the abdomen. There was no projection on the head, as on many other skipper pupae. Adults emerged in captivity within ten to fifteen days. From small caterpillars collected on July 30, adult butterflies were obtained during the last week of August and the first week of September.

This episode indicates the effectiveness of the skipper's lifestyle, living and pupating within a leaf shelter. Of the dozen roadside skipper larvae found, only one was parasitized; the others produced perfect butterflies. In the same stand of giant cane, however, we also found forty-seven pupae and larvae of the southern pearly eye. Fully exposed on the leaves, only three were free of parasitic tachinid flies.

SIZE: 1–1¼ inches.

DESCRIPTION: Dark blackish brown, with light cobweb pattern on hindwing below.

SIMILAR SPECIES: No other skipper in our area has a similar pattern.

SEASON: March–September.

LARVA: Pale gray-green, covered with microscopic pores bearing short hairs; head rusty tan, with black lines; black collar behind head.

FOOD PLANTS: Giant cane.

Common Roadside Skipper
Amblyscirtes vialis
Roadside skipper, Black little skipper

Amblyscirtes vialis is simply called the "roadside skipper" by most authors; however, the North American Butterfly Association has adopted "common road-side skipper" to distinguish it from many other members of the genus collectively called roadside skippers. We subscribe to that policy and apply the latter name here.

Vialis is, indeed, the most common and widespread roadside skipper throughout most regions of the country. It ranges across southern Canada and the United States, and has been recorded from virtu-ally every continental state except Alaska. Its name derives from the Latin *via*, meaning "road." In Texas, however, it approaches its southern limit in the Piney Woods north of Houston. It should be searched for in the wooded sections of northern Harris and adjacent counties, where it frequents roadsides and clear-ings through the woods, often along stream corridors.

Dark blackish brown, with rounded wings, the common roadside skipper has at most a few small white dots in a line near the tip of the forewing. The outer portion of the hindwing below is dusted with violet-gray scales, and the wing fringes are checkered buff and brown. The underside of the hindwing lacks the distinct light spots that characterize Ce-lia's roadside skipper, a more frequent resident of the Houston area.

Vialis flies low, often alighting on bare patches of ground along roadsides and woodland trails. It visits flowers avidly and sips liquid from puddles and stream banks. Various grasses serve as larval hosts, and the caterpillar builds a loose nest by tying leaves with silk. As it ma-tures, however, the caterpillar becomes covered with a waxy white powder that clings to the minute hairs on the head and body. It then may leave its shelter and feed fully exposed on grass blades, perhaps gaining added protection from predators and parasites with its waxy cloak.

SIZE: ⅞–1 inch.

DESCRIPTION: Dark blackish brown above and below, with rounded wings; small white dots near tip of forewing; dusting of violet-gray scales on hind-wing below; fringes checkered tan and brown.

SIMILAR SPECIES: Dusky roadside skip-per is smaller, with pointed wings; pale spots in center of forewing above; fringes white and black. Celia's road-side skipper has scattered light spots on underside of hindwing.

SEASON: March–September; less com-mon in midsummer.

LARVA: Pale green, with tiny green tu-bercles containing minute hairs; head dull white, with red-brown stripes.

FOOD PLANTS: Grasses.

1. Ventral

Celia's Roadside Skipper
Amblyscirtes celia
Creekside little skipper, Roadside
rambler

Celia's roadside skipper is the most common and widespread member of the genus *Amblyscirtes* in the Houston area. It has long been confused with Bell's roadside skipper, *A. belli*, and many authors have listed the latter as a subspecies of *A. celia*. The consensus now is to consider them as distinct species. *Belli* does not occur in our region, instead ranging from north-central Texas northward to Kansas, then east to South Carolina. Because of its distribution, *belli* has been the more studied of the pair, and much remains to be learned about the life history of *celia*.

Range maps in some references confine Celia's roadside skipper to the western and southern portions of Texas and adjacent Mexico. It does, however, occur along the coastal plain to Galveston and Houston, where it wanders frequently into suburban lawns and gardens. It feeds avidly at flowers and perches on tree trunks or on the ground. Paspalum grasses have been listed as larval hosts, and Kendall also reports egg-laying on St. Augustine. Opler notes, however, that the early stages have not been reported in detail.

Like most other members of its genus, *A. celia* is dark blackish brown above, the forewing with the typical small spots near the tip. There is usually another light spot near the center of the forewing. The hindwing beneath is dusted with grayish scales and bears a distinct series of small, light spots. These latter spots are absent on the hindwings of other roadside skippers in this region. On freshly emerged butterflies, the fringes of the rounded wings are strikingly checkered with cream and black, but the fringes quickly wear away with use.

1. Ventral

SIZE: ⅞–1⅛ inches.

DESCRIPTION: Blackish brown; hind-wing beneath with small pale spots and dusted with gray scales.

SIMILAR SPECIES: Other local roadside skippers lack distinct spots on hind-wing beneath. Small, dark skippers of other genera lack gray or violet-gray dusting.

SEASON: May–September.

LARVA: Not fully described.

FOOD PLANTS: Grasses, including St. Augustine.

Dusky Roadside Skipper
Amblyscirtes alternata
Least Florida skipper, Blue-dusted roadside skipper, Dusky little skipper

Amblyscirtes alternata is listed as the "least Florida skipper" by Miller, Opler, and other contemporary authors. The North American Butterfly Association's Standing Committee on English Names, however, has recently chosen "dusky roadside skipper," noting as justification: "This species is a roadside skipper and the committee saw no reason why its name should not reflect this." We concur in this effort to use terms descriptive of close relationships, and we use the NABA name here.

The dusky roadside skipper is smaller than most members of the genus, and its forewings are narrower and more pointed. The white spots near the tip of the forewing are smaller than those of the common roadside skipper, but there are other diffuse, pale spots in the center of the forewing. The hindwing beneath is finely dusted with gray scales. The fringes are white with small black checks, but they are easily worn and may not be present, as is the case in the accompany-ing photograph.

A. alternata ranges from the lower Atlantic Coast through the southeastern states to East Texas. It is not common in the immediate Houston area, but should be looked for in northern Harris and ad-jacent counties. Williams states that it oc-curs "as far west as northeastern Waller Co., the most westerly point of continu-ous woods in the Southeast Texas area." Orr's checklist of the Houston area con-siders it "rare."

The dusky roadside skipper prefers open pine woods and grassy clearings, where it flies close to the ground. Grasses presumably serve as larval hosts, but little is known about the habits or early stages of this tiny skipper.

1. Ventral

SIZE: ¾–1 inch.

DESCRIPTION: Small; forewings narrow and pointed. Dark blackish brown with pale spots in center of forewing; hindwing below dusted with gray; white fringes checkered with black.

SIMILAR SPECIES: Common roadside skipper larger and with more rounded wings; lacks pale spots in middle of forewing; hindwing below with violet-gray scaling; fringes checkered tan and brown. Celia's roadside skipper has pale spots on hindwing below.

SEASON: Probably March–November.

LARVA: Not described.

FOOD PLANTS: Presumably grasses.

Eufala Skipper
Lerodea eufala
Gray skipper

1. Ventral

Lerodea eufala is much grayer than the other small skippers with which it associates. The pale, ashy gray color of the hindwing below can be seen at a considerable distance as the butterfly visits flowers or perches amid the grasses.

The wings above are gray-brown, with three to five small translucent spots near the middle of the forewing. There are usually other tiny white spots that form a short line perpendicular to the leading edge of the forewing near the tip. These latter marks also appear on many other skippers. The underside of the hindwing of the eufala skipper is heavily scaled with gray, and there is often a barely discernible group of pale spots. The overall grayish color serves as the best field mark.

The eufala skipper prefers open, sunny areas, but it occurs in a wide variety of habitats. We have found it in saline coastal marshes and along roadsides through the scenic limestone strata of the Texas Hill Country. It also inhabits agricultural fields, pastures, vacant lots, and lawns and gardens throughout the Houston area. Never as abundant as some other common skippers, it nevertheless occurs through much of the year as the result of several overlapping broods.

A permanent resident of the southern United States, *L. eufala* cannot endure severe winter freezes, but it extends its range widely in the summer. It forms temporary colonies in many of the northern states, particularly through the Great Plains and along the Mississippi Valley. This cosmopolitan species also ranges through Central and South America to Patagonia.

Although it has a rapid, darting flight, the eufala skipper readily visits a variety of flowers, where it can be closely observed. It seems particularly fond of lantana, verbenas, wild and cultivated ruellias, and a number of daisies and asters in the family Asteraceae.

The pale green eggs are laid on a number of different grasses, and the larvae live in nests of rolled leaves. The hosts include lawn grasses such as St. Augustine and Bermuda; weed species like Johnson grass; and cultivated crops of sugarcane, rice, and milo.

SIZE: ⅞–1¼ inches.
DESCRIPTION: Gray-brown above, with three to five small pale spots in middle of forewing; hindwing below pale gray, with faint light spots. Male lacks dark stigma.
SIMILAR SPECIES: Swarthy skipper and other *Nastra* species are tawny or yellow-brown below, never gray.
SEASON: February–November; longer during mild winters.
LARVA: Bright green with white lateral lines; head white with orange-brown spots.
FOOD PLANTS: Numerous grasses.

Twin-Spot Skipper
Oligoria maculata
Twin spot skipper, Three-spot skipper

The twin-spot skipper is dark brown above, with four translucent white spots on the forewing. The most distinctive pattern, however, is displayed on the underside of the red-brown hindwing. Easily seen as this dark skipper perches on flowers or grasses are three oval white spots, the upper one separate, the lower two close together.

Oligoria maculata provides an excellent example of the need to standardize the common names of our butterflies, especially with the growing popularity of butterfly watching. Most authors, including Miller, Opler, and the NABA checklist committee, call this species the "twin-spot skipper," referring to the two paired spots on the hindwing below. We use that name here. Scott, however, calls it the "three-spot skipper," adding the third hindwing mark. To further confuse the novice, there are also a two-spotted skipper and a three-spotted skipper, neither closely related to *O. maculata*. These latter species do not occur in Texas. The scientific name of the twin-spot skipper comes from the Latin *maculatus*, which simply means "having spots."

The twin-spot skipper ranges from coastal North Carolina to Florida and westward along the Gulf to Southeast Texas, straying occasionally northward as far as New Jersey. It prefers pine woodlands and coastal swamps and does not appear to be common in the immediate Houston area. Williams suggests that it can be found at the Armand Bayou Nature Center in southeastern Harris County.

Little is known about the biology of the twin-spot skipper. There are apparently two broods a year in most of its range, with adults appearing in April and May and again in August and September. The larval hosts are probably grasses.

1. Ventral (*photo by George Krizek*)

SIZE: 1¼–1½ inches.
DESCRIPTION: Dark brown above, with four translucent spots; hindwing below red-brown, with three distinct white spots, lower two spots paired.
SIMILAR SPECIES: Obscure skipper smaller, paler, with fainter spots. Larger ocola skipper lacks distinct hindwing spots.
SEASON: April–September.
LARVA: Pale green, with brown head and collar.
FOOD PLANTS: Probably grasses.

Brazilian Skipper

Calpodes ethlius
Canna skipper, Canna leafroller

The robust Brazilian skipper is the largest of our common closed-wing skippers. Dark brown above, it has long, pointed forewings marked with several large translucent spots. The hindwings have three or four more hyaline spots, a pattern mirrored on the red-brown undersurface of the wings.

Most homeowners and gardeners know this large skipper better as the "canna skipper" or "canna leafroller." This is the species whose larvae live within the rolled leaves of cultivated cannas and consume the foliage, sometimes to the point of becoming destructive pests. There is scarcely a patch of cannas in the Houston area without its complement of Brazilian skipper caterpillars.

Scott states that the female preferentially lays her eggs on plants with green leaves and red flowers, seldom utilizing red-leaved cannas or those with yellow blooms. Williams concurs with this observation and notes that "orange blossomed plants with green leaves are also used, but yellow and orange-spotted yellow bloomed plants are never used, in my experience." Ajilvsgi, however, writes that she has never found the skippers to show a preference. In our observations, these butterflies seem to avoid red-leaved cannas, but they freely use those with multicolored flowers. Many of our subjects originated in a canna patch with orange-spotted yellow flowers, a form Williams found unattractive to the species. Some of these differences may be attributable more to location and habitat, or to other variations in leaf chemistry or scent, than to the color of the blooms. In addition to the ubiquitous garden cannas, the Brazilian skipper freely uses powdery thalia as a larval host. This tall, rank plant grows in freshwater ponds and marshes throughout Southeast Texas.

Its taste in cultivated plants aside, the Brazilian skipper can be fascinating to watch. Adults seem almost secretive, perching for a moment and then darting off with their fast, extremely powerful flight. They visit not only canna blooms for nectar, but a wide variety of other flowers as well. They also seem to employ "trap-lining," returning periodically through the day to individual flowers along a carefully selected route.

Females lay their pale greenish eggs singly on leaves of the host, and each newly hatched larva begins almost immediately to fold a small segment of leaf as a shelter. The larger caterpillar rolls an entire leaf into a cylinder, tying it securely with silk. It starts by stretching a strand from side to side, swinging its head back and forth and reaching as far as it can without losing its secure foothold on the upper surface of the leaf. As it repeats its movements, it lays down other strands until they form a silken cable, gradually tightening them to roll the leaf together. Moving up and down the surface, it secures other cables until the roll is securely bound. The caterpillar rests within this protective cylinder through the day and feeds nocturnally, usually eating away at the top of its shelter. Ajilvsgi writes that when a large number of caterpillars are feeding, "their nighttime chomping can be heard for some distance."

If its tent is opened, the disturbed larva has yet another defense. It regurgitates a pool of dark, distasteful liquid, perhaps inhibiting attack by a potential predator. All of these protective adaptations, however, fail to ensure the survival of more than a few of the larval skippers. Parasitic ichneumon wasps and tachinid flies both take a heavy toll, entering the open end of the rolled leaf to lay their eggs within the body or on the skin of the caterpillar. After hatching, their own larva will then eat away slowly at their host, later emerging from the pupal shell. Viruses may also wipe out entire colonies.

1. Ventral

2. Larva, rolling leaf

The Brazilian skipper caterpillar is pale greenish gray, becoming darker green as it ingests leaves; the orange head bears black spots. So translucent is the body that its internal circulatory system is clearly visible, pulsing rhythmically away. The larva pupates within its leafy shelter, the slender green chrysalis fastened with a girdle of silk and dusted with a powdery white exudate. It has a long tongue case that extends beyond the tip of the abdomen and a red-tinged spike on its head.

Resident throughout the year in southern Florida and deep South Texas, the Brazilian skipper occurs in our area from about April until the first frost, usually in December. A tropical species, it also ranges through the West Indies and tropical America to Argentina. Because of its fast, powerful flight, it has colonized many islands and is one of the few butterflies on the Galapagos Islands, six hundred miles off the coast of Ecuador.

With this tremendous dispersal capability, Brazilian skippers also move northward each summer, establishing new colonies among abundant canna plants in cities and suburban areas. Their range then expands through North Texas and as far as Illinois along the Mississippi Valley and New York along the Atlantic Coast. There the females lay their eggs and quickly leave again, winging off to yet another location. The butterflies may scarcely be noticed as they swirl through a flower garden, but their caterpillars can readily be found as they roll and consume the canna leaves.

SIZE: 1¾–2¼ inches.
DESCRIPTION: Larger than most other skippers. Dark brown above, with translucent spots; reddish brown below, with three or four translucent spots on hindwing.
SIMILAR SPECIES: Other common closed-wing skippers are smaller.
SEASON: April–December; occasionally longer.
LARVA: Translucent gray-green; head orange, with black spots.
FOOD PLANTS: Cannas, powdery thalia.

Salt Marsh Skipper

Panoquina panoquin
Panoquin skipper

The salt marsh skipper, as its name suggests, is usually restricted to coastal saline and brackish marshes. The scientific names of the genus and species probably derive from an early Native American term. *Panoquina panoquin* ranges southward along the Atlantic Coast from Long Island to the Florida Keys and around the Gulf of Mexico to South Texas. According to Williams, the species was not known to occur west of Louisiana until the early 1980s, when Rickard discovered it in Texas for the first time. It has since been collected as far south as Padre Island, and we observed an extensive colony on Copano Bay near Rockport. In our area, it can be found in the marshes along the Bolivar Peninsula and should be looked for on Galveston Island and along the fringes of Galveston Bay.

The brownish salt marsh skipper has several translucent white spots on the long, pointed forewing, but it is best identified by the pale yellow veins and short, white dash on the hindwing below. The conspicuous white dash can readily be seen as the skipper perches to sip nectar from a variety of seaside flowers.

Little is known of the biology and early stages of the salt marsh skipper. There are probably three or four broods along the Texas coast, and adults appear from at least April until November. Most references suggest seashore saltgrass, *Distichlis spicata*, as the larval host; a few others mention cordgrass, *Spartina*. The colony we found near Rockport, Texas, in September had stands of both grass species, but we could find no larvae, nor did we witness females laying eggs.

1. Ventral

SIZE: 1⅛–1¼ inches.
DESCRIPTION: Brown, with translucent spots on elongated forewing; hindwing below with pale yellow veins and diagnostic short, white dash.
SIMILAR SPECIES: Obscure skipper lacks white dash; has three pale spots on hindwing below.
SEASON: April–November; possibly longer.
LARVA: Not reported.
FOOD PLANTS: Probably seashore saltgrass.

Obscure Skipper
Panoquina panoquinoides
Beach skipper

1. Ventral

The obscure skipper is closely related to the salt marsh skipper and occupies much the same coastal habitats. Its scientific name, *panoquinoides*, means "similar to panoquin," the specific epithet of the salt marsh skipper. The obscure skipper, however, is smaller, and its forewing spots are reduced or lacking. Three pale spots on the plain brown hindwing below provide the best field mark.

A largely tropical species, the obscure skipper ranges from Florida along the Gulf Coast to southern Texas, as well as through the West Indies and the mainland tropics to Peru. It inhabits salt marshes and adjacent dunes and open fields, where it visits a variety of coastal flowers. Williams reports numbers of adults in Brazoria and Matagorda counties in the spring, and we found the species common near Rockport in Aransas County in September. It should also occur along the Texas coast near Galveston and around Galveston Bay.

Bermuda grass and sugarcane have been documented as larval food plants elsewhere, but such hosts must also include coastal grasses. Seashore saltgrass has been suggested by several authors. The larvae can be very difficult to find, for they live in rolled leaves tied with silk and feed primarily at night.

SIZE: 1–1¼ inches.
DESCRIPTION: Small, brown, with forewing spots reduced or lacking; hindwing below with three diagnostic pale spots.
SIMILAR SPECIES: Salt marsh skipper larger, with well-developed spots on forewing; white dash on hindwing below.
SEASON: April–November; perhaps longer.
LARVA: Green, with white and yellow stripes; head brown.
FOOD PLANTS: Bermuda grass, sugarcane, presumably other coastal grasses.

Ocola Skipper
Panoquina ocola
Long-winged skipper,
Long-wing skipper

Although the ocola skipper is closely related to the two previous species, the salt marsh and obscure skippers, it should not be confused with them. Somewhat larger, it has distinct translucent spots on the forewing, while the hindwing below is essentially unmarked. There may be a faint band of blurred spots across the underside of the hindwing, and freshly emerged females have an iridescent purple wash, but there is no distinct white dash or series of pale spots.

The unusually long forewing provides the best method of identifying the dark brown ocola skipper in the field. At rest, it pulls the forewing down so that it is partially concealed; however, it still projects well beyond the hindwing. This characteristic is reflected in the alternate name, "long-winged skipper."

The ocola skipper ranges from the southeastern states to Texas and southward through the West Indies and most of Central and South America. It is remarkably consistent throughout that range, with little obvious variation. In summer it strays northward through the eastern portion of the United States. Some authors state it prefers low, damp fields and pastures, but it also inhabits woodland edges and city parks and gardens. Grasses, including cultivated rice and sugarcane, serve as larval food plants; adults feed at a variety of flowers, particularly in late afternoon.

Panoquina ocola is one of the few skippers to stage mass migrations. Temporary colonists of the northern states return southward in the fall, sometimes flying in enormous numbers. Penn reports such a flight along the shore of Lake Pontchartrain in Louisiana on October 15, 1950. Thousands of skippers flew from four to

1. Ventral

twenty-five feet above the water and shore; Penn could not estimate the width of the column. He notes that after crossing the bridge spanning the lake, it was "necessary to drive off the highway to clean the car's windshield which was by then covered with squashed skippers." He also stopped to collect a few piled in windrows along the edge of the highway, killed by other passing automobiles.

Closer to Houston, Williams writes of a large flight in southeastern Waller County in September 1987. "Hundreds, perhaps thousands" of skippers were seen along a path bordered by high weeds. We have seen similar, if smaller, concentrations throughout our area. Large numbers of the dark brown, long-winged ocola skippers flock to patches of lantana, mist-flower, and other blooms in September and October. Although it occurs virtually throughout the year in

Southeast Texas, *Panoquina ocola* can be one of the most abundant of Houston's butterflies from late summer into fall.

SIZE: 1¼–1½ inches.

DESCRIPTION: Long-winged, dark brown; distinct translucent spots on forewing; hindwing below without clearly defined markings, although sometimes with faint band of pale spots.

SIMILAR SPECIES: Most other skippers smaller, with shorter forewings, more distinct hindwing pattern below. Similar large *Panoquina* skippers enter South Texas from Mexico but are not expected northward to Houston.

SEASON: Throughout most of the year; especially abundant in fall.

LARVA: Gray-green, with first two segments blue-green; light stripe on each side; head light green.

FOOD PLANTS: Grasses.

Checklist

BUTTERFLIES OF HOUSTON AND SOUTHEAST TEXAS

This checklist covers the butterfly species that occur in Harris County and the neighboring counties of Southeast Texas. Scientific names follow the Lepidopterists' Society's *A Catalogue/Checklist of the Butterflies of America North of Mexico* by Lee D. Miller and F. Martin Brown, published in 1981, and its supplement, edited by Clifford D. Ferris in 1989. Most of the common names follow Jacqueline Y. Miller's 1992 publication, *The Common Names of North American Butterflies*. In some cases, however, we have adopted common names proposed by the nomenclature committee of the North American Butterfly Association where those new names seem to have particular merit.

In compiling this list, we have relied on range maps and records in current butterfly books; Houston-area checklists by Williams and Orr; personal communications from Rickard, Smith, and other area lepidopterists; and our own observations. Some of the species are abundant throughout the region; others occur less frequently. A few claim a place on the checklist by virtue of a single specimen. More butterflies will undoubtedly be added to the Houston list through the years, particularly as strays from deep South Texas.

Although not all species on the list are treated in this book, we believe the accounts and accompanying photographs will serve to identify the vast majority of butterflies observed in Houston. Many less common species are also discussed briefly in the accounts of similar or closely related butterflies. Checklist species omitted in the text are those that are uncommon or accidental to the area and are unlikely to be observed by the casual butterfly watcher.

Checklist key:
Orange Sulphur—Full account and photographs
Cloudless Sulphur—Discussed with related species
(Lyside Sulphur)—Uncommon or rare species, not treated here

SWALLOWTAILS
Pipe-vine Swallowtail
Polydamus Swallowtail
Zebra Swallowtail
Black Swallowtail
Giant Swallowtail
Thoas Swallowtail
Tiger Swallowtail
Two-tailed Swallowtail
Spicebush Swallowtail
Palamedes Swallowtail

WHITES and SULPHURS
(Tropical White)
Checkered White
Cabbage White
Great Southern White
(Giant White)
Falcate Orangetip
Clouded Sulphur
Orange Sulphur
Dog Face
(White Angled-Sulphur)
(Yellow Angled-Sulphur)
Cloudless Sulphur
Orange-barred Sulphur
Large Orange Sulphur
(Lyside Sulphur)
Barred Yellow
Little Sulphur
Mexican Yellow
Sleepy Orange
Dainty Sulphur

GOSSAMER-WINGED
BUTTERFLIES
Harvester
Great Purple Hairstreak
Soapberry Hairstreak
Banded Hairstreak
King's Hairstreak
Striped Hairstreak
Northern Hairstreak
Red-banded Hairstreak

Papilionidae
Battus philenor
Battus polydamas
Eurytides marcellus
Papilio polyxenes
Papilio cresphontes
Papilio thoas
Papilio glaucus
Papilio multicaudatus
Papilio troilus
Papilio palamedes

Pieridae
(Appias drusilla)
Pontia protodice
Pieris rapae
Ascia monuste
(Ganyra josephina)
Paramidea midea
Colias philodice
Colias eurytheme
Colias cesonia
(Anteos clorinde)
(Anteos maerula)
Phoebis sennae
Phoebis philea
Phoebis agarithe
(Kricogonia lyside)
Eurema daira
Eurema lisa
Eurema mexicanum
Eurema nicippe
Nathalis iole

Lycaenidae
Feniseca tarquinius
Atlides halesus
Phaeostrymon alcestis
Satyrium calanus
Satyrium kingi
Satyrium liparops
Fixsenia ontario
Calycopis cecrops

BUTTERFLIES (*cont.*)   Lycaenidae (*cont.*)
Dusky-blue Hairstreak   *Calycopis isobeon*
Olive Hairstreak   *Mitoura grynea*
Frosted Elfin   *Incisalia irus*
Henry's Elfin   *Incisalia henrici*
Eastern Pine Elfin   *Incisalia niphon*
White-M Hairstreak   *Parrhasius m-album*
Gray Hairstreak   *Strymon melinus*
(Columella Hairstreak)   (*Strymon columella*)
Western Pygmy Blue   *Brephidium exile*
Eastern Pygmy Blue   *Brephidium isophthalma*
Cassius Blue   *Leptotes cassius*
Marine Blue   *Leptotes marina*
Ceraunus Blue   *Hemiargus ceraunus*
Reakirt's Blue   *Hemiargus isola*
Eastern Tailed Blue   *Everes comyntas*
Spring Azure   *Celastrina argiolus*

METALMARKS   Riodinidae
Little Metalmark   *Calephelis virginiensis*

SNOUT BUTTERFLIES   Libytheidae
Snout Butterfly   *Libytheana bachmanii*

LONGWINGS   Heliconiidae
Gulf Fritillary   *Agraulis vanillae*
Julia   *Dryas iulia*
Zebra   *Heliconius charitonius*

NYMPHALIDS   Nymphalidae
Variegated Fritillary   *Euptoieta claudia*
Bordered Patch   *Chlosyne lacinia*
Gorgone Checkerspot   *Charidryas gorgone*
Silvery Checkerspot   *Charidryas nycteis*
Texan Crescent   *Anthanassa texana*
Phaon Crescent   *Phyciodes phaon*
Pearl Crescent   *Phyciodes tharos*
Question Mark   *Polygonia interrogationis*
Eastern Comma   *Polygonia comma*
Mourning Cloak   *Nymphalis antiopa*
Red Admiral   *Vanessa atalanta*
American Painted Lady   *Vanessa virginiensis*
Painted Lady   *Vanessa cardui*

NYMPHALIDS (*cont.*)
Buckeye
Red-spotted Purple
Viceroy
(California Sister)
Amymone
(Blue-eyed Greenwing)
Goatweed Leafwing
Hackberry Emperor
Tawny Emperor

Nymphalidae (*cont.*)
Junonia coenia
Limenitis arthemis astyanax
Limenitis archippus
(*Adelpha bredowii*)
Mestra amymone
(*Dynamine dyonis*)
Anaea andria
Asterocampa celtis
Asterocampa clyton

SATYRS, WOOD NYMPHS, and BROWNS
Southern Pearly Eye
Creole Pearly Eye
Gemmed Satyr
Carolina Satyr
Georgia Satyr
Little Wood Satyr
Red Satyr
Common Wood Nymph

Satyridae
Enodia portlandia
Enodia creola
Cyllopsis gemma
Hermeuptychia sosybius
Neonympha areolata
Megisto cymela
Megisto rubricata
Cercyonis pegala

MILKWEED BUTTERFLIES
Monarch
Queen

Danaidae
Danaus plexippus
Danaus gilippus

SKIPPERS
Silver-spotted Skipper
White-striped Longtail
Long-tailed Skipper
Dorantes Longtail
Hoary Edge
Northern Cloudywing
Southern Cloudywing
Confused Cloudywing
(Southern Scalloped Sootywing)
(Scalloped Sootywing)
Sickle-winged Skipper
(White-patched Skipper)
(False Duskywing)
(Sleepy Duskywing)
Juvenal's Duskywing
Horace's Duskywing
Funereal Duskywing

Hesperiidae
Epargyreus clarus
Chioides catillus
Urbanus proteus
Urbanus dorantes
Achalarus lyciades
Thorybes pylades
Thorybes bathyllus
Thorybes confusis
(*Staphylus mazans*)
(*Staphylus hayhurstii*)
Achlyodes mithridates
(*Chiomara asychis*)
(*Gesta gesta*)
(*Erynnis brizo*)
Erynnis juvenalis
Erynnis horatius
Erynnis funeralis

SKIPPERS (*cont.*)

Wild Indigo Duskywing	*Erynnis baptisiae*
Common Checkered Skipper	*Pyrgus communis*
Tropical Checkered Skipper	*Pyrgus oileus*
(Common Sootywing)	(*Pholisora catullus*)
Swarthy Skipper	*Nastra lherminier*
Neamathla Skipper	*Nastra neamathla*
Julia's Skipper	*Nastra julia*
Clouded Skipper	*Lerema accius*
Least Skipper	*Ancyloxypha numitor*
Orange Skipperling	*Copaeodes aurantiacus*
Southern Skipperling	*Copaeodes minimus*
Fiery Skipper	*Hylephila phyleus*
(Meske's Skipper)	(*Hesperia meskei*)
(Tawny-edged Skipper)	(*Polites themistocles*)
(Crossline Skipper)	(*Polites origenes*)
Whirlabout	*Polites vibex*
Southern Broken Dash	*Wallengrenia otho*
Northern Broken Dash	*Wallengrenia egeremet*
Little Glassywing	*Pompeius verna*
Sachem	*Atalopedes campestris*
(Arogos Skipper)	(*Atrytone arogos*)
(Delaware Skipper)	(*Atrytone logan*)
(Byssus Skipper)	(*Problema byssus*)
(Zabulon Skipper)	(*Poanes zabulon*)
(Aaron's Skipper)	(*Poanes aaroni*)
Yehl Skipper	*Poanes yehl*
Broad-winged Skipper	*Poanes viator*
(Duke's Skipper)	(*Euphyes dukesi*)
Dun Skipper	*Euphyes vestris*
Lace-winged Roadside Skipper	*Amblyscirtes aesculapius*
Common Roadside Skipper	*Amblyscirtes vialis*
Celia's Roadside Skipper	*Amblyscirtes celia*
Dusky Roadside Skipper	*Amblyscirtes alternata*
Eufala Skipper	*Lerodea eufala*
Twin-spot Skipper	*Oligoria maculata*
Brazilian Skipper	*Calpodes ethlius*
Salt Marsh Skipper	*Panoquina panoquin*
Obscure Skipper	*Panoquina panoquinoides*
Ocola Skipper	*Panoquina ocola*
Yucca Giant Skipper	*Megathymus yuccae*

Hesperiidae (*cont.*)

Butterfly Organizations and Journals

American Entomological Society
  1900 Race Street
  Philadelphia, Pennsylvania 19013
  Publishes: *Entomological News*

Entomological Society of America
  9301 Annapolis Road, Suite 300
  Lanham, Maryland 20706
  Publishes: *The Bulletin of the*
    Entomological Society of America

The Lepidoptera Research Foundation
  Santa Barbara Museum of
    Natural History
  2559 Puesta del Sol Road
  Santa Barbara, California 93105
  Publishes: *The Journal of Research*
    on the Lepidoptera

The Lepidopterists' Society
  William Winter, Secretary
  257 Common Street
  Dedham, Massachusetts 02026
  Publishes: *Journal of the Lepi-*
    dopterists' Society and *News of the*
    Lepidopterists' Society

North American Butterfly Association
  39 Highland Avenue
  Chappaqua, New York 10514
  Publishes: *American Butterflies*

Sonoran Arthropod Studies
  P.O. Box 5624
  Tucson, Arizona 85703

Southern Lepidopterists' Society
  3820 N.W. 16th Place
  Gainesville, Florida 32605
  Publishes: *Southern Lepidopterists'*
    News and *Southern Lepidopterists'*
    Bulletin

Young Entomologists' Society
  1915 Peggy Place
  Lansing, Michigan 48910
  Publishes: Educational items for
    young people

The Xerces Society
  10 Southwest Ash Street
  Portland, Oregon 97204
  Publishes: *Wings* (newsletter),
    Atala (journal), and Fourth of
    July butterfly count reports

Butterfly Houses and Gardens

Butterfly Exhibit
 Marine World Africa—USA
 Marine World Parkway
 Vallejo, California 94589

Butterfly World
 Port Alberni Highway
 Coombs, British Columbia
 V0R-1M0

Butterfly World
 Tradewinds Park
 3600 W. Sample Road
 Coconut Creek, Florida 33073

Cockrell Butterfly Center
 Houston Museum of
  Natural Science
 One Hermann Circle Drive
 Houston, Texas 77030

Day Butterfly Center
 Callaway Gardens
 Pine Mountain, Georgia 31822

Mercer Arboretum and Botanic Gardens
 22306 Aldine-Westfield Road
 Humble, Texas 77338

Moody Gardens
 1 Hope Boulevard
 Galveston, Texas 77554

Natural History Museum
 Smithsonian Institution
 Washington, D.C. 20560

Papillon Park
 120 Tyngsboro Road
 Westford, Massachusetts 01886

World of Insects Exhibit
 Cincinnati Zoo
 3400 Vine Street
 Cincinnati, Ohio 45220

Bibliography

During the writing of this book, we had at our disposal many different types of butterfly books, including identification guides from various regions, detailed manuals on biology and behavior, and volumes on butterfly gardening and observation. They ranged from the simple and inexpensive to scientific volumes intended more for the Lepidoptera specialist. We also drew heavily from the journal literature, particularly the *Journal of the Lepidopterists' Society*. We consulted standard plant manuals, ranging from volumes on trees to those on grasses, for current food plant names and information and sifted through references on classical mythology to determine the source of many butterfly names. Those publications from which we used information are included here. We have tried in this book to capture the "personality" of each individual butterfly species, discussing behavior, etymology of their names, and other interesting information. We also used individual species to illustrate many of the basic principles of insect ecology.

Ajilvsgi, Geyata. 1990. Butterfly gardening for the South. Dallas: Taylor Publishing.

Bailowitz, Richard A., and James P. Brock. 1991. Butterflies of southeastern Arizona. Tucson: Sonoran Arthropod Studies.

Bitzer, Royce J., and Kenneth C. Shaw. 1983. Territorial behavior of *Nymphalis antiopa* and *Polygonia comma* (Nymphalidae). *Journal of the Lepidopterists' Society* 37 (1): 1–13.

Brewer, Jo, and Dave Winter. 1986. Butterflies and moths: A companion to your field guide. New York: Prentice Hall.

Brown, F. Martin, and Bernard Heineman. 1972. Jamaica and its butterflies. London: E.W. Classey.

Brown, John W. 1990. Urban biology of *Leptotes marina* (Reakirt) (Lycaenidae). *Journal of the Lepidopterists' Society* 44 (3): 200–1.

Clench, Harry K. 1955. Some observations on the habits of *Strymon falacer* (Lycaenidae). *The Lepidopterists' News* 9 (4–5): 105–17.

Correll, Donovan S., and Marshall C. Johnston. 1979. Manual of the vascular plants of Texas. Richardson: Univ. of Texas at Dallas.

Cotterell, Arthur. 1986. A dictionary of world mythology. 2nd ed. New York: Oxford Univ. Press.

D'Abrera, Bernard. 1984. Butterflies of South America. Ferny Creek, Victoria, Australia: Hill House. Daccordi, Mauro, Paolo Triberti, and Adriano Zanetti. 1988. Simon & Schuster's guide to butterflies and moths. New York: Simon and Schuster.

DeVries, Philip J. 1987. The butterflies of Costa Rica and their natural history: Papilionidae, Pieridae, Nymphalidae. Princeton, New Jersey: Princeton Univ. Press.

Douglas, Matthew M. 1986. The lives of butterflies. Ann Arbor: Univ. of Michigan Press.

Durden, Christopher J. 1982. The butterfly fauna of Barton Creek Canyon on the Balcones Fault Zone, Austin, Texas, and a regional list. *Journal of the Lepidopterists' Society* 36 (1): 1–17.

Ehrlich, Paul R., and Anne H. Ehrlich. 1961. How to know the butterflies. Dubuque, Iowa: Wm. C. Brown.

Emmel, Thomas C. 1975. Butterflies: Their world, their life cycle, their behavior. New York: Alfred A. Knopf.

———. 1991. Butterflies. New York: Mallard Press.

Emmel, Thomas C., and John F. Emmel. 1973. The butterflies of southern California. Los Angeles: Natural History Museum of Los Angeles County.

Feltwell, John. 1986. The natural history of butterflies. New York: Facts on File.

Ferris, Clifford D., ed. 1989. Supplement to: A catalogue/checklist of the butterflies of America north of Mexico. Memoir no. 3. The Lepidopterists' Society.

Ferris, Clifford D., and F. Martin Brown. 1981. Butterflies of the Rocky Mountain states. Norman: Univ. of Oklahoma Press.

Forey, Pamela, and Cecilia Fitzsimons. 1987. An instant guide to butterflies: The most familiar species of North American butterflies described and illustrated in color. New York: Bonanza Books.

Friedlander, Timothy P. 1984. Insect parasites and predators of hackberry butterflies (Nymphalidae: *Asterocampa*). *Journal of the Lepidopterists' Society* 38 (1): 60–61.

Gifford, Samuel M., and Paul A. Opler. 1983. Natural history of seven hairstreaks in coastal North Carolina. *Journal of the Lepidopterists' Society* 37 (2): 97–105.

Glassberg, Jeffrey. 1993. Butterflies through binoculars: A field guide to butterflies in the Boston-New York-Washington region. New York: Oxford Univ. Press.

Gould, Frank W. 1975. The grasses of Texas. College Station: Texas A&M Univ. Press.

Gray, P.H.H. 1954. Aristotle's description of the life history of a butterfly (psyche). *The Lepidopterists' News* 8 (5): 145.

Hamilton, Edith. 1940. Mythology: Timeless tales of gods and heroes. New York: Mentor.

Harris, Lucien, Jr. 1972. Butterflies of Georgia. Norman: Univ. of Oklahoma Press.

Hatch, Stephan L., Kancheepuram N. Gandhi, and Larry E. Brown. 1990. Checklist of the vascular plants of Texas. College Station: The Texas Agricultural Experiment Station.

Heitzman, J. Richard, and Joan E. Heitzman. 1987. Butterflies and moths of Missouri. Jefferson City: Missouri Department of Conservation.

Hill, C.J. 1992. Temporal changes in abundance of two Lycaenid butterflies (Lycaenidae) in relation to adult food resources. *Journal of the Lepidopterists' Society* 46 (3): 173–81.

Holland, W.J. 1931. The butterfly book. Rev. ed. Garden City, New York: Doubleday.

Howe, William H. 1975. The butterflies of North America. Garden City, New York: Doubleday.

Israel, Michael L. 1982. Outbreak of *Asterocampa clyton* (Nymphalidae) in Louisiana. *Journal of the Lepidopterists' Society* 36 (3): 234–35.

Johnston, Marshall C. 1988. The vascular plants of Texas: A list, up-dating the manual of the vascular plants of Texas. Austin, Texas: Marshall C. Johnston.

Klots, Alexander B. 1951. A field guide to the butterflies of North America, east of the Great Plains. Boston: Houghton Mifflin.

Knowlton, George F. 1954. Migrations of *Vanessa cardui*, the painted lady butterfly, through Utah. *The Lepidopterists' News* 8 (1–2): 17–22.

Knudson, Edward C. Checklist of lepidoptera (moths and butterflies) of Santa Ana National Wildlife Refuge. Duplicated.

Lederhouse, Robert C. 1993. Territoriality along flyways as mate-locating behavior in male *Limenitis arthemis* (Nymphalidae). *Journal of the Lepidopterists' Society* 47 (1): 22–31.

Macy, Ralph W., and Harold H. Shepard. 1941. Butterflies: A handbook of the butterflies of the United States, complete for the region north of the Potomac and Ohio rivers and east of the Dakotas. Minneapolis: Univ. of Minnesota Press.

Malcolm, Stephen B., and Lincoln P. Brower. 1986. Selective oviposition by monarch butterflies (*Danaus plexippus* L.) in a mixed stand of *Asclepias curassavica* L. and *A. incarnata* L. in South Florida. *Journal of the Lepidopterists' Society* 40 (4): 255–63.

Miller, Jacqueline Y., ed. 1992. The common names of North American butterflies. Washington: Smithsonian Institution Press.

Miller, Lee D., and F. Martin Brown. 1981. A catalogue/checklist of the butterflies of America north of Mexico. Memoir no. 2. The Lepidopterists' Society.

Mitchell, Robert T., and Herbert S. Zim. 1964. Butterflies and moths: A guide to the more common American species. New York: Golden Press.

Neck, Raymond W. 1980. Aberrant specimen of *Chlosyne lacinia* from central Texas resembles tropical form. *Journal of the Lepidopterists' Society* 34 (4): 363–64.

———. 1983a. Causal analysis of a migration of the snout butterfly, *Libytheana bachmanii larvata* (Strecker) (Libytheidae). *Journal of the Lepidopterists' Society* 37 (2): 121–28.

———. 1983b. Significance of visits of hackberry butterflies (Nymphalidae: *Asterocampa*) to flowers. *Journal of the Lepidopterists' Society* 37 (4): 269–74.

———. 1984. On the origin of snout butterflies (*Libytheana bachmanii larvata*, Libytheidae) in a 1978 migration in southern Texas. *Journal of the Lepidopterists' Society* 38 (4): 319–22.

North American Butterfly Association. 1993. English names for North American butterflies: Adoption of policy guidelines and the establishment of English names for butterflies found in the northeastern United States. *American Butterflies* 1 (1): 21–29.

———. 1993. English names for butterflies found in the southeastern U.S. and eastern Canada. *American Butterflies* 1 (2): 27–32.

———. 1993. English names for butterflies found in central and mountain U.S. and Canada. *American Butterflies* 1 (3): 26–31.

———. 1993. English names for butterflies found in the Pacific and southwestern U.S. and Canada. *American Butterflies* 1 (4): 30–35.

———. 1994. English names for butterflies found in Texas. *American Butterflies* 2 (1): 29–35.

Opler, Paul A. 1992. A field guide to eastern butterflies. Boston: Houghton Mifflin.

Opler, Paul A., and George O. Krizek. 1984. Butterflies east of the Great Plains: An illustrated natural history. Baltimore: Johns Hopkins Univ. Press.

Orr, Richard L. 1988. Butterflies of the Houston area. Duplicated.

Orsak, Larry J. 1978. The butterflies of Orange County, California. Irvine: Univ. of California.

Parenti, Umberto. 1978. The world of butterflies and moths: Their life-cycle, habits and ecology. New York: Putnam.

Penn, George Henry. 1955. Mass flight of ocola skippers. *The Lepidopterists' News* 9 (2–3): 79.

Peterson, Charles D., and Larry E. Brown. 1983. Vascular flora of the Little Thicket Nature Sanctuary, San Jacinto County, Texas. Houston: Outdoor Nature Club.

Preston-Mafham, Rod, and Ken Preston-Mafham. 1988. Butterflies of the world. New York: Facts on File.

Pyle, Robert M. 1981. The Audubon Society field guide to North American butterflies. New York: Alfred A. Knopf.

———. 1984. The Audubon Society handbook for butterfly watchers. New York: Scribner's.

Rickard, Mike A. Letter to authors, 6 April 1994.

Riley, Thomas J. 1980. Effects of long and short day photoperiods on the seasonal dimorphism of *Anaea andria* (Nymphalidae) from central Missouri. *Journal of the Lepidopterists' Society* 34 (4): 330–37.

———. 1988. Effect of larval photoperiod on mating and reproductive diapause in seasonal forms of *Anaea andria* (Nymphalidae). *Journal of the Lepidopterists' Society* 42 (4): 263–68.

Ritland, David B. 1990. Localized interspecific hybridization between mimetic *Limenitis* butterflies (Nymphalidae) in Florida. *Journal of the Lepidopterists' Society* 44 (3): 163–73.

Robbins, Robert K. 1980. The lycaenid "false head" hypothesis: Historical review and quantitative analysis. *Journal of the Lepidopterists' Society* 34 (2): 194–208.

Rutowski, Ronald L., and John Schaefer. 1984. Courtship behavior of the gulf fritillary, *Agraulis vanillae* (Nymphalidae). *Journal of the Lepidopterists' Society* 38 (1): 23–31.

Sandved, Kjell B., and Jo Brewer. 1976. Butterflies. New York: Abrams.

Sandved, Kjell B., and Michael G. Emsley. 1975. Butterfly magic. New York: Penguin Books.

Sbordoni, Valerio, and Saverio Forestiero. 1985. Butterflies of the world. New York: Times Books.

Schneck, Marcus. 1990. Butterflies: How to identify and attract them to your garden. Emmaus, Pennsylvania: Rodale Press.

Scoble, Malcolm J. 1992. The Lepidoptera: Form, function and diversity. New York: Oxford Univ. Press.

Scott, James A. 1986. The butterflies of North America: A natural history and field guide. Stanford, California: Stanford Univ. Press.

Sedenko, Jerry. 1991. The butterfly garden: Creating beautiful gardens to attract butterflies. New York: Villard Books.

Shapiro, Arthur M. 1981. Phenotypic plasticity in temperate and subarctic *Nymphalis antiopa* (Nymphalidae): Evidence for adaptive canalization. *Journal of the Lepidopterists' Society* 35 (2): 124–31.

Shields, Oakley. 1989. World numbers of butterflies. *Journal of the Lepidopterists' Society* 43 (3): 178–83.

Shull, Ernest M. 1987. The butterflies of Indiana. Bloomington: Indiana Academy of Science.

Smart, Paul. 1984. The illustrated encyclopedia of the butterfly world. New York: Chartwell Books.

Smith, James L. Letter to authors, 20 December 1993.

Stamp, Nancy E. 1983. Overwintering aggregations of hackberry caterpillars (*Asterocampa clyton*: Nymphalidae). *Journal of the Lepidopterists' Society* 37 (2): 145.

———. 1984. Foraging behavior of tawny emperor caterpillars (Nymphalidae: *Asterocampa clyton*). *Journal of the Lepidopterists' Society* 38 (3): 186–91.

Stokes, Donald, Lillian Stokes, and Ernest Williams. 1991. The butterfly book: An easy guide to butterfly gardening, identification, and behavior. Boston: Little, Brown.

Tekulsky, Mathew. 1985. The butterfly garden: Turning your garden, window box or backyard into a beautiful home for butterflies. Boston: The Harvard Common Press.

Tilden, James W., and Arthur C. Smith. 1986. A field guide to western butterflies. Boston: Houghton Mifflin.

Toliver, Michael E., edited by Richard Holland. 1991. Distribution of butterflies in New Mexico (Lepidoptera: Hesperioidea and Papilionioidea). Duplicated.

Tveten, John, and Gloria Tveten. 1993. Wildflowers of Houston. Houston: Rice Univ. Press.

Tyler, Hamilton A. 1975. The swallowtail butterflies of North America. Healdsburg, California: Naturegraph Publishers.

Van Hook, Tonya, and Myron P. Zalucki. 1991. Oviposition by *Danaus plexippus* (Nymphalidae: Danainae) on *Asclepias viridis* in northern Florida. *Journal of the Lepidopterists' Society* 45 (3): 215–21.

Vane-Wright, R.I., and P.R. Ackery, eds. 1989. The biology of butterflies. Princeton, New Jersey: Princeton Univ. Press.

Venables, B. Adrienne B., and Edward M. Barrows. 1985. Skippers: Pollinators or nectar thieves? *Journal of the Lepidopterists' Society* 39 (4): 299–312.

Vines, Robert A. 1960. Trees, shrubs and woody vines of the Southwest. Austin: Univ. of Texas Press.

Waller, D.A., and L.E. Gilbert. 1982. Roost recruitment and resource utilization: Observations on a *Heliconius charitonia* L. roost in Mexico (Nymphalidae). *Journal of the Lepidopterists' Society* 36 (3): 178–84.

Watson, Allan, and Paul E.S. Whalley. 1975. The dictionary of butterflies and moths in color. New York: McGraw-Hill.

Whittaker, Paul L. 1984. Population biology of the great purple hairstreak, *Atlides halesus*, in Texas (Lycaenidae). *Journal of the Lepidopterists' Society* 38 (3): 179–85.

Williams, Stephen G. 1990. The butterflies and skippers of Southeast Texas: An annotated checklist. Duplicated.

Xerces Society/Smithsonian Institution. 1990. Butterfly gardening: Creating summer magic in your garden. San Francisco: Sierra Club Books.

Zimmerman, J.E. 1964. Dictionary of classical mythology. New York: Bantam Books.

Index of Larval and Nectar Plants

Index of Butterfly Species

Blue (*continued*)
Mexican, 96
pygmy, 90
Reakirt's, 96
solitary, 96
southern, 95
striated, 92
striped, 93
tailed, 97
tropical striped, 92
West Indian, 92
western pygmy, 90
western tailed, 97
Blue-dusted roadside skipper, 255
Blue-eyed grayling, 189
Blue-gray skipper, 228
Blue swallowtail, 20
Blues, 69
Bordered patch, 133
Branded skippers, 206
Brazilian skipper, 259
Brephidium exile, 90
exilis, 90
isophthalma, 90
pseudofea, 90
Broad marsh skipper, 247
Broad-winged skipper, 247
Broken dash, 242
northern, 242
red, 242
southern, 242
Brown, gemmed, 184
Brown dusky wing, 219
Brown tailed skipper, 211
Browns, 179
Brush-footed butterflies, 129
Buckeye, 158
common, 158
dark, 158
mangrove, 158
tropical, 158

Cabbage butterfly, 41
Cabbage white, 41
Calephelis virginiensis, 106
Callophrys gryneus, 82
henrici, 84
niphon, 86
Calpodes ethlius, 259
Calycopis cecrops, 79
isobeon, 80
Campestris skipper, 246
Canadian tiger swallowtail, 28
Canebrake roadside skipper, 251
Canna leafroller, 259

Canna skipper, 259
Carolina satyr, 178, 185
Carolinian satyr, 185
Cassius blue, 92
Cedar hairstreak, 82
Celastrina argiolus, 98
ladon, 98
Celia's roadside skipper, 254
Ceraunus blue, 95
Cercyonis pegala, 189
Charidryas gorgone, 136
nycteis, 136
Checkered skipper, 226
Checkered white, 39
Checkerspot, gorgone, 136
lacinia, 133
silvery, 136
streamside, 136
Chioides catillus, 211
Chlosyne lacinia, 133
nycteis, 136
Closed-wing skippers, 206
Clouded skipper, 233
Clouded sulphur, 48
Cloudless giant sulphur, 53
Cloudless orange, 55
Cloudless sulphur, 53
Cloudy wing, 214
northern, 214
Cloudywing, confused, 214
northern, 214
southern, 214
Cobweb little skipper, 251
Cobweb roadside skipper, 251
Colias cesonia, 51
eurytheme, 48
philodice, 48
Comma, eastern, 147
Common blue, 98
Common buckeye, 158
Common checkered skipper, 226
Common hairstreak, 87
Common mestra, 166
Common roadside skipper, 253
Common white, 39
Common wood nymph, 189
Confused cloudywing, 214
Copaeodes aurantiacus, 237
minima, 237
minimus, 237
Coppers, 68
Cosmopolitan, 155
Cosmopolite, 155
Creekside little skipper, 254
Creole pearly eye, 182

Funereal duskywing, 222
Fuscous skipper, 230

Gemmed brown, 184
Gemmed satyr, 184
Georgia satyr, 181, 186
Giant swallowtail, 26
Giant yucca skippers, 206
Glassywing, little, 244
Goatweed butterfly, 168
Goatweed leafwing, 168
Goggle eye, 189
Gold rim, 20
Gorgone checkerspot, 136
Gossamer-winged butterflies, 67
Graphium marcellus, 22
Gray hairstreak, 66, 87
Gray skipper, 257
Grayling, blue-eyed, 189
Great blue hairstreak, 71
Great purple hairstreak, 71
Great southern white, 43
Green-clouded swallowtail, 31
Gulf fritillary, 114, 118

Hackberry butterfly, 171
Hackberry emperor, 171
Hairstreak, alcestis, 73
   autolycus, 77
   banded, 74
   beon, 80
   cedar, 82
   common, 87
   dusky-blue, 80
   dusty-blue, 80
   Edwards', 74
   gray, 87
   great blue, 71
   great purple, 71
   hickory, 74
   King's, 74
   melinus, 87
   northern, 77
   olive, 82
   red-banded, 79
   soapberry, 73
   southern, 77
   striped, 74
   Texas, 77
   white-M, 72
Hairstreaks, 68
Harvester, 70
Harvesters, 68
Heliconiidae, 115
Heliconius charitonius, 123

Hemiargus ceraunus, 95
   isola, 96
Henry's elfin, 84
Heraclides cresphontes, 26
Hermes satyr, 185
Hermeuptychia hermes, 185
   sosybius, 185
Hesperiidae, 205
Hesperiinae, 206
Hickory hairstreak, 74
Hoary edge, 209
Hop merchant, 147
Horace's duskywing, 219
Hunter's butterfly, 153
Hylephila phyleus, 238

Incisalia henrici, 84
   irus, 85
   niphon, 86
Indigo dusky wing, 224
Iulia, 120

Jeweled satyr, 184
Julia, 120
Julia's skipper, 232
Junonia coenia, 158
   evarete, 158
   genoveva, 158
   nigrosuffusa, 158
Juvenal's duskywing, 218

King's hairstreak, 74

Lace-winged roadside skipper, 251
Lacinia checkerspot, 133
Large orange sulphur, 55
Large wood nymph, 189
Laurel swallowtail, 33
Leafroller, canna, 259
Least Florida skipper, 255
Least skipper, 235
Least skipperling, 235
Leptotes cassius, 92
   marina, 93
Lerema accius, 233
Lerodea eufala, 257
Lethe, 182
Libytheana bachmanii, 111
   carinenta, 111
Libytheidae, 109
Lilac-banded longtail, 211
Limenitis archippus, 163
   arthemis arthemis, 161
   arthemis astyanax, 161
Little glassywing, 244